PENGUIN BOOKS

DREAMERS AND UNICORNS

Abhijit Bhaduri is a Talent Management practitioner with global experience across various sectors. As Chief Learning Officer for Wipro, a role he worked in for seven years, Abhijit oversaw global initiatives across several countries. As an alumnus of PepsiCo, Colgate and Tata Steel, he has been exposed to globally acknowledged best practices in leadership, talent management and culture building. He heads Learning and Development for Microsoft globally. He has close to a million followers on social media who follow his articles and sketchnotes. His newsletter on LinkedIn has more than 280,000 subscribers.

Follow him on LinkedIn, Pinterest, Instagram and Twitter @abhijitbhaduri
Email: abhijitbhaduri@live.com

DREAMERS *and* UNICORNS

How Leadership, Talent *and* Culture *are the* New Growth Drivers

ABHIJIT BHADURI

PENGUIN BOOKS
An imprint of Penguin Random House

PENGUIN BOOKS

USA | Canada | UK | Ireland | Australia
New Zealand | India | South Africa | China

Penguin Books is part of the Penguin Random House group of companies
whose addresses can be found at global.penguinrandomhouse.com

Published by Penguin Random House India Pvt. Ltd
4th Floor, Capital Tower 1, MG Road,
Gurugram 122 002, Haryana, India

First published in Westland Business, an imprint of Westland Publications
Private Limited in 2020
Published in Penguin Books by Penguin Random House India in 2023

10 9 8 7 6 5 4 3 2 1

ISBN 9780143459347

Typeset by SŪRYA, New Delhi

www.penguin.co.in

To
Nandini Bhaduri
for the dreams we have chased together

Contents

1

Before Corona (BC) and After Disaster (AD)

We have to look at the equilibrium of work-working-workers to understand why changes in one impact the other two. When 'work' changes, new business models are created. These need leadership styles to attract workers with these skills. The new culture of work fosters new norms and cultures of work. That's what happened in the first and second industrial revolution. The pandemic changed everything overnight. The new equilibrium between work-working-workers is still evolving. The new design principles are clear.

Digital Transformation—BC or AD?

In 2016, I wrote *The Digital Tsunami* to explain how firms would have to transform themselves or risk losing relevance. But nothing had prepared us for what we saw unfolding in 2020.

In early 2020, I started writing about my experiences with various organisations, chief executive officers (CEOs) and human resources teams I have consulted with. That was the genesis of *Dreamers and Unicorns*. I wanted to address how the key drivers of growth have shifted to softer aspects like leadership, talent strategies and organisational culture. I wanted to explore what turns a startup into a market shaper with a trillion dollars of market capitalisation.

Then, in the first quarter of 2020, even as this book was still being written, COVID-19 was declared a pandemic. Everything that we knew about the world of work changed forever. In the middle of this chaos, *Dreamers and Unicorns* was conceived and then reconceived.

Convergence of Many Shifts

Writing about the business landscape today is a complex affair. A company that was once the darling of the stock market suddenly goes bankrupt. Fortunes are built and destroyed on social media. It is a difficult battleground where real news and fake news are often hard to distinguish. Social media remains a great source of great information and misinformation. Facebook has been accused of refusing to label, moderate or remove content that promotes extremist views or remove misinformation spewed by powerful authorities. Then Twitter decided to fact-check content and call out contentious content. It also disallowed forwarding such content. Should one assume that all content is now fact-checked, unless labelled otherwise by Twitter? If we step back and observe the media industry, it is going through convulsive changes—especially print.

Two newspapers in India suspended operations in the first quarter of 2020. Five print publications, two news television channels and two news websites went under in 2019. Hundreds of journalists have lost their jobs.[1]

Beyond the loss of jobs and the closing of the print business, this also has sharp second-order implications in the long term for how people get multiple perspectives, how they learn and, of course, how people view the functioning of a democracy. This is a convergence of many shifts that will trigger many more.

It is an equation with many variables. There are political, economic, social, technological and other changes (the acronym PESTO) that are changing consumer segments, purchasing patterns and consumption models. To address these changes, new business models will have to be made. New skills have to be acquired at a scale that has never been done before.

The stock of Tesla is trading higher than Exxon Mobile or Toyota.[2] The credit does not go only to Elon Musk. There are many forces at play. The stock price reflects geopolitical shifts. It means renewable energy is going to replace dependence on fossil fuel. That could be driven by environmental activists or just plain awareness. The Tesla stock's rise may be triggered by its or Elon Musk's other ventures—Space X, The Boring Company etc.

Space X successfully launched astronauts into space for the first time on 30 May 2020. The test flight, called Demo-2, is also the first crewed launch to orbit from the United States since the space shuttle programme ended in 2011.

One of the things I have learned is that life is an equation with hundreds of variables. It is not unlike untangling a set of wires patiently before you can use those earphones.

It's Complicated

Talking of which, the AirPod earphones made by Apple sold nearly 60 million units in 2019, grabbing 71 per cent of totally wireless headphone revenue that was $6 billion already. The AirPods division is a unicorn when we look at it as part of Apple's twelve-month turnover of $267.981 billion as of March 2020. To reduce its dependence on China, Apple plans to assemble wireless earbuds in Vietnam and produce iPhones in India and Mac Pro computers in the US. Apple has started manufacturing one of its flagship devices, the iPhone 11, at Chennai's Foxconn plant. Is that a sign of a more diversified supply chain? For the moment, the status message would read 'It's complicated'.[3]

When businesses were drawing up their plans for 2020 and beyond, very few strategic planning teams would have imagined the crisis that COVID-19 precipitated. Some said it was a 'Black Swan' event, while others pointed to Bill Gates's TED talk as evidence that 'microbes, not missiles will kill us'. In January 2020, 'change is the only constant' was a cliché. Leaders had told us in conferences to 'expect the unexpected'. And that 'we live in a VUCA world'. Then it actually happened. COVID-19 changed the world of work forever.

During the initial phase of the lockdown, the most common phrase used was 'unprecedented'. Then we switched to calling it the 'new normal'. Not knowing whether we are at the beginning, middle or end of the pandemic makes decision-making very complicated. Much depends on the development of the vaccine, its distribution, the easing of tensions between the US and China, the recovery of businesses, the skills, the forex reserves of each country and its bargaining power …

In short, 'it's complicated'.

We Then Experienced the VUCA World First Hand!

VUCA, an acronym first used in 1987 stands for volatility, uncertainty, complexity and ambiguity, and draws on the leadership theories of Warren Bennis and Burt Nanus.[4]

On 24 March 2020, India shut its $2.9 trillion economy, closing its businesses and issuing strict stay-at-home orders to more than a billion people. Air, road and rail transport systems were suspended. Businesses scrambled to figure out how to run their operations during this twenty-one-day lockdown that was subsequently extended to more than sixty days. As soon as the lockdown was lifted, people threw caution to the wind and a fresh wave of infections and death was unleashed. As a result the lockdown was reintroduced. This cycle would continue in an infinite loop.

It is hard to make decisions until we know if 'we are at the end of the tunnel or the beginning'. That in itself depends on so many other factors.

'Unprecedented' Rapidly Became a Cliché

The closures sharpened the digital divide. Some businesses thrived. In the US, Amazon added 100,000 new jobs for warehouse workers and drivers. Walmart added 150,000 positions to keep up with booming demand, and 7-Eleven hired 20,000 people to deal with what executives said was an 'unprecedented crisis'.[5]

The rest were not that lucky. In 2019, retailers announced a record 9,300 store closures amid widespread bankruptcy filings. In 2020, the prediction was that 15,000 stores were likely to announce closures. In July 2020, Brooks Brothers, the 202-year-old maker of business suits, and one of the last with factories located in the US, filed for bankruptcy. A business that was older than the California Gold Rush and had survived the World Wars, surrendered to the pandemic. That is truly unprecedented.

People experienced scenarios they had never encountered or imagined. The word 'unprecedented' appeared in every speech and every article. This was also an opportunity to build trust with colleagues and customers alike. Some employers decided to support employees during these difficult times. Others used this opportunity to price-gouge.

New stories were added to every brand's folklore. A large insurance provider in India realised that they had kept payroll and performance data on their intranet, which the lockdown prevented them from accessing. PeopleStrong, their HR platform provider, had to get a team to work for forty-eight hours at a stretch to ensure salaries were not delayed.[6]

One thing is for sure: many of the 63 million small businesses in India will not survive this catastrophe.

Workplace Norms Demolished

When the lockdown was announced, schools were closed and teachers had to move their classes online. Working parents struggled to keep their children busy and many ended up giving them unlimited screen time. It was as if summer vacations had been declared a few months early. Disney moved up some of its summer releases by three months and released them on OTT platforms. Even an Amitabh Bachchan movie was released on Amazon Prime. That opened the floodgates for many others to follow. More than a dozen theatrical releases were done digitally. Cinema and multiplex owners watched helplessly as the film makers' dependence on theatrical releases—a hundred-year-old relationship—simply dissolved overnight. This will most likely mean a complete change in studio economics.

WFH—the New Acronym

Until recently, working from home was a privilege reserved only for the trusted few. That norm had to be revisited.

Overnight, even junior employees were reluctantly given the privilege to work from remote locations. Some employees struggled with poor connectivity. Rules and norms had to be formulated in a matter of hours. Business continuity mattered. There was no playbook. There was no time to consider whether the decision was right. There was no time to pause and reflect on precedents and ethics, and sometimes leaders wondered if the decision they just took was even legal.

Every role that we play at work will shape our IDENTITY

It was not about offering laptops to employees. Their work allocations and productivity had to be maintained. The managers had no idea how to manage projects without a co-located team. Hurried webinars and coaching classes were conducted to tell them how to connect with clients on video calls. Employees complained about being fatigued due to long-drawn video calls. As if work-related calls were not enough, some managers were told to take their teams out for 'virtual dinners' to keep employees engaged even as employees groaned.

The chief human resources officer (CHRO) of an IT services giant spoke to me about procuring 4,000–5,000 laptops for employees in order to enable them to work from home. The shift-to-home scenario introduced complications that are hurting many multinational companies.

Ninety per cent of the 4.1 million workers in the Indian IT and business-processing industry—which generates $180 billion in annual revenue—were working from home after the country announced a nationwide lockdown in the last week of March 2020. In the Philippines, where the IT and business process management industry employs 1.2 million people, companies scrambled to distribute computers and install high-speed internet in employee residences.[7]

Online forums were awash with questions about how to conduct virtual onboarding, performance appraisals, employee engagement and even do layoffs over a video call. HR leaders were asking others if the lockdown period could be squared off against the annual leave entitlement in case the employee did not have connectivity where they were staying.

Human beings are adaptable creatures—at least most of us are. At the end of April 2020, fundraising went online. One Nation India, an online event brought together renowned YouTube creators, musicians, sportspeople and entertainers to help raise funds. The 11.5-hour marathon show featured singing, dancing and cooking, reaching 18.4 million views.

But for some issues, there were no immediate solutions. Students at several Ivy League business schools complained that replacing classroom lectures and one-to-one tutor meetings with YouTube videos and group calls on Zoom had compromised their learning experience.[8]

Professors in colleges and teachers in schools grappled with video cameras and managed to deliver their lectures but failed to engage the students. Did the teachers lack the skill to teach online or did the students fail to adapt?

That would mean mayhem, and most small colleges (the equivalent of MSMEs in education) will collapse, never to open again.

Scott Galloway says, 'There's a recognition that education—the value, the price, the product—has fundamentally shifted. The value of education has been substantially degraded. There's the education certification and then there's the experience part of college. The experience part of it is down to zero, and the education part has been dramatically reduced.'[9]

VUCA in the Workspace

The lockdown was a time when all four elements—volatility, uncertainty, complexity and ambiguity—combined to change the ecosystem of work.

V = Volatility: Decisions that would have taken days and weeks were all taken in minutes and hours. Every decision risks becoming a precedent that the leaders may regret in the future. No one has the luxury of time to deliberate. The lockdown announced with four hours' notice in India triggered the biggest migration on foot since Partition. The announcement caught about 120 million migrant workers unprepared to stay in urban areas without their daily wages.[10]

Without buses and trains plying, they were unable to go back to their villages. Flipkart, Amazon, BigBasket, Swiggy, Zomato, as well as logistics companies such as Delhivery and Rivigo, all faced a shortage of blue-collar workers.

U = Uncertainty: No one knows when the situation will return to 'normalcy'. Experts are as clueless as the most ignorant. The global economy is in the sharpest downturn since the Great Depression.[11]

Businesses are unable to plan how long they will need to operate in the 'lockdown' phase. Uncertain times lead us to go wrong in our estimates of resources needed, the speed of response and the extent of disruption. In short, the past is no longer a predictor of the future.

C = Complexity: Leaders are having to make choices that are complex. Social distancing and keeping people indoors contains the disease but is hard on the economy.[12] Should the business lay off people or reduce salaries across the board to save jobs? It is a choice between saving lives and livelihood. Some political parties pressed for waiver of school fees as a relief measure for families dealing with job losses. But unless schools collect fees, they cannot pay their teachers.

A = Ambiguity: Everyone is experiencing moments which have no precedent. People are watching the funerals of loved ones on video, unable to travel.[13] Video conferences are forcing colleagues to peek inside the homes of their managers and team members. Children, pets and the elderly compete for the mind share of the overwhelmed employee who is often dealing with lack of connectivity even as she jumps from one video conference to another.

One Size Does Not Fit Even Peers

Even when the trigger is the same, responses vary (even for businesses in the same industry). IndiGo announced a pay cut of up to 25 per cent for its senior employees while Vistara announced compulsory leave without pay of up to three days for its senior employees in March. SpiceJet also initiated pay cuts stating that its employees' salaries would be reduced between 10 to 30 per cent. Similarly, Air India announced a 10 per cent cut in allowances for every employee, except cabin crew, for three months. GoAir also initiated salary cuts, laid off its expat pilots and introduced leave without pay for employees on a rotational basis.[14]

Business leaders were making decisions and hoping they were right. Employees were watching their employers' moves in a world filled with uncertainty about the future. During times of stress and uncertainty, we begin to question ourselves and the relationships that surround us.

We feel isolated because we worry about going out to meet friends and family. Spending time with friends at a coffee shop seems like a luxury that is no longer affordable.

Equally, we worry about our jobs. First it was about losing our jobs to robots and algorithms. After the pandemic, with so many businesses closing shutters, there is unspoken fear. What if I lose my job? How will I meet my financial commitments? What if I can't ...

In the hierarchy of human needs, suddenly the whole world was forced to shrink their time horizons to the short term. Everyone worried about the air they were breathing and wondered if the other person was getting too close. More importantly, was he/she infected? We also wondered if we had been infected and just don't know it yet.

Our relationship with work changed. So did our relationship with colleagues. The workplace ... did we need it at all? Work and relationships at work define our identity. We introduce ourselves to strangers by declaring what we do for a living. When people lose their jobs, the vacuum they face is one of loss of identity. Yet, the pandemic is also an opportunity to redefine our identity.

It is time to find meaning in our relationships.

Hierarchy of Needs

5
4
3
2
1

1. PHYSIOLOGICAL
AIR, WATER, FOOD, SHELTER
2. SAFETY
SECURITY, EMPLOYMENT, MONEY, HEALTH
3. LOVE AND BELONGING
FRIENDS & FAMILY
4. SELF-ESTEEM
STATUS, RECOGNITION, FREEDOM
5. SELF-ACTUALISATION

ABHIJIT BHADURI

The Rise of Relationships

Some definitive shifts took place across every organisation around the world, shifts that the lockdown forced us to consider.

From rigid structures to fluidity

It is a generational thing at work too. If you want to understand these shifts, talk to someone who found their first employment in the Eighties and compare it with the views of someone who is starting work in this decade. The way they look at roles, hierarchies and boundaries will be sharply different. The greatest contrast in their views will come up when you ask them, 'Why do you work?'

Work is an increasingly important shaper of our identity. We work not just to earn a living but to discover and fulfil our potential. A promotion is an anchor that lets us establish a milestone in shaping our view of ourselves. In a collectivist society like India, a promotion earned by a member of the family enhances the status of the entire family.

For centuries, in India, the caste system dictated what work we did. It was a rigid structure. The roles and the boundaries of the role were defined and so was the hierarchy. Everyone knew where they stood in the pecking order. Unique skills were closely guarded by the family or the 'gharana'. Rigidity provided certainty but it was also constraining. Sometimes the son of the priest or blacksmith did not want to continue the family profession. Work also impacted social mobility. Giving up the family tradition was hard and relationships outside the professional circle were harder to form.

The workspace is also where individual identities get formed. When we move away from a pre-defined path, we can chart our own course. That needs intense exploration and the risk of getting lost. When there is no road map, it is stressful. When we are in a well-defined structure, we want to break free to seek our own individual identity. When we feel alone, it is time to focus on relationships. Human beings form relationships by balancing their need to collaborate and compete.

From one caste system to another

Today, work is an opportunity to cross social and economic boundaries. Skills have become the passport. As a result, another caste system has emerged in the workplace. Studying in an elite institution (especially for engineers and MBAs) gives the person an edge at work. Certain people have become the 'upper caste' and enjoy privileges of being given extra coaching to prepare them to lead the rest. But that has meant that good education has become the opportunity only the rich and privileged are able to access. The Indian middle class understands this and invest in their children's education. Education gives people a chance to take up more cognitively complex work.

Making Place for Emotions and Relations at Work

The workplace that we inherited in the second industrial revolution is the one that constituted the offices we worked in, pre-pandemic. That workplace was a factory aimed at standardised products, built on an assembly line where workers did not need time to think and engage with others. Employers believed that workers were looking for excuses to slack off. If you could not measure it, you ignored it, because it was too fuzzy.

Modern work is anything but standardised. The stress is on innovation. The firms that were considered benchmarks even two to three decades ago have disappeared. New kinds of business models and job roles have emerged. What matter now are soft skills. In the analogue world, the firm's value came from tangible things that could be counted, measured and seen. The real estate a firm owned, its buildings and machinery, were the greatest components of value.

Now the value of the firm comes from its intellectual property, talent acquisition, databases, content development, software, brands, customer contracts, supply-chain partnerships, training, the leadership team, the talent they have access to and the culture that either slows down or speeds up innovation, agility and collaboration. It is a winner-takes-all market. Just fifty cities that account for 8 per cent of the world's population are home to the headquarters of nearly 50 per cent of the 5,750 companies. These cities have the ecosystem to become centres of global finance, trade, governance and technology.[15]

Experience Makers Are Your Competitive Advantage

On 19 June 2020, I logged into my Twitter account @abhijitbhaduri to discover that I could now create a 140-second audio tweet. I was delighted and created my first audio tweet. Then, one day I noticed the feature was missing. I requested Twitter to restore the feature that I loved. Twitter restored it. But critics quickly noted that it didn't permit captioning, making it useless for deaf people. I had not considered that. A terrific feature that I applauded Twitter for was not inclusive.

Three hundred million people live with colour blindness worldwide. Zoom used to have a red text on black for the 'leave meeting' button. As the user base of Zoom exploded, besides improving the technology and encryption, they decided to use white text on a red background to make the button easily visible to users. Apple's iOS Color Filters setting addressed that issue in 2016.

That is exactly why firms need to hire experience makers in large numbers. A firm's competitive advantages no longer come just from writing complex algorithms but from understanding the emotions of users. Experience makers are high on empathy. Technology can be cloned. But experience makers are unique. Two companies can provide the same ride-sharing cab service. But in the post-pandemic world, a cleaner cab with the smell of disinfectant, with a sanitiser bottle at hand can change the experience of being in a cab. Experience makers are the competitive advantage.

Soft Skills and Mental Health

Machines are increasingly getting better than humans at any task that is predictable and rule-bound. A new era is emerging in the workplace—the rise of the relationship worker. According to LinkedIn, the five most important soft skills in demand today are: creativity, persuasion, collaboration, adaptability and time management.[16]

The knowledge worker now has to co-exist with the relationship worker. When the nature of work changes, the skills portfolio needed to do that work also changes. Google's fonts, for instance, are designed in cross-functional teams where coders work with psychologists to design fonts that will be more attractive to users. Google needs anthropologists who will help understand how a user behaves and thinks. Their insights become useful inputs for designing and continuously tweaking the company's products and services.

Working in transdisciplinary teams will mean that knowing how to manage people and coordinate with others are skills that will be valuable in the job market. Routine problems will get solved by algorithms. Human beings who can solve complex problems will be valuable. Being able to leverage data, form a hypothesis, present the idea to others and convince them will be important.

Creative people who are skilled in working with others to solve complex problems will be flooded with opportunities. If accomplishing the task becomes more and more dependent on others, we will need to work more closely with others. None of these skills can be learned by taking a class. They have to be built through interactions and feedback. We will need others to be able to succeed.[17]

Emotions in the Workplace

Doctors and healthcare workers wore face masks and protective equipment as they worked through the pandemic. Some of them printed smiling photos on their masks as they visited patients in the wards. That smiling photo gave the patients hope even as they struggled to breathe. Such is the power of emotions.

Work from home too brought the importance of relationships to the forefront. Two managers from a client organisation achieved very different results. One focused on not letting productivity drop. He would micromanage and the net result was that team members felt overworked and cramped because they were hesitant to take initiatives.

Relationships and emotions are the new WORKPLACE LANGUAGES

The other manager told them on day one, 'I am struggling. I have never run a day-care centre, an old-age home and a business from my kitchen. How do you think I should organise my work?' The crisis brought the team together. They all celebrated their successes by giving one another an extra day off and everybody did a little bit extra to make sure the productivity did not drop while the team member took time off.

People who are quarantined are very likely to develop a wide range of symptoms of psychological stress and disorder, including low mood, insomnia, stress, anxiety, anger, irritability, emotional exhaustion, depression and post-traumatic stress. Low mood and irritability specifically stand out as being very common according to a study by the *Lancet*. The invisible element of mental health is going to become a lingering problem for every country just as people are getting back to work.[18]

Strong human bonds, in which one experiences psychological safety, can be the antidote to this. Relationships and emotions must create the fabric of the new workplace that has so far been limited to focusing on the cognitive and tangible.

The lockdown has shown the world that we do not need to go to the workplace to get work done. What people missed about the workplace were the relationships. The banter with colleagues, griping about the boss (even our gripes are about relationships), the politics of promotions and rewards, the absurdity of rules ... it is all about our relationships. Connecting over video calls is not the same. Video conferencing is efficient. It is really like being well fed but still feeling hungry. Relationships are like comfort food. We need to go to workplaces not only to work but also to build and nourish our relationships. The post-pandemic workplace has to solve the problem of recreating the intangible benefit of the nourishment humans get from meeting other people and the emotional support that we have taken for granted. Now that it has been taken away, we are craving to fill that vacuum.

References

1. The media is going through convulsive changes. https://www.thecitizen.in/index.php/en/NewsDetail/index/4/19003/Skeletons-in-Media-Cupboards
2. It is a vote for what the future of transportation looks like. https://www.bloomberg.com/news/articles/2020-06-30/tesla-overtakes-exxon-s-market-value-in-symbolic-energy-shift
3. Airpods if combined with Apple's Augmented Reality apps could be the next S Curve for Apple. https://www.cnbc.com/2019/12/20/airpods-a-6-billion-business-for-apple-will-be-bigger-next-year.html
4. The VUCA world—the history and origin made popular by Warren Bennis and Burt Nanus. Bennis ascribed it to his time with the military. https://en.wikipedia.org/wiki/Volatility,_uncertainty,_complexity_and_ambiguity
5. While many retail stores are struggling, there is no better time to become a digital business. https://www.washingtonpost.com/business/2020/03/21/economy-change-lifestyle-coronavirus/
6. Those who kept their payroll data 'secure' on their intranet were unable to access it during the lockdown. https://abhijitbhaduri.com/2020/04/09/healing-the-workplace-with-trust/

7. The outsourcing industry has to work extra hard to build trust with customers. https://www.wsj.com/articles/coronavirus-sends-outsource-workers-home-causing-a-ripple-effect-11585738803
8. Students from top B Schools want a refund because the experience of learning online is not good enough Are they right? https://www.ft.com/content/d093664c-0381-487f-99e6-027230e2104f
9. Always entertaining, part attention grabber but always thought provoking Scott Galloway's ideas on education do make sense. https://nymag.com/intelligencer/2020/05/scott-galloway-future-of-college.html
10. The migration of workers from the unorganized sector that accounts for more than 90 per cent of India's workforce is the largest movement India has seen since the Partition in 1947. http://www.aajeevika.org/labour-and-migration.php
11. The comparisons with the Great Depression are not unfounded. https://www.ft.com/content/19d2e456-0943-42fc-9d2d-73318ee0f6ab
12. Social distancing is a choice between saving lives and livelihood. https://www.bloomberg.com/news/articles/2020-03-31/store-hotel-and-restaurant-collapses-prove-distancing-s-bite
13. Live streaming funerals in times of Corona. https://www.nytimes.com/2020/04/02/opinion/coronavirus-funeral-livestream.html
14. The airlines are all grounded. They are all dealing with it in their own way. Benchmarking peers is no longer a valid strategy https://www.peoplematters.in/article/employee-relations/air-deccan-halts-operations-employees-to-go-on-sabbatical-without-pay-25232
15. McKinsey refers to them as 'superstar' companies. In my parlance, they would be market shapers. https://www.mckinsey.com/featured-insights/innovation-and-growth/what-every-ceo-needs-to-know-about-superstar-companies#
16. LinkedIn 2019 Global Talent Trends https://news.linkedin.com/2019/January/linkedin-releases-2019-global-talent-trends-report
17. The era of the relationship worker is here. Being able to understand other's emotions and regulate one's own is how relationship workers operate. https://yourstory.com/2016/10/relationship-worker-era
18. Being isolated after an exposure to a communicable disease can have several mental health challenges. https://www.thelancet.com/journals/lancet/article/PIIS0140-6736(20)30460-8/fulltext

2

Five Shifts to Watch For

A dynamic equilibrium exists in the relationship between work, workers and workplaces. A change in the way work is done results in a new set of skills and norms that govern the workplace. When factories switched to electricity, they were able to introduce a new method of work, i.e. assembly lines. The workers then needed to develop new skills to negotiate the assembly line. Electricity allowed people to work in shifts. That led to regulations about shift work and the role of the shift supervisor emerged.

The Work, Worker and Workplace Equilibrium

The smartphone created a new kind of work—app development. Thousands of business models were born and industries were shaken up. The workplace moved to the mobile phone and created a new workplace that was virtual. That in turn allowed for remote working. The need existed to have team leaders learn how to manage working with a remote workforce. Since most firms did not want to invest in that training, they were caught unprepared when the pandemic forced the transition to remote work. The work, worker and workplace equilibrium must once again be established.

When humans and machines started to work together, it led to the creation of new jobs, which required new skills. Now we are working with many different kinds of technology, and so the skills needed have to change quickly. When someone wants to be a hologram character designer, it needs a unique combination of skills that no university or school offers. This is the first time when all three elements of the equilibrium have changed for the whole world simultaneously.

Understanding Exponential Changes

We are mourning the loss of the modern workplace. The world of work Before Corona (BC) was a patchwork of norms and mindsets that were no different from what prevailed in the second industrial revolution. The sequence has always remained the same. The nature of work changes and demands new skills from the workforce. The workplace creates rules and regulations to manage this new configuration and change happens over time. This new change, however, has been shocking in its suddenness and universality. No country has been spared. This is what exponential growth means in any sphere.

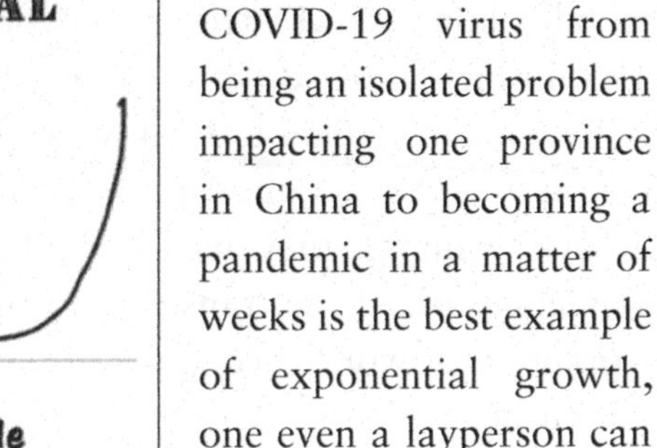

The growth of the COVID-19 virus from being an isolated problem impacting one province in China to becoming a pandemic in a matter of weeks is the best example of exponential growth, one even a layperson can follow.

Manish Sabharwal, co-founder of Team Lease, says his favourite question to students is to ask them to choose between getting Rs 1,000,000 now versus one paisa doubling every day for a month. Most choose to get the million today. One paisa doubling every day for thirty consecutive days is Rs 10,800,000. But until the twenty-seventh day, you are better off taking the million rupees. The magic of exponential growth kicks in only after that.

This principle of exponential growth pays off just as strongly in knowledge, relationships, health and businesses. Not taking a second helping and adding on the extra calories over ten or twenty years has a similar compounding effect. Reading a book a week for twenty-five years can have an exponential impact in shaping someone's world view, knowledge and ideas. Most great companies take twenty to twenty-five years to build. A twenty-five-year plan is not a patchwork of twenty-five annual plans. Similarly, in relationships, aiming for cognitive diversity really pays off. Your best ideas come not from strong ties, but from the 'weak' ties—those who are at the fringes of your network.

The same exponential change has happened in the world of work. The human mind finds it hard to comprehend the size and scope of impact, unprepared for the sheer scale of it. Until the pandemic struck, our conversations and debates were limited to speculating about how technology would put humans out of work. The impact was on work and workers. But the pandemic made us question what a workplace really meant and if we needed a workplace at all. Did we need to be co-located?

Never before has every living human being wondered about the same questions. What will be the new world of work? Are there design principles that can help me plan the way forward?

The workplaces of the future will have five different characteristics.

Shift 1: Boundaryless, Digital and Can Be Run from Anywhere

The Coronavirus starts by attacking the old and the vulnerable. I mean businesses (not people). People realise that they can do without a certain product or service. The lockdown may have forced them to try some new form of behaviour. When asked, 'What business are we in?', analogue businesses define it as the sector they compete in—automobiles, pharmaceuticals, retail etc. Digital leaders

When businesses move from an offline model to online, they often continue to THINK in terms of offline models and only use technology in some areas.

A common error is to not invest adequately in HR technology that lets employees collaborate seamlessly as they run the digital business.

If a restaurant has to serve clean, hygienically prepared food to customers, the kitchen has to be squeaky clean and the employees have to be healthy. Investing in technology that enables great customer experience needs HR tech that enables great employee experience.

answer the same question by saying, 'We are where the consumer is. We are where there is growth and profitability.' Zoom went from 10 million to 300 million daily users, and Zoom, Google Meet and Microsoft Teams combined have more call volume than the entire US mobile network.

Amazon started off selling books. Today they are into publishing (they have published this book), logistics, movies, hardware and are toying with healthcare, space travel and more. So what business is Amazon in? Businesses that can be scaled up or down in a few days are digital and their employees can work wherever they want and when they want to.

When businesses build their organisation around one single product line, they run the risk of losing everything when the business landscape or consumer behaviour changes. This period of forced adoption and experimentation by the customer or consumer is going to kill many businesses because they were holding their breath during the lockdown, waiting to go back to the Before Corona (BC) days.

By mid-April 2020, more than 28,000 workers at news companies in the US had been laid off, furloughed or had their pay reduced.[1] Some publications that relied on ads had shut down. In India, newspapers found that their print circulation had dropped overnight. Newspaper delivery teams were down to a trickle. The launch of a major business newspaper's conference was entirely taken online. But advertisers pulled back because they believed that it was a substantially diluted opportunity. Could each journalist bring their skills to an open marketplace? Or become a freelancer like so many others? Or would they keep waiting for another newspaper to employ them—which is unlikely. As readers got used to not reading the newspaper every morning, the printed news media

Media Viewing Habits are Getting Recast

- People are watching more video of all kinds—Netflix, TikTok (before it was banned), cable TV and YouTube. They are watching it during the day—not 7 p.m. to 10 p.m. as they have done for years, says Bloomberg. So, perhaps 'prime time' is officially dead.
- People are watching more videos as compared to audio-only content like music and podcasts. Spotify as a market shaper has launched video podcasts. When the consumer starts multitasking, the audio will continue.
- Communicating digitally must become part of leadership development curriculum. Background noise, poor lighting and poor quality sound on video conferences is a recipe for boredom. How to engage people online is a new skill everyone needs to learn.

was on life support. The pandemic simply speeded up the death of the sector.

Unbundle the Conference

After the lockdown, several organisers were forced to hold conferences online. Most had the speakers record their videos at home and mail it to the organisers. Why not reimagine everything from speakers to networking and coffee with random groups of attendees and speakers? Here are some ideas:

1. The audience approves the speakers: Get the speakers to do a short one-minute video of the topic they wish to speak about. Share the names of the speakers and their video 'pitches' on the conference website. Let people vote for the topic and the speaker. Some keynote speakers are notorious for recycling old slide decks. Worse still, some stalwarts of the speaking circuit (especially those who are sponsors) do not prepare and rehearse their talks adequately. They meander on. The audience that is paying for the conference can vote and decide on which speakers are worth their while. Also, allow the audience to pay to listen to selected speakers. You don't need to buy the album, just a single track.

2. Audience votes for the key themes and topics: Conference organisers can post the key themes they wish to explore. The audience can suggest specific issues they would like discussed by the speaker. These questions can be a useful guide for speakers to keep their talk sharp. Conference organisers too will know in advance which sessions have fewer takers and can assign them a smaller 'room' that is just right. The speakers who have no takers are best forewarned. They could get in a few additional participants through their own networks. Needless to say, conference organisers would welcome the additional funds.

> **3. Simultaneous webcast across platforms:** Some speakers are a huge draw. For these speakers, the organisers can webcast across multiple platforms. Those who are watching the conference live, on say Facebook, can use a pay-per-view option to join specific sessions. It allows more people to join the conference and is not an all-or-nothing choice for a participant who may wish to listen to specific speakers or topics.

There was another adjacent digital business that was thriving. I decided to start a weekly newsletter, and in no time had it going at https://abhijitbhaduri.substack.com.

They send me weekly statistics, much like Google analytics does for my website. Only, this is simpler. I can write text, add sketchnotes, format my columns and even add a podcast if I like. The site offers the option to create a paid subscription should I want to. Why could my newspaper not be as instinctively designed and customised?

When work from home became the norm around the world, conferences began to be held online. Outsourcing companies had to invest in technologies that allowed sensitive data of customers to be encrypted and protected. Work–life balance took on a whole new meaning. CEOs were running their companies, a crèche and elder care from the same room at home. Everyone's world was boundaryless! Overnight.

During video meetings, Flipkart encouraged working parents to bring their young kids to greet colleagues, who were more than happy to see them. This built a strong sense of togetherness during the lockdown.

There are many examples of ordinary people who began reimagining their jobs in the post pandemic world.

A wedding photographer offered to shoot front-porch photos on a telephoto lens. A waitress at a restaurant joined a NGO that provided food for the homeless. She made one-third the money but more than made up for the loss through greater job satisfaction. Faced with the closure of her hair salon for many months, a hair stylist turned the space into a studio. She used a grey screen, lights and an iPhone camera to shoot a video tutorial on washing and maintaining curly hair. She performed on a mannequin to adhere to social-distancing norms.[2]

Developing a portfolio of options as a career instead of having a linear view may help people adapt better to the sudden collapse of employment opportunities. Hobbies could turn into career options, for instance, and collaborating with 'weak ties' may create unique and fulfilling opportunities too.

From business models to career strategies, boundaryless thinking will enable people to thrive in this new world of work. Reimagine your business as a digital offering. Maybe try out a different product or service. Make it easy for people to discover you. Make it easy for customers to rate and evaluate your services—it builds trust. Simplify the way they can pay for your services and pay special attention to your returns policy. Make it boundaryless. Make it digital.

Shift 2: Balancing Polarities

Do you think e-books have killed the paperback market? Not really. Both co-exist. When we travel, the e-books library goes with us. But then there are times when we like to curl up in bed with a paperback and a cup of hot chocolate. Most things operate along a continuum. The pandemic has only sharpened the polarities that we must manage in every decision. While 2020 saw a global slowdown and recession, the Initial Public Offering market turned out to be the biggest ever.

The Polarity Challenges at Work

Work is done by humans and machines. In some places, the machines augment the work of humans. In some cases, they replace humans. While working from home, employees had to manage their work responsibilities while taking care of elderly people at home, their children and pets.

Did the remote working experience during the lockdown make businesses adopt remote working as the norm? Of course not. It will be an 'and' world. Remote working will certainly get adopted by more businesses with the intention of being better prepared for business continuity. People have become more comfortable using video for some kinds of meetings.

Balancing Offline and Online

Online shopping and e-commerce got a massive boost during the lockdown. So did telemedicine. Once things started to ease back to normal, we started to enjoy going back to the shopping malls and window shopping. The retail industry too heaved a sigh of relief that their long-term leases would not go to waste. When you look at the process of buying through the eyes of the consumer, they do not distinguish between online and offline retail. They just know what is convenient for them and what is not. A consumer will try out a piece of clothing in a store and then order it online. If they wish to return the product, they would like to have the flexibility of choosing to return it at the store or online, whatever is convenient.

> **Japan's '&' Work Culture**
>
> Japan is an interesting case of an '&' culture. While they are known for their tech-savvy products, their offices still prefer paper over digital documents.
>
> You can expect to see files, fax machines, business card exchanges and a clear preference for face-to-face meetings and strict norms of hierarchy.
>
> Work from home is frowned upon. Those who telework are afraid of losing favour with their bosses.

The '&' Challenges in Education

When MOOCs (Massive Open Online Courses) became mainstream, it was heralded as the model that would put academic institutions out of business. During the lockdown, several students expressed disappointment with online classes. The professors were not as effective in their online avatars as they were in class. The result is a poor 'experience' of education.

The content has to be not just relevant but also interesting. Students are used to consuming hours of engaging short form video content. When they compare that with each webinar being a 'live telecast' from the home of a professor, often with poor lighting, slides that are static and with zero peer interaction, the result is a sub-par experience.

Students don't just pay for education, but the experience of learning.

Education is not just about content transfer, which an online course can do very well but it also needs a teacher, or in case of an organisation, a manager to set the context that makes all learning translate to improved job effectiveness.

So which one is better—online or offline education? Both need to exist in tandem. It is not one or the other. Online education is especially efficient in the teaching of subjects like accounting, finance or anything that does not require another person while implementing. I could do a course online and become a terrific coder or business analyst. But to improve my soft skills, I would have to work with others. It is possible to read all the rules and legal requirements to prepare oneself for becoming a driver. But you need to actually drive a car for a period to be able to respond not just to your car but to other drivers on the road. Education has to be imagined as an '&' experience.

Rethinking Talent Management Polarities

Collaboration tools are getting better every day and that allows people to work not just from home but from anywhere. A greater percentage of people can now avoid paying high rents and talent is truly going boundaryless. Take it a step further, if co-location is no longer a precondition for people to work on a project and apply for any internship or project anywhere, suddenly it throws open the possibility that someone sitting in a small town in India will be able to work in Silicon Valley without having to board a plane. No visas needed.

Talent management has eternally worried about this choice—is it better to build talent or simply hire someone who is ready to do the job? When it comes to jobs that have been around for a while, and have a defined set of tasks that everyone understands, external hires could suffice because everyone understands what the role entails. When organisations create jobs with unconventional job titles (for example, Chief Storyteller) in an otherwise conventional business, external hiring might be a recipe for failure.

Build platforms where internal job postings are visible to everyone. The conversation has to move from jobs/positions to skills. Skill development strategy must be a Board agenda. Shift to agile operating models and leverage a portfolio of internal and external resources to build a skill bench. Plan for a Disaster Recovery Plan for the critical skills.

When the past is no longer a predictor of the future, developing people from within is a smarter talent management strategy because the internal candidate understands the culture of the organisation. Internal hires come with a network built and nurtured over the years. Somebody coming in from the outside will spend a long time building that trust and goodwill.

The Polarity Challenge for Leaders

Leaders have to balance short-term requirements with long-term strategy. Without meeting short-term results every quarter, they cannot remain in power long enough to fulfil their long-term vision and strategy. Brian Chesky launched Airbnb four different times before it was a success. Getting people to travel and share their homes with strangers may have seemed like a crazy idea before the launch of Airbnb; now it sounds far-fetched. During the pandemic, Airbnb had to drop marketing spends, freeze hiring and constantly shore up the confidence of its 'hosts'—people who rented out their homes for short-term stays. Chesky's time horizon shrunk to addressing every day as it unfolded.

Leaders need to keep their ears to the ground to understand what employees feel, but they also need to stay connected to the external world. When leaders no longer have an outside-in view, they become too insulated and focus only on dealing with what is going on inside the organisation. The changes that are happening at a rapid pace outside do not give them enough time to prepare their organisations to deal with it effectively. If leaders lack confidence, they cannot make bold decisions. But when they are over-confident, they stop listening and become arrogant.

The Most Fundamental Polarity in the Workplace

Humans have two conflicting needs as social animals. They need to collaborate with others for sheer survival. Simultaneously, they also want to have their individuality recognised—and so, everyone wishes to get ahead. Both instincts are necessary. Just as we need to fit in with the crowd, and get safety in numbers, we also need to have our uniqueness identified to stand out from the crowd. The most effective individuals understand the emotions of the other person almost as well as they understand their own. Polarities are part of the experience of working with others. As the workplace becomes more human, the polarities will become sharper and part of every role far more prominently.

One of the biggest challenges in the workplace would be to understand what the experience of work itself will be. That is a role where HR will have to take the lead and help reimagine work as an experience much like we have designers imagine the customer journey. Managing the polarities will be the new challenge for leaders. Some employees may want to meet in person. Others may be comfortable working from remote locations. It is an AND work. Design for that.

IDEA FOR DREAMERS & UNICORNS

Build an Employee Research Unit

Think of HR in the new world of work as going through a product–market fit. Better still, as Brian Halligan of Hubspot says, an 'experience–market fit'. While he speaks of product building experience as a differentiator, I would take that to focus on leadership, talent and culture. There is no way to redesign the workplace experience without research.

I would recommend having HR teams engage in qualitative research because many things in human behaviour are hard to quantify. It is the language of emotions. To hire experience makers for this new world, invite the best ethnographers and social scientists to come and study your employees and understand what matters to them.

Shift 3: From Tangible to Intangible

Upskilling Choices

JobsForHer is a platform that enables women to start, restart and rise in their careers. This platform connects 1.8 million women across India with top reskilling and upskilling partners who provide online courses, specialisations and degrees. Women can choose courses like data science, digital marketing, big data, data analytics etc. to update themselves in new technologies and be job-ready for new challenges post pandemic.

UpGrad is an online platform that offers educational services. UpGrad's range of programmes consist of digital marketing, product management, entrepreneurship, data analytics, data-driven management, and digital technology management. It offers industry insights and student support services.

Udacity Nanodegree programmes provide credentials earned through a series of online courses and projects in an array of subjects from self-driving cars and AI to data science and digital marketing. Udacity collaborates with more than 200 global employer-partners including AT&T, Google, Facebook, Mercedes-Benz and NVIDIA to close talent gaps.

Asset-lite and idea-intensive is how the biggest and most profitable firms are today. McKinsey analysed 6,000 of the world's largest public and private firms, each with annual revenues greater than $1 billion, that together make up 65 per cent of global corporate pre-tax earnings.

All of these superstar firms shared some common attributes: fewer fixed capital and labour imports, more intangible inputs, and higher levels of digital adoption and regulatory oversight than other sectors. These firms also made more investments in R&D. Brands, patents and software made up the competitive advantage of the superstar firms.[3]

Health and Wellness

During the pandemic, the automobile major Mahindra launched a series of activities for the well-being of employees, which involved interactive sessions with nutritionists as well as an exercise regime.

Johnson & Johnson rolled out a telemedicine programme globally to help employees and their families with questions about their physical and mental health. They had digital mindfulness tools, virtual fitness sessions, home workout apps, access to health experts and regular knowledge-sharing to ensure their workforce stayed motivated, healthy and mindful.

Flipkart encouraged employees across the organisation to take a 'Digital Chai Break' and guided them in scheduling their work day.

Even Money Is Becoming Invisible and Intangible

In 2018, India ranked second globally on fintech adoption, with its percentage of fintech users at 57.9 per cent, behind

China's 83.5 per cent, but ahead of many developed countries where it is at 34.2 per cent.[4]

Since the launch of schemes like Jan Dhan Yojana (2014) and Direct Benefit Transfer (2013), there has been a marked rise in awareness and adoption of financial services products. The traditionally unbanked and underbanked population is now embracing this technology. Fintechs now serve this segment across the country with their low-cost and digitised products which the incumbent have not been able to offer.

Employer Brand and Talent Brand

The voices of the leaders of an organisation shape the perceptions of people about the business. This can often come from the stances taken by the leaders on issues that impact stakeholders.

In 2013, ExxonMobil was bigger than Apple or Walmart in terms of market capitalisation. That has eroded by 60 per cent and in August 2020, Exxon along with Pfizer and Raytheon was removed from the list of thirty companies that make up the Dow Jones Industrial Average (DJIA). Exxon had been a part of the DJIA for more than 100 years.

Starbucks aims to slash the greenhouse gases it emits and the waste it sends to landfills by half over the next decade. It is also committing to conserving or replenishing 50 per cent of all the water it draws for its operations and coffee production by 2030. That impacts its employer brand.

Investing in the brand is an important element of building trust, which has now become the fundamental currency of the workplace.

Being able to build trust means investing a lot in the communication skills of people managers. Managing teams that are not co-located needs very sharp skills in being articulate and engaging.[5]

Integration of content, commerce and talent is important for every business. The CHRO and the Chief Marketing Officer (CMO) must work together to be growth drivers of the business, by building both the employer brand and the talent brand. That means using data to generate insights but telling the story in a manner that creates the experience. Customers and employees both expect the firms to treat them like they have been friends their entire lives.

'Brand trust is on par with quality, value, convenience and ingredients as a purchase consideration'
Edelman's Trust Barometer 2020

The talent brand comes from the voices of the employees when they share what it feels like to work in the organisation. They often share their opinions on sites such as Glassdoor. These insights from 1.2 million employee reviews is now the largest repository of corporate culture data in the world. The nine values that have the greatest impact on results are: agility, collaboration, customer, diversity, execution, innovation, integrity, performance and respect.

Brands must provide a reliable product and a rewarding customer experience. But consumers are looking for many more things before they can trust a brand. They want to be sure that the brand is doing the right thing even if it means taking a hit on the profits. Corporate reputation encompasses everything from the supply chain, reputation, acknowledging marginalised talent, environmental impact and the way it treats employees and customers. Brands have to be involved in social issues and not operate solely based on an obsession with shareholder value and market share.

In short: can consumers trust a brand to do the right thing? During the lockdown, Amazon prioritised 'essential' items such as cleaning products, health-care items and shelf-stable food. The mandate resulted in Amazon temporarily not accepting shipments of items that accounted for 58 per cent of its sales.[6]

To operationalise this, leaders have to set personal examples. People expect brands to do what is right for all stakeholders until the world has offset the damage done by the pandemic. That could mean shifting the product mix to create products that could help people stay healthy

HP donated 3D printers to hospitals to produce masks

TCS promised no retrenchment for its 450,000 employees. They are funding this initiative by not giving any salary hikes for a year.

The company said it will honour each of its commitments on new hires by taking each one of the 40,000 people who have been given offers, on board.

Azim Premji Foundation and Wipro Enterprises together committed an aid of Rs 1,125 crore. These sums are in addition to the annual CSR activities of Wipro, and the usual philanthropic spends of the Azim Premji Foundation.

Ford, GE and 3M are partnering to build ventilators and protective equipment.

Inditex, owner of the retail store Zara, announced that it will donate masks to health officials in Spain.

and safe. Offering free or low-cost products to healthcare workers or those in the front line who are at risk, or to the needy, is an expectation that consumers have of every brand.

These intangible initiatives have a measurable impact on results. Businesses have worked on the premise that if something cannot be measured, it has to be ignored. In the new workplace, the most powerful measures that impact results are all intangible.

In the analogue world, the value of an organisation came from its tangible assets—the building, the land, factories, machineries etc. Land, labour, capital and entrepreneurship were the factors that drove businesses alongwith customer satisfaction, quality of business processes, customer relationships, human capital, reputation of brand, strategic decision-making, strategy execution, patents, robustness of supply chain etc. Advertising and public relations agencies have long been run very differently from other businesses. When I worked at Mudra Communications, an ad agency, the saying was, 'Our assets walk out of the door every evening. Treat them right so that they want to come back tomorrow morning to give their best ideas.'

Shift 4: Emotions Matter at Work

The workplace has always been driven by logic and rational behaviour. Showing any emotion at work was considered a weakness. This was also driven by the nature of work that was expected. Analytical thinking and high IQ have been common to most leaders of corporations. In such a scenario, emotions were seen as a hindrance, and the show of emotions at work was often labelled as 'unprofessional'.

Understanding the 'Emotional Diaries' of Your Team

Psychologist Esther Perel speaks of the 'emotional diary' everyone brings to the workplace.[7] The messages that we have internalised of the world around us determines whether we work well in a team or not. If the message while growing up has been 'nobody will ever help you and you are for yourself', then it is easy to understand why he or she would be looking out for himself or herself in the workplace. On the other hand, if the person has grown up in an environment of interdependence, he or she is likely to have understood that relationships are not transactional. They are built over time by investing our emotions. Yet, in the workplace, relationships are kept at an extremely superficial level. This is the biggest area of opportunity in creating the new world of work. To make it human, focus on the emotions.

To make the workplace
HUMAN,
focus on the
emotions

Happiness Makes Money

Employee-engagement activities are meant to ensure that the employee stays productive, not from a genuine concern for happiness. The Society for Human Resource Management (SHRM) defines employee engagement as 'the strength of the mental and emotional connection employees feel toward their places of work'.[8]

'People leave bosses, not organisations' simply means that attrition is triggered when someone wants to get out of a toxic workplace relationship. The toxic relationship could be with the boss, the work itself or the culture of the workplace.

Companies with high engagement bring in 2.5x more revenue than companies with lower levels. Highly engaged employees are 87 per cent less likely to leave their companies than their less engaged counterparts. Organisations with high employee engagement outperform those with low employee engagement by 202 per cent. Highly engaged business teams result in 21 per cent greater profitability.[9]

Interdependent Teams Need 'Psychological Safety'

Team members feel secure when they are sure their idea, even if it is outlandish, will not result in them being seen as ignorant, incompetent, negative, or disruptive. This is what Google found when they tried to figure out what makes a team effective. When members can speak their mind without fear of authority or ridicule, the team can come up with innovation that is truly out of the ordinary.[10]

Mental Health

Vedanta put employee well-being ahead of productivity issues and offered psychological counselling helplines to people facing anxiety and stress-related problems, along with online meditation and fitness sessions as well as a series of engagement activities during the work-from-home phase to keep their employees motivated and engaged.

The prime minister of New Zealand was as battle weary as any of the world leaders during the COVID-19 crisis. She announced (like most country heads) that, other than essential services workers, everyone would have to stay home. When a child enquired if the Easter Bunny was considered to be an 'essential worker', the prime minister responded on national television saying, 'You'll be pleased to know that we consider both the Tooth Fairy and the Easter Bunny to be essential workers.' It may be an early indicator of a model of leadership that comforts and builds courage during times of crisis. Emotions matter even more.[11]

The world celebrates leaders who are comfortable with their emotions and vulnerability. We are in an age that celebrates emotions and relationships.

Shift 5: Perpetual Beta

After Windows 95 came Windows 98. Then Windows 2000. The old belief was that you built a complete product and only then shipped it to the customer. Software developers do not wait for the final product anymore. They create a minimum viable product (MVP for short) with the express intent of observing the customer as they are using the product or service. This allows the developers to keep improving the product features and remove the ones the customer does not use.

Amy Webb lists eleven sources where a change could either create a short window of opportunity or sow the seeds of irrelevance. They are: wealth distribution, education, infrastructure, government, geopolitics, economy, public health, demographics, environment, media-telecom and technology. These are the sources of change that every leader must monitor.[12]

What stops people from expecting and adopting perpetual beta as the state to be in? It is exhausting. Imagine having to watch your back at every step. It is stressful. At times of stress, our mind and body are on high alert. Continued stress is corrosive and impacts our mental as well as physical health.

I hosted a podcast called 'Dreamers and Unicorns' where I invited eleven dreamers who had worked their way into becoming unicorns in their own fields. It was interesting to see that each one of these achievers juggled multiple interests. They found time to coach and inspire others while seeking to reinvent themselves all the time professionally.

No one seemed to be resting easy because they had achieved a certain degree of success. Organisations that adopt this mindset are continuously innovating across boundaries.

Think of the impact of COVID-19 on mobility. Public transport usage has dropped between 70 to 90 per cent in major cities. Operators have to take fewer passengers to avoid overcrowding while also maintaining hygiene and safety requirements that drive up operating costs. Ride hailers have also experienced declines of up to 60 to 70 per cent, and many micro-mobility and carpooling players have suspended their services.

Regulatory frameworks have to balance the polarity of keeping some guardrails intact while allowing for innovation. It may need someone like Elon Musk to challenge our

The Dreamers & Unicorns Guest List

1. Pankaj Bansal (CEO and co-founder of PeopleStrong);
2. Anita and Harsha Bhogle (online education and sports commentary);
3. R. Balki (film director);
4. Renuka Ramnath (founder-CEO of PE firm Multiples);
5. Joshua Karthik (celeb photographer);
6. Anuj Kacker (president and executive director at Aptech);
7. Shantanu Moitra (Bollywood music composer);
8. Ravi Venkatesan (former chairman of Microsoft India & author);
9. Pratik Kumar (CEO of Wipro Infrastructure & board member of Wipro) and
10. Sairee Chahal (entrepreneur and founder CEO of SHEROES, a community platform for women)

assumptions about what mobility ought to be. Solving such a problem may need someone who can question every assumption we hold sacred.

Tech writer Kara Swisher says, 'What they do share is a proclivity for what is perhaps the most important element of all truly legendary makers of important things: creative destruction.' She's writing about the unlikely comparisons drawn between Elon Musk and Steve Jobs. Musk is managing three unsolved problems of humanity—electric cars, space exploration and urban transportation. Yet, his tweets have often put Tesla, SpaceX and The Boring Company in the cross hairs of regulators and adversaries. Lack of sleep can impede the executive function of the human brain—even if you are Elon Musk.

Musk told Kara Swisher in an interview, 'I haven't counted exactly, but I would just sort of sleep for a few hours, work, sleep for a few hours, work, seven days a week. Some of those days must have been 120 hours or something nutty. You're gonna go a little bonkers if you work 120 hours a week.'[13]

When NASA announced its plans to launch the first crewed mission in a decade, what caught everyone's attention was that the rocket and spacecraft were both developed by private company SpaceX—a company that bears Elon Musk's stamp of persistence and resilience to achieve the unachievable. Tesla, SpaceX, The Boring Company are all products of being in perpetual beta. They are always improving. They are always works in progress.

Ideas for You to Try Out

- Instead of a work-from-home strategy, ask how you could imagine your company as a born-remote (people working from remote locations where there is poor connectivity). What would be the processes you would design? Create this plan for every function, business unit and geography where people are located.
- How would you create skill-building opportunities for people who wish to work on a thirty-day project for a company in Silicon Valley?

To increase adaptability to changing circumstances, organisation have to be rethink their roles, structures and processes around outcomes rather than tasks. Hospitals are facing skill shortages because experienced doctors are also the ones who are most vulnerable to the COVID-19 virus. What if the future holds a scenario where people who have the most critical skills are the ones most impacted?

One tip: When your business does scenario planning for the future, invite a creative fiction writer who can help you conjure a course of events that logical thinkers cannot. The pandemic is proof of that possibility.

References

1. The print media was struggling everywhere even before the pandemic struck. The lockdown shaved off even the razor thin margins from print and with no newspaper delivery happening, the print business had to make way for digital news. https://www.nytimes.com/2020/04/10/business/media/news-media-coronavirus-jobs.html
2. A crisis could trigger panic or creativity. From wedding photographers to lawmakers many people are reimagining their work. https://www.wsj.com/news/collection/makingitwork-aec5a7ef
3. McKinsey calls them the 'Superstar' firms. It is the intangible assets that gives them the competitive advantage. https://www.mckinsey.com/featured-insights/innovation-and-growth/superstars-the-dynamics-of-firms-sectors-and-cities-leading-the-global-economy
4. After demonetisation in November 2016, India has been quick to adopt digital payments. https://www.pwc.in/assets/pdfs/consulting/financial-services/fintech/publications/emerging-technologies-disrupting-the-financial-sector.pdf
5. During the lockdown people have watched hours and hours of high-quality video that has now become the standard of communication. That will impact how communication happens in organisations. https://www.bloomberg.com/news/articles/2020-04-14/how-is-coronavirus-changing-the-way-people-use-media
6. Amazon worked hard to ensure people were dissuaded from ordering anything which was non-essential, even if it meant a revenue loss. People do not trust brands which do price gouging during a crisis. https://www.wsj.com/articles/amazon-retools-with-unusual-goal-get-shoppers-to-buy-less-amid-coronavirus-pandemic-11587034800
7. Work is not just a source of livelihood. It is an integral part of our identity. It must allow us to become a better version of ourselves. https://www.ft.com/content/aaa3b29a-ffb0-11e9-be59-e49b2a136b8d
8. Employee Engagement is a measure of the 'experience' of work—the feelings generated while working. https://blog.shrm.org/blog/defining-employee-engagement
9. Employee engagement definitely impacts the bottom line. Here is proof. https://giveandtakeinc.com/blog/employee-engagement/a-roundup-of-2019-employee-engagement-facts-and-statistics/
10. What makes a team effective, especially when the task demands a very high degree of interdependence among the team members. https://rework.withgoogle.com/print/guides/5721312655835136/
11. A leader who can show the vulnerable side is far more trusted than someone who seem to be infallible. Authenticity is in. https://www.

bbc.com/news/av/world-asia-52189013/jacinda-ardern-tooth-fairy-and-easter-bunny-are-essential-workers

12. Eleven sources of change that every leader must monitor. https://sloanreview.mit.edu/article/the-11-sources-of-disruption-every-company-must-monitor/
13. Elon Musk is a man who needs to save his own companies from himself despite his brilliance. https://www.vox.com/2018/11/2/18053424/elon-musk-tesla-spacex-boring-company-self-driving-cars-saudi-twitter-kara-swisher-decode-podcast

3

Life Is a Series of S-Curves

Change management is all about planning for one element that is changing. Think about it like the Y2K challenge. We knew what to do and just how much time was left. When water turns to ice or vapour, it has gone through a transformation. Water, ice and vapour are not like each other in any way. Transformations happen through S-curves and exponential changes. Everything changes and at an ever-increasing pace. The human brain finds it incredibly challenging to handle S-curves.

In the world of work, the shadow of the second industrial revolution is a long one. If the first industrial revolution was all about steam power and textiles, the second industrial revolution was all about standardisation and mass production using electricity. It was a new method of work that needed a new set of skills.

Compared to the first industrial revolution, the second was an S-curve, where the changes were slow and spaced out over time in the beginning. That made the curve flatter at the beginning. The convergence of several factors then cause the curve to rise sharply in the middle. As the changes were adopted, the curve flattened out towards the end.

A company can launch a product with slow adoption in the beginning, a sharp rise after some time and taper off as consumers switch to other products. Strategy gurus always say that when the first product is hitting its growth phase, that is the best time to begin the next S-curve.

Workplaces must change whenever the way we **work** changes and a new **'worker'** emerges.

By 1914, the S-curve of the second industrial revolution was tapering off and new workplace legislations were also being enacted. By the early twentieth century, many states in the US had passed laws regulating child labour, minimum wages and working conditions.

The new method of doing work created a new class of workers who were regulated by a new set of norms for the workplace. There were many changes in the way people worked with machines, supplementing manual labour and creating new jobs with new skills.

Reskilling the workforce becomes harder with each quantum shift in the method of working. During the first industrial revolution, the shift from farm labour to skills needed in a factory was not significant. The machines were rudimentary and so were the skills needed to run them. The second industrial revolution saw electricity powering the factory and the rise of new skills needed on the shop floor. It was about mass production, standardisation and automobiles, mining, railways—all of which needed more sophisticated engineering skills. Fast forward to the rise of computing power, the rise of super specialists, the inability of the education system to teach the skills that are relevant and you can see the skill gap brewing.

The 'Modern' Workplace Practices Are Ancient

Electricity made it possible to run factories round-the-clock and introduced the system of shift working. New roles were created, like that of the 'shift supervisor', and many principles of modern business management can be traced to the second industrial revolution. UK, Germany, France, US, Italy, Japan and some other countries progressed industrially. Much of the world's infrastructure, like transportation systems, manufacturing, electrification, paper, petroleum and automobiles, began to take shape. Engineering colleges and business schools came up to feed the demand for people to run these enterprises.

Then complacency set in. We continued to run workplaces in the digital age with the norms and mindset of the analogue world. The transformational shifts of workplace norms that were overdue, simply erupted during the COVID-19 crisis. We realised that the modern workplace is actually quite ancient.

The transformational shifts of workplace norms that were overdue simply erupted during the COVID-19 crisis.

A set of businesses rose (and disappeared) at the turn of the century. Social, Mobile, Analytics and Cloud (SMAC for short) laid the foundations for the digital era. Social media turned every individual into a broadcasting powerhouse. Companies like Amazon (1994), eBay (1995), Netflix (1997), Google (1998), JD.com (1998), Salesforce (1999) and Alibaba (1999) were formed to take advantage of the shift. These business models were market shapers because they changed the way we lived and worked.

SMAC created new businesses and business models (work) and with it many new kind of workers. But workplace norms remained stubbornly resistant.

The iPhone launched in June 2007 was a game changer. It was the beginning of a whole new S-curve. With the launch of apps, new categories of work and workers entered the market. The mobile became a device that was personal to everyone, and made everything accessible from entertainment to commerce. The first cracks in the world of work came up as the world got hyper-connected. Being able to work from anywhere gave rise to a new worker whose workplace was actually in the cloud. Most employers did not change enough to create new ways of working. Most contemporary workplace practices remained rooted in norms that were in urgent need of a rethink. While some businesses experimented with new cultural practices, many of them were gimmicky and came apart quickly.

Case: Everlane

Everlane was a San Francisco startup that was a direct-to-consumer fashion company. Michael Preysman, the founder and CEO, promised 'radical transparency' by disclosing pricing markups, its ecological footprint and information about its suppliers. That promise was a great differentiator and, in five years, Everlane valued itself at more than $250 million.

When Everlane rushed to show support for the Black Lives Matter movement, its employees exposed the inauthenticity of the move, and Everlane's culture of racism, bias and inequality. A company that claimed to sell 'ethical clothing' had an organisational culture that was inconsistent with the image being sold.[1]

Analytics created the ability to see patterns in data that had not been possible previously. Predictive analytics and prescriptive analytics made it possible to look ahead to the future and also do what a machine was advising. Cloud technologies made it possible to replace physical storage with virtual. Facebook (2004), Twitter (2006) and Uber (2009), which worked on these technologies, started heading Fortune 500 lists and signalled the start of the digital era.

One company that started its life in 1982 by selling its iconic software in boxes caught the S-curve and made its transition to a Fortune 500 company. When Shantanu Narayen became the CEO of Adobe in 2007, it was already on the peak of the S-curve. In 2011, Adobe moved its entire suite of products to the cloud and got a new lease of life. By 2013, Adobe killed boxed software and moved entirely to the cloud. That allowed its users to update the product in real time and build in Artificial Intelligence (AI) capabilities that keep growing.[2]

Along with changes in business models, workplace norms should have moved to the next S-curve, but they did not. We just continued with the norms that we had inherited from the pre-World War I days.

In 2011, Erik Brynjolfsson and Andrew McAfee described the interaction of digital technology, employment and organisation in their book called *Race Against the Machine: How the Digital Revolution Is Accelerating Innovation, Driving Productivity, and Irreversibly Transforming Employment and the Economy.* They pointed out that in industry after industry, businesses were substituting machines for people at an exponential pace. In this book, they viewed machines as complementary to human effort.

Three years later, they wrote *The Second Machine Age*, where they warned that machines were now capable of substituting humans. 'Software that grades students' essays more objectively, consistently and quickly than humans' and 'news articles on Forbes.com about corporate earnings previews' were 'all generated by algorithms without human involvement', they said.

The Workplace in India

In India's social structure, caste was the deciding factor in determining an individual's profession. The system was rigid but it made life very predictable. The first set of opportunities for Indians to break out of this mould emerged after Independence in the government and the public sector, which were the biggest employers. Jobs were for life and people rarely had to travel to another city to look for a job.

Family-owned businesses have always been another aspirational option in the job market. Tata, Birla, Bajaj, Kirloskar, Ambani, Piramal, Lalbhai, Murugappa, Escorts, Hinduja, Godrej, Oberoi, Mahindra, Wipro and many others offered attractive careers across several sectors.

Even in 2016, fifteen of the top twenty business groups were family-owned. Together, they controlled 84 per cent of the combined assets of the top twenty business groups. Bharti, Adani, GMR, HDFC and the Jaypee group came up post liberalisation. As software started impacting every sector, it saw the rise of Infosys and Wipro.[3]

With the liberalisation of the economy in the '90s, for the first time, mobility across jobs and sectors became mainstream. Sanjeev Bikhchandani founded an Indian job search engine, Naukri.com, in March 1997. People sitting in internet cafés began uploading their resumes to Naukri.com. The job market had gone online and boundaryless across all locations in India.

Global multinationals started hiring from the Indian talent pool and it was possible for a certain set of people to have careers across continents. In 2002, a company called LinkedIn was set up in Silicon Valley. It invited people to post their résumé on the platform. Indian talent now became accessible to companies everywhere. India became a hunting ground for managerial and engineering talent for the world.

危机

The Chinese word for crisis is made up of two characters: danger and opportunity

Then came the next wave in the workplace when young entrepreneurs fresh out of engineering colleges and business schools launched the startup boom in India. Credentials were no longer the reason why somebody could not switch careers. The workplace was ready for an overhaul.

Why the Work-Worker-Workplaces Equilibrium Needs to Be Re-established

Even before the pandemic, it was clear that the marketplace was getting sharply divided between the digital haves and have-nots. The digital giants tend to be tech companies that operate without much competition, are most likely replacing industries that have employed millions and often employ an army of tax lawyers who minimise their tax liabilities through loopholes in the law.

Most incumbents (explained in detail later in the book, but dominant companies in their space to put it briefly) are at the peak of the S-curves of their industry and are led by leaders who take decisions that have short-term payoffs and hollow out the company in most cases. The story is not just about winners and losers. There are shades of grey.

Exponential Changes

Humans understand linear change. When you fill fuel in your vehicle, the indicator of the fuel gauge moves up at a rapid pace, but it is still linear. We know how to deal with linear shifts. The human brain does not know how to deal with exponential changes.

The rapid escalation of the virus left every country and business leader stumped. That was an example of exponential change. If left unchecked, it could overwhelm the hospital system of any country.

It took seventy-five years for landline phone usage to reach 50 million users, while mobile phones did that in just twelve years. That was linear change.

A game like Pokémon GO reached 50 million users in just nineteen days. Connectivity makes it possible to roll out a service to a billion people in twenty-four hours. Google's mail service Gmail rolled out Smart Reply to a billion+ Gmail users overnight.

According to CNBC between January and February 2020, Zoom added 2.22 million users. In 2019, they added 1.99 million users during the entire year. Zoom gets 300 million users daily who use its meeting app. The company moved rapidly from being a unicorn to becoming a market shaper with its global popularity. In April 2020, hackers exposed Zoom's vulnerabilities. Many organisations and government bodies issued directives to uninstall Zoom. Market shapers may have mastered tangible markers of success like growth and profitability, but they usually struggle with intangibles like trust and reputation. Boeing, once a market shaper, now is just another incumbent whose leaders created a culture where employees worry about flying in their own planes.

Crisis and Opportunities for Sectors

Travel and tourism was severely hit by the travel ban and lockdown. It changed the fortunes of the airlines industry. Delta, American Airlines, United, Southwest and Alaska have spent $44.9 billion on share repurchases and dividends since 2015. When a large percentage of the cash flow is spent on share buybacks, it boosts the share price but leaves the businesses with no liquidity. CEOs are rewarded for the increase in share prices. Shareholders are happy because they get better dividends. But there is very little cash reserve to tide over periods of low demand or shutdown. This is the corporate version of what happens to an individual who does not have money in the bank to pay the rent and EMI until he finds another opportunity or job that pays enough. When the pandemic struck, companies that had done share buybacks had no liquidity to pay employees' salaries even for a month. After all, 'customers pay salaries—not shareholders'.

Over the last five years, the airlines had already shed thousands of jobs. Running an airlines is a complex business. They say the fastest way to become a millionaire is to be a billionaire and start an airline. With travel bans across the world during the lockdown, airlines all headed towards bankruptcies. Between these five airlines, i.e. Delta, American, United, Southwest and Alaska, 750,000 jobs are at stake. Should the government bail out an industry that wasted money in good times?[4]

Even Richard Branson's airline was not immune. He pledged to mortgage his home and luxury holiday resort in the British Virgin Islands to save Virgin Atlantic.

Even before the lockdown, some airlines in India were gasping. Air India had reported a record loss of Rs 8,556.35

crore in 2018–19, compared to a net loss of Rs 5,348.18 crore reported for 2017–18. It has not reported a profit since its merger with Indian Airlines in 2007. The cash-strapped carrier's accumulated losses in the past decade stood at Rs 70,000 crore approximately.[5]

At its peak, Jet Airways had 119 aircrafts in its fleet and used to operate about 600 flights a day. It also ran the most successful international operations by an Indian airline. In 2010, Jet Airways had a 22 per cent market share and was the largest airline in India. In April 2019, Jet Airways shut its operations with losses totalling Rs 15,000 crore. Almost 16,500 employees lost their jobs as did thousands more who were working in ancillary services.

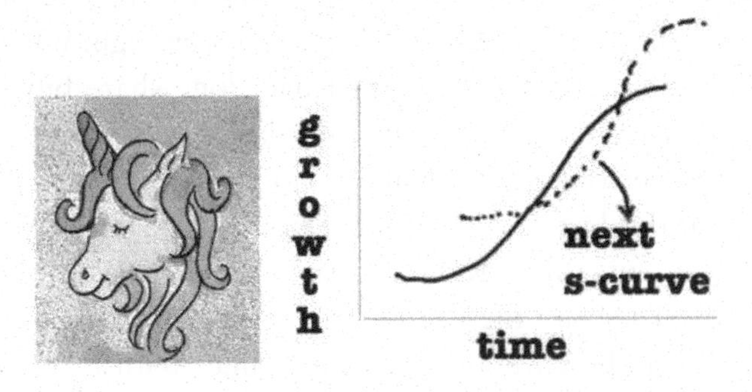

Beyond inefficient business models, there was the biggest disruptor—technology. During the second industrial revolution, electricity was the game-changer. AI is doing just that in the world of work today.

Three shifts that were visible in the early days of the lockdown were:

1. Revenue drop from the current portfolio.
2. Customers switching to low-cost options and substitutes or delaying purchases.

3. Hiring freezes leading to talent-acquisition engines getting stopped.

The pandemic is as good a disruption as any. It will create new behaviours and new choices in the market. Businesses that are able to get market share in this new space would have created moats around their customers that would be hard to replicate.

The pandemic also created some unexpected opportunities. People were cooking more at home, leading to mixed fortunes for companies like Unilever. Sales of Ben and Jerry's ice cream in major markets like India and China dropped because of the lockdown. But it was compensated for by enhanced hand-washing and cooking at home. It created opportunities for brands like Knorr soup and Maggi.

Telemedicine has faced concerns in the past about privacy and physician liability. The travel ban forced greater usage of telemedicine, especially to respond to patients in India's rural areas. Platforms like DocsApp, mfine and Practo allow patients to connect with doctors and schedule virtual consultations.

Suddenly, some technologies appeared to be heaven-sent in a world of social distancing and challenges of last-mile delivery.

Robotics company Nuro has been using electric, self-driving vehicles to deliver groceries to retail giant Kroger's customers in Phoenix and Houston in the US. Their services now extend to delivering pizza from Domino's in the same area.

Japanese retailer Uniqlo runs an automated warehouse with 90 per cent of its workers replaced by warehouse robots. They work twenty-four hours a day, doing the most tedious jobs, e.g. inspecting and sorting clothes. Fashion retailers like Zara and Bonobos are also using robots in their warehouses.

Drones are routinely being used by photographers to take aerial shots for weddings or recording photographs of rallies and crowds. Oil companies are using drones to look for leaks in oil pipelines that stretch for thousands of kilometres across barren lands. Geologists use drones to photograph inaccessible spots like volcanoes. Wildlife poachers are tracked by drones to protect animals from being hunted. Terrorists use them to launch attacks. Every technology is equally available to the good guys and the bad. The problem is not the technology, it is the human being.

3D printing is being used in medicine to customise, prototype and manufacture personalised prosthetics. It is used to print tissues and organs and to prepare precise doses of medicine. But 3D printing of guns causes a massive problem for lawmakers because they do not have tracking numbers.

The falling prices of computing power is a powerful example of exponential growth. Full genome sequencing can now be done for a few hundred dollars, as opposed to the thousands required in 2015, or the millions in 2006, or the billions that were spent on the first full sequence in 2003. This is making personalised medicine a reality that will soon be affordable even in the poorest countries.

The real game changers are when we combine exponential technologies to solve a problem. Boston Dynamics is a robotics design company that combines robotic hardware systems and sensors with computing, communications, and cloud services. When combined with AI, Boston Dynamics robots can climb stairs, do back flips, open doors and dance.

The use cases that are possible with these robots are mind boggling.*

Why Do Leaders Miss the Opportunities that a Crisis Creates?

Having the right strategy is just a small part of responding to a crisis or disruption. Executing the strategy needs great leadership that can balance polarities (short-term needs versus long-term). It needs investment in building employee skills to enable them to execute things they have not done before. When leaders take decisions to respond to a crisis, they have to rely on their own judgement and hence the organisational culture has to be comfortable with failure and course correction.

1. Data is not everything: When the past is not a predictor of the future, the analysis of the past is unlikely to generate insights. Taking decisions based on data is a challenge at a time like this. Not all the data gathered in the pre-pandemic era may be relevant today. Leaders are so used to relying on past trends-based data that they do not know how to navigate a situation like this. During an unprecedented crisis or disruption like COVID-19, there is no data to fall back on. Leaders must then rely on their own ability to connect the dots based on stories, images and metaphors. The leaders' time horizon can determine whether they will be taking a short-term view or a long-term approach. It is a

*In software and systems engineering, a use case is a list of actions or event steps typically defining the interactions between a role (known in the Unified Modeling Language (UML) as an actor) and a system to achieve a goal. The actor can be a human or other external system.

complicated mix of their personal values, risk appetite and how they respond under stress. For small- and medium-sized companies, the transaction volume for something like hiring is limited. A conference module about using Big Data in HR would be irrelevant to them.

2. They cannot rely on customers to guide them either: Customers' opinions are useful when there is an existing product in use. There are opinions and suggestions that can be used to improve the user experience. If it is a product that does not exist, then surveying customers is not helpful because they often do not have a way of articulating what they need. Generating these insights needs a high degree of skill in qualitative research—unfortunately, most businesses are paralysed when it comes to taking a decision without tangible data to fall back on.

It needs judgement, which is dependent on the personality of the final decision maker.

Decoding Judgement

1. **The way you learn:** Prefer words and pictures or numbers (data)

2. **Decision-making :** Based on data or intuition. Short-term or long-term focus. To avoid risks or get gains.

3. **Openness to feedback:** Defensive or open. Accept failure and shift or refusal to change.

Source: http://www.hoganjudgment.com/

Solving for cybersecurity in a medical 'device'

Is a health tracker a medical device since it tracks the exercise and sleep patterns. An Apple watch can check your heart rate. Is that a medical device? Patient safety can be impacted by security features and software used in the medical devices like pacemakers or insulin pumps used by diabetics. Recalling a pacemaker is a huge expenditure for the patient, but hackers have demonstrated that they can reverse engineer a pacemaker (if it does not have enough cybersecurity built in) remotely and drain out the battery. Can the device information be encrypted? Yes, it can, but that makes the device expensive.

For a long time, regulatory bodies believed that, since there was no money to be made by draining pacemaker batteries, there was no incentive. So security in medical devices was not prioritised. But we know that money is not the only reason for the commission of a crime. Revenge and causing harm are equally popular motives.

Getting a medical device to the market is a three- to five-year process. Then it is available for twenty to thirty years. Putting security patches in a device needs doctors, technology people and device makers to update the devices. Negligence is hard to prove because some doctors erase the device logs making it impossible to reconstruct the cause of death.

The complexities of the problem make it hard to be solved but some things can no longer be left to chance.[6]

The Crisis in Jobs and Skills

We have all grown up with a three-stage world norm—learn, earn and retire. Once we completed our education, we found a job. It was time to 'settle down', parents advised their children. For many years, a government job spelt job security. For years, the public sector offered the same job security. Even if the public sector enterprise made losses, it was kept alive because closing it would be a political landmine. Getting laid off was a matter of shame not only for the employee, but also for the family.

LOOK AT YOUR LIFE AS A SERIES OF S-CURVES

'What do I do with my life?' That is the question that keeps coming up at different times of our life. Circumstances may change; and answers will differ because we are optimising for different things at every stage of our careers.

A. Early career

Be a learning machine. Learn about everything around you and about yourself. Figure out what you are good at and what you enjoy. Learn by trying many things.

Establish a reputation for excellence through sheer hard work. Doing a great job consistently is so rare that you automatically start attracting opportunities as your reputation spreads.

Avoid a victim mindset. Stop blaming the world for your circumstances. Take responsibility and develop a 'growth mindset'.

B. Mid-career

This is when you begin to sense your mortality. There is a younger generation behind you that is gaining ground. You have a short window to do that something big you want to do. Experiment with many new ideas.

This is when you also are at the highest risk of becoming obsolete and irrelevant. Mid-level managers in many companies have not stayed relevant. In today's world, you could have a hard landing.

Reinvent yourself every few years. Look at your life as a series of S-curves. Walk away from success and start all over again. Start a new S-curve.

Interview with Ravi Venkatesan, ex-Chairman of Microsoft, India

The pandemic-hit sectors, like IT, aviation, media, and tourism, employ millions of people in India's organised sector. The real tragedy was faced by 136 million non-agricultural jobholders. Most of them were casual labourers who did not have formal employment contracts and worked for small companies or were self-employed.

For a country without social security, this is a frightening problem.[7]

Over 1.5 lakh people across India's various information technology firms face an uncertain future because 75 per cent of this sector's revenues come from the US and European markets that are deeply impacted by the Coronavirus. Even India's largest IT firms will not be immune to wage freeze, pay cuts and layoffs.[8]

In the pre-Corona world, AI startups were seen to be the most aspirational jobs where funding was abundant. The pandemic was unkind to them, as customers of these startups became cash-strapped. Half of Britain's companies plan to furlough their workers, threatening to overwhelm the UK's aid programme.

Accenture, Lincoln Financial Group, ServiceNow and Verizon put together an employer-to-employer platform called People + Work Connect, which brought together companies laying off people with others in urgent need of workers.[9]

Succession Planning Is a Game of Assumptions

The COVID-19 crisis showed us that the best scenario-planning teams were unable to anticipate the business risk from a situation like this.

But then truth can be stranger than fiction. What is the likelihood of losing the sales director and the CEO within the span of a fortnight? That is just what happened to BMW India. Their sales director Mihir Dayal passed away on 7 April 2020 and, on 20 April 2020, the company announced the demise of their CEO Rudratej Singh.

What if your entire leadership team were to be away for a strategy conference at a remote location with no connectivity and a lockdown is announced for some reason? How would the business run? Please don't dismiss it as unlikely. A virus (and not a computer virus) bringing the business down, keeping everyone at home? Naah … that is just a figment of your imagination. It is highly unlikely to happen. Right?

While most companies struggled to hold on to their existing talent and just stay afloat, companies with deep pockets found it easy to acquire cutting-edge startups that were gasping. 'Acqui-hiring' will be the opportunity for cash-rich giants seeking to cherry-pick the best talent.

Job opportunities may dry up for most people who are laid off, but it may actually be the golden time for those with cutting-edge skills. This may be a time when businesses will move from hiring for jobs to hiring for skills.

In India, parents typically push children to find jobs that are predictable and seem to be in high demand today. Career is rarely a straight path. It is only in hindsight that I can connect the dots. It evolves. The parents assume that their child will grow up to love the chosen field, e.g. engineering or being a lawyer (pick your own version of this). The field itself may change. Learning and Development did not exist as an area of specialisation when I started my career. There was a training department, which I liked but was not madly in love with. A book by Peter Senge, called *The Fifth Discipline*, triggered my interest in organisational learning.

Then the themes of leadership, talent and culture began to emerge as key drivers of organisational success. That is what I work with today and I love it. I use my love for writing and drawing seamlessly to create a cocktail that gives me a high. The visuals help me to simplify complex ideas. All of it converges in the book that you are reading.

Source: Li Jin, Andreessen Horowitz

The field has changed, I have changed, my unique combination of experiences at work shaped my world view, my drawings and writing helped me connect the dots, and taking the plunge to be an entrepreneur created the client base and variety I wanted.

When I started my tiny boutique advisory firm, the portfolio of work I offered was based on the experiences I had working with businesses in various sectors around the world. Four years later, my work in coaching leaders and businesses discover their personal brand, and B2B marketing through social media are the fastest growing segments of my work.

Jobs evolve. Skills evolve.

Jobs Are Temporary Assignments

As technologies are developed and new applications are found, each field is transformed. From agriculture to education, technology is being used to create new possibilities. Technology allows every job to be broken into tasks. Each task can be done either by a machine or an algorithm. If the work is to be done by humans, the company has to decide whether the tasks can be distributed to outsourcing partners in countries where wage costs are lower or given to an expert community or to a freelancer or gig worker.

If most tasks in a job can be done by a machine, or by someone more skilled or cheaper, that job becomes dispensable, and during a crisis, it is the first one to get axed.

Many jobs are becoming like temporary assignments done by humans until the machine (or a more skilled human) learns to do it.

Boundaryless Jobs—Jobs Without Fixed Descriptions

Google's Threat Analysis Group (TAG) report in May 2020 highlighted an interesting emerging trend: hackers for hire. They are like gig workers but for projects that have questionable ethics. Many 'hack for hire' operations are now increasingly being done by formally registered firms. They target senior elected officials, businesses and journalists. Their targets could be based anywhere in the world. The world of hackers is also riding the digital tsunami.[10]

A job description tells you where the job fits in the hierarchy of the organisation, its boundaries and, of course, the accountability of the person doing it. If the job description has not significantly changed over the last few years, chances are that it is already obsolete. Job descriptions often lead to siloed behaviour in organisations. People use it to protect their turf and prevent others from learning enough to be able to do that job.

Many jobs are becoming like temporary assignments done by humans until a machine learns how to do it.

In a post-pandemic world, job descriptions are likely to become more meaningless as the world shifts towards jobs that are boundaryless. If you had one person who can fix the plumbing and be good enough as an electrician-cum-carpenter, you are likely to pay that person a premium. That is what boundaryless jobs are all about. They are individual versions of what digital businesses are trying to do. Market shapers redefine markets and their own capabilities continuously.

Think of boundaryless jobs like Lego blocks that can be added to create new dimensions to the role. Boundaryless jobs can be crafted in two ways:

1. Adjacencies: In case of an 'adjacency', there are commonalities that make it easy for a person to move from one function to another. For example, someone working as a compensation specialist could leverage their analytical ability to also understand some other elements of finance. The adjacency is created by the core skill of analytical thinking that is common to compensation and finance.

2. Leaps: Encouraging people to use online courses to build their skills in a completely different function would be an example of a leap. Someone in brand management building skills that help in understanding the supply chain would be an example of a leap.

Adjacencies and leaps can be created by working across sectors or in related industries. Working at different points of the supply chain in one industry, say telecom, can give a marketing or sales (or any other function) professional a broader understanding of the sector and the role marketing plays, and how it depends on the size of the firm, its market share or profitability. Working with a telecom provider and then a handset maker is another possibility of broadening one's value to an employer.

Working across geographical boundaries offers exposure to different cultures and markets. This can be a priceless perspective to gain at every stage of one's career.

Automating Continuous Feedback

Case: Dockabl's app

In October 2019, in a product design war room, the Dockabl team arrived at a pivotal conclusion, to build a new app that they would call Clink. The app would make it easy for people to get feedback from their colleagues. Feedback, if done well, can dramatically improve productivity and employee engagement. It helps people build their skills.

The insights came from primary research done with 20,000 active users over two years. They supplemented this with fifty in-person interviews done as they built the prototype. One of the key asks was to make the feedback process simple and on platforms that support integration with other workflows.

Feedback is valuable when it is accepted and available in real time. It must provide actionable insights. Continuous performance remained an inadequately solved challenge for HR tech firms. There is a need to build a culture of sharing feedback to encourage continuous performance.

Clink was an app built to solve the fundamental human need to continuously become better at one's profession. Becoming better at anything depends on getting feedback that can be in the form of encouragement or course-correction. In the post-pandemic scenario, it is even more valuable as a B2B productivity tool.

'Hybrid Jobs' and 'Purple Squirrels'

A boundaryless job builds on adjacencies and one leap skill. Hybrid jobs often combine multiple leap skills (often across multiple disciplines) which often seem like polar opposites. They combine technical expertise with soft skills. It is a combination of left-brain and right-brain competencies.*

This combination of the right- and left-brain competencies makes these jobs much harder to automate. While 42 per cent of all jobs can be automated, only 12 per cent of hybrid jobs can be automated. Take, for instance, app development. These apps need coders who not only write the code but can also design the User Experience (UX) and User Interface (UI) and understand how to market the app given budget constraints and a very competitive scenario.

These hybrid jobs are becoming precious. Marketing managers who know SQL, for example, make 41 per cent more money than those who do not. Hybrid jobs will grow by 21 per cent over the next decade, more than twice the 10 per cent growth rate of the job market overall, according to Burning Glass, which has been tracking these jobs since 2015.[11]

People who combine the critical thinking of STEM (Science Tech Engineering and Math) and creative problem-solving that we generally associate with the liberal arts are of great value. Recruiters call individuals who possess these skills 'purple squirrels'. Take, for instance, a marketing professional who not only knows how to build a brand, but also understands data strategy and SEO. This purple squirrel

*A 'competency' is a combination of knowledge skills and attitudes that go into making someone visibly and measurably more proficient at a task.

could probably give the creative team a few tips on how to use Photoshop and Premier Pro to edit the video. Using Augmented Reality (AR) to create amazing experiences in the storefront would come easy to this purple squirrel.

Would the Leader Need to Be a Polymath?

I have always been fascinated by Leonardo da Vinci. The Italian polymath lived during the Renaissance. He had a wide range of interests, from drawing, painting, sculpture and architecture to science, music, mathematics, engineering, literature, anatomy, geology, astronomy, botany, paleontology, and cartography. He is hailed as one of the greatest painters of all time, even though only fifteen of his paintings survive.

A polymath usually excels in at least three seemingly unrelated fields. Maya Angelou excelled as a poetess, playwright, author, singer, composer, dancer, actor, filmmaker, journalist, polyglot, historian and activist.[12]

Skill Building Could be the Biggest Perk the Employer Offers

Amazon will spend $700 million over six years turning warehouse floor workers into IT technicians and low-level coders into data scientists. As robots get better at doing various jobs in the warehouse, the workers who learn new skills will continue in Amazon.

They will retrain about 100,000 employees by 2025. A programme called Amazon Career Choice pays 95 per cent of the tuition and fees for certificates and degrees in high-demand fields such as nursing, work that could take staffers outside

> of Amazon. It is no longer about disappearing jobs but about having skills that are marketable—whether the market for the skills is inside Amazon or outside.
>
> When the shelf-life of skills is ever diminishing, businesses must start viewing skill building as a talent-retention device.

Could the new workplace see the rise of a leader who is a polymath?[13] Someone who is comfortable balancing the polarities of multiple disciplines and able to juggle the short term and long term? A leader who can look within as easily as look at the world outside?

Organisations have to continuously refine their business models, create new products and services and find new markets. The speed of business growth is constrained by the skill base inside organisations.

Skills and Education—Both Must Shift

The world of work continues to change. The way we manufacture, hire, sell and innovate are all different from how it has been done for a century. The changes in our world today come from the convergence of several shifts. It is easy to understand the link between skills, technology and education to the world of work. But some other shifts, like wealth distribution, are harder to link directly to that world. It is never a straightforward cause-and-effect but a complex web of forces that impacts the world of work directly and indirectly.

Inequities can impact access to healthcare, nutrition and access to digital connectivity to name a few connections. The impact of the pandemic on global wealth distribution is yet to be understood. So many school-going children are learning at home during the most formative years of their lives, deprived of interaction with other children, for instance. The impact of this will be felt when these children join the job market.

Over the past decade, wealth distribution has been concentrated in the US and China. The United States is home to 40 per cent of dollar millionaires worldwide. In 2019, China overtook the United States this year to become the country with most people in the top 10 per cent of global wealth distribution. The United States added 675,000 newcomers (about 50 per cent) to the millionaires list. Japan and China added 150,000 each while Australia lost 124,000 millionaires following a fall in average wealth. In India, 78 per cent of the adult population has wealth below $10,000. India has 827,000 adults in the top 1 per cent of global wealth holders with almost 1,800 people having more than $100 million.[14]

Shrinking Shelf Life of Skills

The workforce in India will grow from 473 million to 600 million by 2022, with barely 10 per cent of the jobs being in the organised sector. It is a workforce heavily dominated by men. About 67 per cent women graduates in rural India do not work. They will need skills—not jobs. If they have skills, they will find opportunities in either the organised sector or the unorganised. Or even turn into entrepreneurs who create jobs for others.[15]

Exponential technological change resulting from AI and automation, coupled with the growing talent pool and the

A Vision for Education

Educator 4.0's role should foster a mindset and culture around integrating multiple skills among both students and faculty. Adopting an integrative-discipline approach can make this possible. The *integrative-discipline* approach focuses on the ability to bring together not only technical and soft skills but also on tying together multiple and diverse disciplines to offer a broad solution. The Educator 4.0 is expected to play a key role in creating a suitable environment for the design and implementation of an *integrative discipline*-based curriculum.

Source: 2019 Deloitte Dean's Summit

gig workforce, will likely shrink the shelf life of skills, due to which the nature of jobs will change. A vast majority of the 4 million jobs in India's IT and ITES industry today will likely change over the next five years.

Some roles, like data entry operators, financial analysts, telemarketers, customer service executives, computer support and retail sales, are getting automated. The jobs that are now emerging need individuals to have the ability to continuously learn and challenge their own views.

The McKinsey Global Institute predicts that up to one-third of the American workforce will have to switch to new occupations by 2030. Already, more jobs involve working with advanced software or machines, even in fields that might not have traditionally required digital acumen.

Employers, right from corporates to the armed forces, now look for adaptability, cultural competence, 360-degree thinking, intellectual curiosity and empathy when they hire someone. Hard skills tend to be deep but narrow. Their half-life is getting shorter. The more specific and concrete the skills, the more they are prone to being automated or significantly transformed by advanced technologies such as AI, making it necessary for workers to be flexible enough to keep adapting to continuing changes in the workplace.

Retirement Is a Century-old Concept

Retirement, or the practice of leaving one's job or ceasing to work after reaching a certain age, has been around since around the eighteenth century. Older people would slow down assembly lines and were prone to falling sick more often. If the nature of work has changed drastically, does it still make sense to have someone retired based on their birthday or should it be based on their ability (and willingness) to contribute?

What is the right age for a person to retire? Should retirement be a function of someone having relevant skills? Is retirement a function of one's bank balance? Should the age of retirement be common across jobs or should it be a combination of the person's skills and motivation to continue working? Is retirement driven by the need to carve out opportunities for the next generation, or is it a function of the employer's liquidity? Should men and women have a common age for retirement?

It Is a Complex Equation

Retirement is usually the age at which certain benefits like superannuation and, in many countries, some form of state pension, come into the picture. Economists usually consider the demographic mix, average cost of healthcare, life expectancy, nature of profession, supply and demand of the skill etc. while deciding the retirement age.

Retirement is at fifty-five in Sri Lanka and fifty-nine in Bangladesh. In Libya, you would have to be seventy to retire. Men and women retire at sixty-six in Australia. The retirement age in China currently is sixty for men and fifty-five for female civil servants and fifty for female workers. Vietnam and Venezuela have fifty-five as the retirement age for women and sixty for men.

In some professions there is no age for retirement. The oldest serving prime minister of India was Morarji Desai (eighty-one years). The oldest member of parliament was Rishang Keishing who was ninety-four when he passed away in August 2017.

1. A hundred-year-old question: Lynda Gratton, professor of Management Practice at London Business School, speaks about the '100-year life'. Half of the babies born in countries like the UK, the US, Japan, Germany, Italy, France, Canada in 2007 or later will live to be between 102 and 107.[16]

That, of course, means that we need to rethink retirement, because most people will not be able to stretch out their savings and pensions so far. So, people will have to plan to earn enough to fund their life, assuming they will live to be a hundred. It is not that difficult to imagine if you consider that the life expectancy of Indians in 1947 was approximately thirty-two years. In 2012, it was sixty-five years and it is hovering at about seventy now.[17]

Dr Olivia Mitchell, a professor at the University of Pennsylvania's Wharton School of Business says actuaries (the people trying to figure out how long beneficiaries will live) are now projecting that people entering the workforce could live up to 125 years.[18]

2. Work is a source of identity: Work contributes to improved mental and physical health. During the lockdown, people were isolated in their own homes. While work continued through email and video calls, what people really craved for was the human connection. Having coffee with colleagues is a different experience when it is done together in a café or even around the worktable. Watching colleagues sipping coffee in little tiled boxes on the computer screen is no different from the security officer of a prison keeping an eye on the inmates while sipping coffee alone.

Technology allows work to be sliced and diced like a pizza and shipped across the world. The scattered pieces of work are then reassembled by someone before being sold to the consumer. If the nature of work changes, it is only logical that a new breed of workers will emerge who can work in this fragmented manner. Work is a source of meaning and identity and it is no surprise that, post retirement, individuals suffer from mental health breakdowns as much as physical health challenges.

The real value of work is not just economic. It is also psychological. What we do is an important element of our identity. Continuing to 'work' even after retirement is a simple path to a longer life with a lower risk of dementia, depression and obesity. The desire to 'not retire' is not just economic but also psychological. But finding work may be solely dependent on having skills that the marketplace needs and values.

3. The employed and the vulnerable: The labour market has always had two sectors—organised and unorganised. Retirement is a luxury available only to the workers in the organised sector.

The majority of the blue-collar workers are in the unorganised sector. The lockdown laid bare their stark vulnerability, with no health insurance or savings to fall back on. What was not talked about enough was the plight of 15 million freelancers who do some form of white-collar jobs. They operate on a similar vulnerability—low margins of savings and no health insurance—and the lockdown pushed many of them to the brink of poverty. The top six countries accounting for the majority of online workers are India, Bangladesh, United States, Pakistan, Philippines and the United Kingdom.[19]

4. The maze at the end of the tunnels: The only way to work (even if no one is employing you) is to have skills that are valuable. We will have to constantly learn new skills and keep trying out many different projects. Some of them may take off and others may not.

Without stable incomes and health-care coverage, freelancers are as vulnerable as the illegal immigrants in the world of work.

Being an entrepreneur today is infinitely easier. Technology is creating new possibilities. Mastanamma, 107 years old, was YouTube's oldest star, with a million subscribers who enjoyed watching her cook.

On my podcast, 'Dreamers and Unicorns', Ravi Venkatesan, ex-chairman of Microsoft India likened careers in his father's generation to tunnels—you entered an organisation when you found a job and emerged only when you retired (from the same employer).

We may be at the start of an S-curve where automation is going to create jobless growth. There will be exciting opportunities for a few highly skilled workers, while the less skilled may face a bleak horizon. People nearing forty must seriously think of their portfolio of marketable skills because, after that, with each passing year, a person's cost outweighs the value their work creates. Younger people are more eager to work and certainly cost a lot less.

From the mid-Nineties, job-hopping became more common. People switched employers. So, instead of one tunnel, the person navigated a few different tunnels throughout one's career. In the digital world, careers are full of twists and turns and looks more like a maze. One has to think of life as a series of projects lasting a few years and then do something different. Just as organisations have to keep reinventing themselves or die, individuals have to stay relevant or else wither away without stable jobs.

Navigating the S-Curves

It is a great time to be an entrepreneur

NASSCOM's report on the 'Indian Tech Startup Ecosystem: Leading Tech in the 20s' underlines how the Indian startup ecosystem continues to expand and how various elements of the ecosystem are coming together in a symphony to create an orchestra of innovation—right from government support (state and centre), evolution of the investor landscape, increase in participation from corporates, growth of national digital infrastructure, to incredible global exposure. The startup base in India continues to grow at 12–15 per cent, and was at 9,300 startups before the pandemic.

'Careers are not about education and previous experience anymore.'

'Education does not guarantee the kind of work you will do,' says Jayesh, my Uber cab driver. He graduated as a civil engineer from Nagpur. He was working with the Jaypee group and got laid off after eight years. He moved to Mumbai and his friend told him to apply to Uber. He started driving on days when he did not have job interviews to go to. After seven months of going to job interviews without success, he has now started enjoying driving. 'I always liked driving. I sit in an air-conditioned cab and get to talk to interesting people. On the construction site, I had to stand in the sun. This is better and pays almost the same.'

The pandemic would have been harsh on Jayesh, with commuters avoiding cabs.

While COVID-19 was hard on the startups that were nearing the end of their funding cycle, there is no doubt that entrepreneurs will be back. They may have a larger talent pool to pick from, given the number of people who were left without jobs in the organised sector.

The emergence of startup hubs, availability of deep tech and a greater risk appetite among the youth, who are inspired by success stories of entrepreneurs, creates a heady concoction that continues to draw more and more people. India is the third largest startup hub in the world, with twenty-four 'unicorns' (a company valued at more than a billion dollars).

More than 250 venture capital (VC) firms make it easy for the right idea to get funded. There are incubators and accelerators. Schools in Delhi are experimenting with offering entrepreneurship classes to students in high school. There is no doubt that this is the golden time to be an entrepreneur in India.

Career 3.0 Means Navigating Multiple S-Curves

Career 1.0

In Career 1.0, educational qualifications defined the kind of employment one found. Employment was for life. A qualified engineer remained an engineer all through life. An engineer could change employers and join another firm, but only as an engineer, though maybe at a higher salary or a greater job responsibility.

Career 2.0

Career 2.0 looks something like Jishnu Dasgupta's career track. He graduated from XLRI Jamshedpur, a b-school. He got a job offer on campus from ITC. He joined them and enjoyed his role in sales and marketing. While on campus, Jishnu used to play the bass guitar for the campus band, Bodhi Tree.

A few years of work convinced Jishnu that he wanted to be a full-time musician. He quit ITC and joined the indie band Swarathma as a bass guitar player. This is now his full-time job. The band meets at a studio every morning to rehearse for concerts and to write new songs. 'It is no different from doing a job.'

In Career 2.0, there is the possibility of an individual moving to a completely different profession that the person may/may not have formal credentials for. But the person builds up the skill and expertise by learning on his own.

Career 3.0

Career 3.0 goes something like this. Freelancers bring all their skills to the marketplace. A person can work with competing buyers for each of the skills and get paid at different price points. When an engineer quits a job to open up a restaurant, they are on their way to Career 2.0. Maybe that person learns to play the guitar, and starts teaching the neighbourhood kids math and music. Maybe, one day, the videos that he had been posting on Instagram and YouTube start bringing in revenue and that completes the transition to Career 3.0. In Career 3.0, the person brings in all learning, formal and informal, to monetise skills in different marketplaces.

The way to manage these transitions is to build your life as a series of 'S-curves'. When you learn a new skill, any skill, you feel that progress is painfully slow. When I enrolled in a class to learn photo-editing, I was clearly the oldest person in the institute. Every professor was younger than me. The first few classes were embarrassing, to say the least. I was the slowest learner in the class. I had to go back home and spend hours practising the skills. I must confess there were days when I had wanted to quit.

As time went by (and I persisted), I moved to the second stage of the S-curve. I started enjoying the classes. I would occasionally be praised for the new things I was creating. And as I got better at the software, I was often able to teach my peers a trick or two (and learn many more from them). I should have quit after the course was over, but I did not.

I did something weird. I enrolled for another class at the institute. I signed up for video-editing. I am at the first stage of the S-curve as far as this skill is concerned. It is frustrating. I assumed that I would find video-editing easier, what with having understood photo-editing. But no, this is a different animal. I wonder if I should have stuck to photo-editing. I could have mastered one software. I think I missed the thrill that comes from moving across stages of the S-curve.

In retrospect, the pattern is familiar to anyone who has passed through a career transition—becoming an employee after being an entrepreneur, or the other way round. I became a freelancer after many years in the corporate world. As an entrepreneur, you don't move up from stage one to stage two of the learning S-curve, because this is a 'fluid environment'. You have to keep learning different things every single day. Here are three lessons I learned:

1. Adapt: You career journey is made up of some factors within your control, especially the amount of effort you put in. Much depends on how you adapt to the new scenarios and grab the S-curves that are in the early stages. But then you also inherit 30–40 per cent of your personality based on a combination of genetics and also the environment in which you grew up. Then there are factors outside of your control, e.g. the family, country and the year you were born in. Being able to adapt to opportunities helps. That is within your control.

2. Have some hobbies: We pursue hobbies because they fit in with our natural inclinations. But, in these times, it is also possible to monetise your hobbies, especially through digital platforms, e.g. by becoming a professional YouTuber or Instagrammer. These were not options that were available earlier. Try them out. Hobbies like reading literary fiction help you learn about emotions. That is invaluable in a world where emotions form the basis of so many professions that are just starting out on the S-curve.

3. Build your skills, before you look for passion: Unless you can drive a car reasonably well, it is impossible to be passionate about it. Your enthusiasm is overshadowed by the fear of hurting someone on the road or getting hurt yourself (maybe both). As you build your skills, you can enjoy driving without getting stressed every time you see someone driving towards you. The same goes for any skill that you learn. You cannot be passionate about doing something without being reasonably ahead on the S-curve.

Your career graph is the biggest research project you will undertake. The more self-awareness you have, the more wisely you can choose opportunities that come your way and the ones you seek out. Once I discovered that I had a sweet tooth, it was easy for me to zero down on the options available and know that it was dark chocolate I craved. Career is all about discovering dark chocolate with each new S-curve.

References

1. Everlane's culture was inconsistent with the image it was selling said its employees. https://www.nytimes.com/2020/07/26/fashion/everlane-employees-ethical-clothing.html
2. Adobe could've become irrelevant in the era of the cloud. By embracing the change and killing its still profitable business, Adobe entered its next S-curve. https://www.engadget.com/2013-05-09-adobe-creative-or-cloudy.html
3. Indian business houses have always played a significant role in the world of work in India. https://www.rediff.com/money/report/special-in-india-15-of-the-top-20-business-groups-are-family-owned/20160818.htm
4. When the government is using the taxpayers' money to bail out airlines as an industry, it raises many questions on whether the current challenge was brought out by board decisions by leaders. Without a bailout 750,000 jobs will be at stake and no politician can afford that in an election year. https://www.theguardian.com/business/2020/mar/18/america-airlines-bailout-shareholders-coronavirus
5. Air India net loss at all-time high of Rs 8,550 crore in FY19, says aviation minister https://www.businesstoday.in/current/corporate/air-india-to-post-highest-ever-net-loss-in-fy19-says-aviation-minister/story/391590.html
6. Medical devices can be used by hackers to cause harm. https://a16z.com/2020/07/22/security-hacking-medical-devices/

7. While layoffs in the formal sector get more media coverage, the biggest tragedies are with people in the informal sector. https://scroll.in/article/959485/battered-by-covid-19-lockdown-indias-formal-sector-is-resorting-to-massive-layoffs-and-pay-cuts
8. The bigger firms tried to avoid layoffs by using furloughs, wage freezes and paycuts. https://www.business-standard.com/article/companies/indian-it-firms-set-to-defer-annual-wage-hike-plans-but-say-no-layoffs-120041701338_1.html
9. Platforms connecting companies that are hiring with people who are getting laid off. https://economictimes.indiatimes.com/tech/ites/accenture-verizon-and-other-cos-build-hiring-platform-to-connect-businesses/articleshow/75147945.cms
10. Canadian watchdog Citizen lab found that India is becoming an outsourcing hub even for hackers. https://www.livemint.com/technology/tech-news/how-india-became-a-hack-for-hire-hub-11595768182875.html
11. These Hybrid Jobs are super specialised jobs and are growing at a rapid pace. They are specialist roles e.g. data scientist and require a wide set of skills from different fields (design, user experience, data analysis etc). https://www.burning-glass.com/wp-content/uploads/hybrid_jobs_2019_final.pdf
12. This book provides an excellent perspective on who is a polymath and what makes them so. Waqas Ahmed, *The Polymath: Unlocking the Power of Human Versatility*, John Wiley and Sons, 2019.
13. Michael Arakis and I connected on LinkedIn over a shared interest in the subject of polymathy. https://youtu.be/k_u_zIliodc
14. The Credit Suisse Wealth Report 2019 describes the shifts. https://www.credit-suisse.com/about-us/en/reports-research/global-wealth-report.html
15. Wheebox India Skills Report 2019. https://wheebox.com/india-skills-report.htm
16. The challenge http://www.100yearlife.com/the-challenge/
17. India's record since independence. https://blogs.wsj.com/indiarealtime/2013/08/15/indias-record-since-independence/
18. If longevity increases to 125 years then retirement as a concept has to end. https://www.wsj.com/articles/the-end-of-retirement
19. The freelancers and gig workers are the most vulnerable segment of the workforce. https://indiamicrofinance.com/freelancers-income-2018.html

4

It Is All About Human Relationships

The virus tends to kill the weak and the vulnerable. Some researchers describe the scenario as TUNA i.e. Turbulent, Uncertain, Novel and Ambiguous. Each one of these conditions renders much of the wisdom of frameworks and models inadequate since there is no past data to analyse. The leader has to create a narrative that is powerful enough to energise the ecosystem because the organisation does not exist in isolation. The new organisation will be built on relationships and emotions and should not be a transactional clinical workplace that everyone hates but works in to pay the bills.

This is our chance to build a workplace we own and love.

One of the most popular questions leaders are asked during a crisis is, 'What is keeping you awake at night?'

We seem to have imbibed from the environment that during a crisis we must stay awake and fret about the issue. Research actually shows us that during a crisis, it is important for leaders to be well-rested so that they are able to think through issues. Their decisions should not be knee-jerk reactions. Poorly written responses or becoming irritable when asked questions, leading to erosion of trust is often traced to lack of at least seven hours of deep sleep. Lack of sleep makes our reactions slow down. We start looking at broad strokes and miss the nuances and have a much lower ability to control our emotions.

A tweet worth $14 billion: Who knows it better than Elon Musk? Tesla's share price has surged in 2020, taking the electric carmaker's value close to $100 billion, a mark that would trigger a bonus payment of hundreds of millions of dollars to the entrepreneur. Putting in 120-hour weeks month after month resulted in Elon tweeting that Tesla was overpriced, leading to a $14 billion drop in its price. It must be the most expensive tweet resulting from lack of sleep.[1]

Even decent leaders are more likely to engage in unethical or abusive behaviour if they are sleep-deprived. Unsurprisingly, there is a strong link between having good quality sleep and good quality leaders—and lacking both can be particularly destructive. Sleep tends to act like a cleanser of toxins that accumulate in the brain and prevent us from remembering information clearly or being able to access it when needed.[2]

A well-rested brain may be the best answer to these novel setting in which we are living now. It requires the well thought through 'System 2' response. People who do not come in well rested can create toxic cultures.

When you ask people, 'What's the opposite of fragile?,' they tend to say robust, resilient, adaptable, solid, strong. That's not it. The opposite of fragile is something that gains from disorder.

Nassim Nicholas Taleb

Stop Thinking 'When Will It Go Back to Normal?'

One of the most commonly asked questions during a crisis, 'When will things go back to normal?' We want to go back to the familiar environment where we had figured out our life. Familiarity is comforting because we can operate with just our instinct. When we think of the future, we tend to think of it as a slightly modified version of our current setting (i.e. Before Corona) that we have always had. Maybe we will need to wear masks to work. Maybe offices will be emptier than before. Think of all the 'experts' who had predicted in the early days of the pandemic that it would take several weeks for things to return to normal. More than six months later, nothing is yet normal. The reality is that the best futurists and scenario planning experts had no clue how to deal with this.

Hybrid models of going digital: Some of us recreate the physical world online. While there are others who repurpose this as a new way of doing things which have only a faint resemblance with the pre-lockdown office. All of us are novice-experts trying to make sense of this novel world of work. It will be hard to predict how people will behave. They will probably make choices and then change their mind many times over till they find something they adopt. Don't be in a hurry to declare that you have discovered the 'new normal'.

In 2020, more than 171,000 people from 164 countries, regions and territories attended the nearly week-long Consumer Electronics Show (CES) before the pandemic set in. The 2021 version will be done online. Would that mean that more people will be able to attend the show since it does not need any travel or would it mean that the coolest tech will be used to reimagine CES?

Leadership behaviour: Should a leader cry in public? The answer to that a few years back was, 'I don't want someone who cries, to have the permission to press the nuclear button'. Today the people say, 'I don't trust the nuclear button with someone who does not cry.' What a shift it is in what is acceptable behaviour as a leader. Leaders must lead with empathy and build a different level of trust with employees. Purpose and social impact must shape the decisions leaders take as tech gets more and more embedded in businesses.

Don't be in a hurry to declare that you have discovered the 'new normal'.

Survival of the most adaptable: Health has always been something that individuals have had to worry about. But in the post-pandemic world, issues of health, sanitation and safety will become far bigger concerns. Checking everyone who enters the workplace could mean long queues. We will need to rethink elevator etiquette and norms. Maybe we will need to rethink air-conditioning in the workplace. The role of facilities management teams and the skills they will need to add to their team to be able to operate in this new setting will change. Fear of infection could mean smaller lines in office cafeterias. Thinking of colleagues as possible sources of a life-threatening condition could change behavioural norms at work. This may be a signal that we need to rethink the norms of work, the people who will do the work and of course, workplace norms itself.

Many luxury hotels have lost 70 per cent of the business that came from international travellers. After a brief set back, hotel chains like Accor, Hilton and Conrad listed in-house restaurants on food-delivery platforms Swiggy and Zomato. Taj Hotels began offering takeaways. Sheraton Grand in Bangalore began offering laundry services. Being adaptable is the key to survival.

Iconic Brands Go Bankrupt Too

From automobiles to showbiz, every sector is experiencing convulsive changes. The recording company HMV, started in 1921, had iconic musicians like the Beatles and still filed for bankruptcy not once, but for the second time in December 2018. Its failure was attributed to the 'tsunami of challenges' retail was facing. Digital music revenue overtook sales of physical formats like CDs and records for the first time in 2012. Since then, online shopping, downloads and streaming provided by platforms such as Amazon, Spotify and Netflix, have continued to eat into the sales of physical music. We do not need to buy DVDs or CDs to watch a film or listen to music. Personal libraries of movies and music are bound to be limited. A monthly subscription for the price of one DVD can get one a month's worth of unlimited access to digitally mastered content.

Paul McGowan, executive chairman of HMV said: 'Even an exceptionally well-run and much-loved business such as HMV cannot withstand the tsunami of challenges facing UK retailers over the last twelve months on top of such a dramatic change in consumer behaviour in the entertainment market.'[3]

Blurred Lines of the Workplace

When businesses had to shut down offices and let everyone work from home during the lockdown, they tried to replicate office norms in the new setting. Then it was discovered that not everyone had high-speed connectivity and a quiet place from which to join endless video calls with colleagues. People reluctantly let colleagues get a view of their home—a complete breakdown of privacy and choice. The crisis resulted in the employers of 4 million IT workers in India having to make the transition to work from home, in the shortest possible time!

India's largest IT employer Tata Consultancy Services (TCS) used the crisis to rethink where work could be done even after the lockdown was lifted. It decided that 75 per cent of its 4.48 lakh employees globally (including 350,000 in India) would work from home, up from the industry average of 20 per cent today. The new model required only 25 per cent of its employees to be in the office.[4]

IMPLEMENTATION CHALLENGE

Creating a Business Continuity Plan

- What investment in technology will enable EVERY employee to work remotely and still be as effective as being physically present in the office? Start with functions like sales and HR that are high touch.
- Ask an insurance provider to validate the risk assessment for your business and see what they come up with that you missed.
- What would it take to move every employee from a Work From Home (WFH) to a Work From Anywhere (WFA) model?

Challenge Your Assumptions about Your Business Model

Can you wake up one morning and decide that you want to compete with Usain Bolt's timing at the Olympics? Incumbents are faced with such a challenge. They are working with legacy systems, inadequately skilled workforce and a leadership team that is unable to visualise what it means to compete with a digital born company. Nike decided to create a direct-to-consumer model of selling from a model that had almost 40,000 retailers.

The pandemic crisis has challenged many business models and supply chains. Sophistication of components, manufacturing processes that require specialists and the need for flexible capacity has led to the practice of subcontracting. Supply chains were built with assumptions of cheap labour, and low cost of logistics. Businesses were built on the assumption that it would be impossible to replace China as a low-cost manufacturing hub for the world.

Apple had asked its suppliers to manufacture a low-cost iPhone in the first half of 2020. The Foxconn complex in Zhengzhou employs 200,000 workers. Many of those workers come from other towns in the vicinity. When they were asked to stay away as the virus spread through China in early January 2020, the supply chain was broken. Three-fourths of Apple's top suppliers have at least one manufacturing unit in China.[5]

When India banned TikTok (and fifty-eight other Chinese apps) on grounds of 'national security', TikTok called it unfair. China has banned Facebook, Twitter and Google and replaced it with their versions of these services. That is non-negotiable, says China. Yet they wanted the Chinese apps to be restored. What if China offered to house mirror sites for Amazon Web Services data centres? Would that impact the buyer's trust?

TikTok's parent company, Bytedance, has tried to dissociate from the 'Chinese' part of the company by changing the name from Douyin as TikTok is called inside China. TikTok is based in Silicon Valley and had an American CEO in Kevin Mayer who was hired from an organisation that is as American as it gets—Walt Disney. (Mayer, who was the head of Disney Plus became the CEO of TikTok in May 2020 and resigned in August 2020.) But TikTok's founder is a Chinese national and the engineering team is in China, subject to direct Chinese state influences.

This may be a good time to also question the assumptions we had about our customers and consumers. Estimate what is the inventory you will need along the value chain (including the spare parts and stock kept for after-sales) and you will get a sense of how vulnerable your business continuity plan is. The recession may lead to a new set of behaviours about spending. Some businesses may need to invest more heavily in their technical infrastructure, data gathering and production technologies, cyber security etc.

A US-based global giant in the consumer goods space created a global business services hub in Hyderabad. Letting the employees work from home during the crisis has encouraged them to ship more of the jobs to lower cost locations like India. Could this be a new surge of business for the outsourcing industry or will it mean businesses will try to keep their supply chain closer geographically?

IMPLEMENTATION CHALLENGE

Create a Risk Map

- Where do you have high dependence on a few firms?
- Create a product risk map. What if your biggest product or service is not available? What would make your customer's work continue uninterrupted?
- What new tasks will need to be added to the existing roles to ensure hygiene, safety, cybersecurity etc.? What new roles will need to be created that are not already present?

Build a Platform

The seven biggest companies—Apple, Microsoft, Alphabet (Google's parent company), Amazon, Facebook, Alibaba and Tencent—had a combined market capitalisation of $6.3 trillion in January 2020. They were all platforms.

Platforms like Airbnb, Didi Chuxing, Ola, Uber, TapChief, Internshala, Freelancer, TaskRabbit Dunzo, Zomato etc. have used platform strategies to launch the gig (or sharing) economy. They enable transactions. Apple iOS, Google Android, SAP DreamWeaver, IBM Watson etc. are 'innovation platforms' because they facilitate many other innovations that can be built on these platforms. Some like Amazon, Apple, Google, Microsoft etc. combine the ability to innovate and carry out transactions. They are hybrids. Many of the hybrid platforms offered cutting-edge tech that can be used to create new business models.[6]

IMPLEMENTATION CHALLENGE

Using a Platform

- What new product or service could you create using one of the transaction platforms or innovation platforms?
- KFC, Pizza Hut, and Taco Bell in China focus on customisation and localisation to maintain their market dominance. The menu on KFC's app suggests items to customers based on their ordering patterns and local demographics. That cuts the time taken to serve the customer. Data related to transactions

by each store enables better forecasting and lowers waste. Better margins mean the stores do not need to raise prices. Can you implement this technology for your cafeteria to avoid queues?

Use Constraints to Your Advantage

Constraints often encourage people to be creative. Panera is an American chain store of bakery-café fast casual restaurants with over 2,000 locations in US and Canada. They were impacted by the pandemic and suffered lower revenues. During one of their brainstorming meetings, the leadership team spoke about the challenges of buying fruit, vegetables and dairy during the lockdown. Panera Grocery then became strategised how to deliver a part of what they were procuring to the consumer. From idea to execution was done in a fortnight. This was not something that they had ever done, but they had not faced a pandemic either.

- What could your business do to solve a problem that you are aware of? Do it as a way of making your business more agile.

Challenge Your Assumptions about the Workforce

Talent acquisition as a function is in a tizzy, with many employers having frozen or slowed down hiring altogether. During the pandemic, Microsoft has almost halved its job openings in three weeks and its subsidiary LinkedIn reduced vacancies. Google put a freeze on hiring for the rest of 2020. They had hired 20,000 employees in 2019.

What does a talent acquisition team do when external hiring is on hold? This may be a great opportunity to build relationships, understand future trends in talent and build the brand. Several industries like hospitality and entertainment are letting go of their top talent. This may be the time to cherry pick and engage such people with the brand.

Compensation and benefits teams could use the opportunity to re-craft the choices employees may have in a post-pandemic world. Healthcare, insurance and upskilling are likely to be top of the mind issues for people returning to work. Responding to that could be a great opportunity to delight.

IMPLEMENTATION CHALLENGE

- Ask the talent acquisition team to identify startups or other businesses that are letting go some of their employees. This is a great time to hire talent you would otherwise have no access to. They could provide a perspective that someone from your peer group would never have.
    - For example, with hundreds of journalists and content creators out of jobs, it is time to create a kickass team that can create content for your website. And teach your employees to create content.
    - Could the skills of someone with deep experience in hospitality coach the sales team on relationship selling?
- McDonald's uses an AI algorithm to serve digital menus that continuously change in response to

factors such as time of the day, days of the week, restaurant traffic and weather. If you hired someone from that team, what would they recommend doing in your business?

- Domino's uses computer vision technology in its Australian and New Zealand stores to do a quality check on every pizza. Where could you use this technology in your business to create value? You could do the same with any technology like 3D printing or face recognition etc.

Rethinking Time and Space in Workplaces

Norms and policies have to be redesigned for the new workplace. That means taking a fresh look at the assumptions that lie behind our choices. In a multi-locational business, having a city strategy or a country strategy would be more appropriate and create the flexibility needed to respond to black swan events in future. By definition, a black swan event describes the disproportionate role of high profile, hard-to-predict, and rare events that are beyond the realm of normal expectations in history, science, finance and technology.

During a crisis we usually make three kinds of errors:

1. Accurately estimating how long something will take to be completed.
2. Estimating cost of resources and alternatives.
3. The extent of disruption.

In the world of work, workers and workplaces, the digital tsunami has already driven several shifts. Whether it is in the business model or the way they build the product or service or their go-to-market strategy, digital technology is at the heart of it. It enables them to scale globally and at a speed that was considered impossible in the erstwhile analogue world. Customer experiences are personalised and engaging. Technology and data are empowering brands to build direct, emotional relationships with consumers that are changing the way businesses operate forever. Customer-centricity is magnifying an organisation's structural, cultural and technological barriers that shape data management, customer experience delivery, and ultimately business success.

Questions to Ask When You Move Online

When we take any behaviour that has not been done online, it is a good opportunity to rethink the basics.

For example: Using video interviews to hire people

1. *What is the behaviour you wish to achieve?* Are you doing it so that neither interviewers nor candidates can travel to the office? Is it to eliminate human bias that is inevitable, for instance, the belief that 'a candidate from a top tier college is more likely to be successful in our firm'? In which case you could have picked any random student from the college and the outcome would not be impacted (unlikely). Is it to ensure the candidate is 'better' than the other existing team members? If so, how would you assess existing candidates to establish the benchmark? Or is it to establish a more diverse candidate pool to choose from?

2. *What tools can help you do that?* In the hiring example, using an algorithm with a set of rules can help improve

'cognitive diversity'* of the pool of candidates. What are the limitations of the tool? What are the possibilities? For example, a recording of an interview can be viewed at any time (asynchronous). Not having to travel anywhere can make the talent pool really wide.

3. *What are the new skills needed by the user?* That may involve training the interviewers to follow standardised questions in the interview, for starters. Many interviewers hate using standardised phrases.

4. *Think of the social elements:* Think of all the relationships that were using the in-person experience. What are the ways to build the human connect? What are the experiences that people will miss? For instance, reading a book on an app like Kindle could mean that the reader will miss the feel of turning a paper in the app, but it can be recreated. How can we build in the ability to share ideas, reviews and engage with other users to be able to build a user community?

5. *Would the considerations shift if the product was aimed at the enterprise or the individual employee?* Just as the online versus offline choice is meaningless, so is the enterprise versus employee debate. The product may be introduced by the enterprise, but if the employees find the experience cumbersome, it will fail to get traction. Think of it as E2E—enterprise to employee.

---

*How individuals think about and engage with new, uncertain, and complex situations.

IMPLEMENTATION CHALLENGE

Predicting What Customers and Employees Need Next

- Google uses AI to predict what people may be searching for. LinkedIn composes short responses in its mailbox. Netflix predicts what you are likely to enjoy watching given your viewing history. Amazon uses it to suggest your next purchase. Facebook uses it to feed you news that aligns with your political leanings. What can you predict about your employees' needs and aspirations? What HR tech will let you delight your employees?
- Twitter lets people compose an audio tweet. How can that feature be used by your talent acquisition team or the marketing team? LinkedIn lets you tell people how your name must be pronounced. How could that feature be used to improve the candidate experience?
- As Google starts using voice enabled search, it has changed the way people use search. On the web, we can get multiple possible search results to a query raised on Google. Using voice search we get a single response to a query. What if you put all data—sales, finance, supply chain, HR etc. in one big pool and use AI to simply answer any queries that may arise? That would probably be the new digital approach for businesses.

Engage the 'Creator Consumer' and 'Creator Employee'

In an interconnected world where everyone with a smart phone is creating content, social media is a way to create trust between your current and potential stakeholders. It is the way people engage with each other as they go about their daily life. Opinions, ideas, facts and fake news all rub shoulders to create a pot-pourri that has millions hooked. These millions include your employees, potential hires, board members and all stakeholders. It is giving everyone a voice that is hard to ignore. Unlike traditional media, this one is a two-way street. It is only by creating content that you can get the benefit of social media and that makes it very different from traditional.

It is a Way to Shape Your Brand Experience

Experiences shape brands. In the digital world, the organisation's brand is shaped by what people say about the organisation online. The pandemic forced many businesses to cut down on their workforce. What made news on social media was the way it was done. If it is not done for an employee's lack of integrity or violation of a code of conduct, separations are some of the biggest shapers of an organisation's brand.

In a connected world, even if an organisation doesn't say anything about itself, others will. That will shape the brand. Not being on social media is the equivalent of saying one does not know how to use the telephone. What is cooler than talking about your company on social media? Creating the most interesting and relevant experiences for the customers that gets them to share their experience online.

Frog Design offices in San Francisco have a flipchart next to the cubicle of a new hire labelled 'new frog in the well' where older hires are encouraged to stop by and discover one interesting piece of information about the new hire that they add to the flip chart (e.g. the person's hobbies). With each interaction the cumulative knowledge about the new hire keeps building up on the flipchart for everyone to read.

Germans call them 'geisterspiele' or 'ghost games'. They are played in empty stadiums and minus the cheering of the crowd. The soccer experience amid social-distancing rules has taken a beating. NBC Sports, Sky Sports and BT Sport are adding crowd sounds to their soccer broadcasts. Disney is offering its Florida Disney World Resort as an isolated bubble where NBA will play its basketball matches. The players are being put up in hotels where the shower heights can match the heights of the players. What the players will miss are the fans.

IMPLEMENTATION CHALLENGE

Is your marketing team savvy enough to qualify as a digital marketing team? Is social media marketing a part of your business plan?

Relevant and Interesting

Content is one of the most powerful way for individuals and brands to attract attention in a crowded world. The content must be interesting enough to stand out in the crowd and make the reader pause. Everyone speaks of short attention spans but fails to explain what makes someone binge watch the entire season of a show. This is the golden age of storytellers who can keep a distracted audience at the edge of their seat or couch! The organisation's employer brand is built by the leadership team's ability to create content which value adds to others. The talent brand of the organisation is built by the employees. It is important to build both. Enterprise and employee both need to learn to communicate on various social media platforms and shape the brand. It is E2E in the eyes of the readers.

I have found it a better approach to work with the leaders first to help them understand how social media works and the need for two-way communication and engagement. And then work with employees who have been using social media and support them on content creation etc.

In 2017, Ford partnered with a pizza company to check if customers would be interested in having their pizza delivered by an autonomous car. That company was Domino's. They have since been working on many such partnerships with self-driving cars and the customers want to try out what it means to get a driverless car come up and deliver a hot pizza. The look on the customer's face when the driverless car pulls up with the pizza is shared on social media. You can imagine what happened. Yes, the world paused and watched and shared the video—that is free marketing for Ford and the pizza company.[7]

What makes the story go viral? It needs to be relevant and interesting. Most people understand how to say something which is relevant. When millions of people create relevant information, it is the interesting story that gets our attention. In case of the Ford-Domino's story, it is not the technology but the human element of surprise and delight that goes viral.

You shape your reputation online by your digital presence. Every click, every swipe, every website you visit is part of the enormous set of data points that add up to your online reputation. But even as you shape it, what people say about you and your posts also adds to your reputation. Your future employers look up (often through agencies which carry out social media scanning) your social media presence (and most of it is publicly available) before you are even called for that interview.[8]

Tickle the Creative Gene

The iconic Apple ads are made by the agency TBWA. They launched Apple's first branded Instagram handle, to showcase the 'Shot on iPhone' community. The handle attracted five million followers in the first nine months, resulting in 2.5 million new instances of Instagrammers tagging images #ShotoniPhone. TBWA has its own cultural insights organisation (Backslash), its own strategic consulting practices (Disruption\Lab and Disruption Consulting), its own product design group (\Quantum and Q Lab), and its own innovation database (10x). No surprise that Apple ads go viral. Unless you are a Korean pop star, Momo. Then Momo's fans can make her videos trend more than an Apple launch event.

Jack Phan talks about the ability of Korean pop music fans ('stans' in the K-Pop world) to self-organise and taking over trends for the love of their idols—from hashtags and fan art to group orders, birthday events and beyond. Businesses can cultivate 'stans' and give them the content that they would love to make viral. Business leaders would do well to study this phenomenon.[9]

Should you let customers shape your brand on social media? For instance, Adidas lets customers play with the brand and have created separate Instagram and Twitter accounts to highlight the contributions of their influencers and customers called Adidas Originals. Interestingly, these accounts actually have more followers than the main accounts. 'We Are Originals' is the tagline Adidas uses to promote user-generated content. It also showcases unique partnerships with Instagram influencers. By creating content and messaging for each influencer they partner with, Adidas is able to foster a more genuine relationship between the brand, the influencer and their followers.

IMPLEMENTATION CHALLENGE

1. Identify opportunities for your users and employees to create content about your product or service or business. Ask employees to design a contest that would engage their colleagues. At the end of the year, the person who got the most responses can be rewarded.
2. Ask the employees to come up with ideas on how to build a social media strategy for your business. Invite some freelancers to work with you for a day and see the magic that happens.

3. Can you trust your employees enough to be able to let at least a few of them represent your organisation on social media? If a country can trust its citizens to manage the country's social media handle, I am sure your organisation can do it as well.

Create the Guidelines When You Hand Over Controls

Sweden allowed control of the country's official Twitter account, @Sweden, to one citizen each week. They ran this experiment for seven years. Their guidelines were simple:

'Do not violate Swedish law, do not promote commercial brands and do not present a security threat. Curators are also asked to mind their language, respect other people's views and refrain from sharing racist, sexist or homophobic sentiments.'[10]

This hyperconnected world now communicates in real-time through social media.

While you may not be able to always influence what others post about you, you can certainly be thoughtful about what you post on social media. Social media is not just a megaphone you use to announce your (or your company's) achievements to the world—it is, as most social media experts will tell you, where your customers, talent and competition come to listen and get a pulse of what is happening in your field, from the people who are influencing the domain.

In his book, *Be Social*, author Karthik Srinivasan shares a formula, which can help you make the most of social media by just spending fifty minutes on it. He suggests spending ten minutes to listen to the chatter on social platforms.

Another ten minutes should be spent sharing your own ideas and views. Spend another five minutes every day to connect with two or three different people in your network. Spend five minutes to listen and engage with others at five different times through the day.

The operative word in social media is 'social', not media. So, how does one get social?

IMPLEMENTATION IDEAS

Social media is very different from print media because it is two-way. Remember, whatever you say can be fact-checked by anyone even years later. There is no delete button on the internet. If you are seen as being narcissistic or pushing your own agenda, it slows your acceptance on social media (these rules often don't work with celebrities. If you are a celeb, skip this section).

Being spontaneous and authentic on social media builds trust. But it also heightens the possibility of errors.

Embrace the risk. Chances are that millions before you have made errors that are far worse than what you could make. To regain trust, acknowledge your error. People are reasonably forgiving if they see it as a one-off error. Understanding this paradox should be part of every leader's playbook. Here are some ideas to think about:

1. Understanding social media is an integral part of building your reputation: Relevant and interesting content is a great way to add value to readers. Towards this end, there are three Vs that any leader needs to master as a way of building employee engagement: video, visuals and voice. Building content that conveys your message in an engaging manner can be powerful. Ask for volunteers in your organisation who can reverse mentor you. They will be delighted.

2. Build social selling skills: Social selling always begins with social listening. This is an important way to know how stakeholders are impacting your reputation. People routinely comment about their leaders and company culture on sites like Glassdoor. Listening to the feedback and suggestions helps to build trust among employees and other observers. The best content creators are authentic and share ideas and respond in real-time. Help B2B sales teams to build social selling skills. In her blog on the Hootsuite website, Christina Newberry, an award-winning travel, lifestyle, and digital marketing writer, defines social selling as 'the art of using social media to find, connect with, understand, and nurture sales prospects. It's the modern way to develop meaningful relationships with potential customers so you're the first person or brand a prospect thinks of when they're ready to buy.'[11]

The City Police on Social Media? That's Funny.

Bangalore City Police @BlrCityPolice sent out a tweet on 30 Dec 2019 to tell people, 'Dear Citizens, Pls Don't invite us to your upcoming #NewYear2020 parties, we are happy to be away from your celebrations. We are even more happy when your parties are peaceful and safe #BCP2020'

When Lawrence Police Department @LawrenceKS_PD absolutely had a zero-tolerance stalker policy, a citizen @sburson85 asked them on Twitter, 'Are you at Maine and 6th?'

@LawrenceKS_PD responded, 'That's creepy Sandy don't do this to us.'

My all-time favourite would be Bangalore City Police @ BlrCityPolice commenting on the infamous slow-moving traffic in Bangalore.

'Ashes to Ashes, Dust to Dust

If Bangalore Police doesn't catch you

Bangalore traffic must.

You can't run after a crime.'

3. Build an in-house social media team: In 2015, Zomato started an in-house team to handle social media, films and internal and external brand communication. What it did was to speed up response time from idea to execution. Since then many other startups like BookMyShow, Swiggy, PaperBoat, Byju's and Dunzo have set up their in-house teams. Vaidehi Murthy, a copywriter at Dunzo, has a fan following, courtesy her endless supply of puns and one-liners. When U2 had a concert in Mumbai, her tweet read, 'The U2 concert is obviously pro Bono.'[12]

4. Leverage social recruiting: Engaging the audience is one of the first principles of social media. Having a sense of humour is one of the most powerful ways to build an audience. The passive job seeker must feel curious enough to stop and read your message. What if you had just that one chance to engage the candidate. What would be the most authentic value proposition you would share with your dream candidate? Would this message make someone pause and want to send you their resume?

5. What differentiates you: Talent acquisition company Belong.co published a coffee table book, *Outbound Hiring,* about which Aadil Bandukwala, one of the authors told me, 'It carries a curated set of quotes from business leaders, data and insightful narratives, talent frameworks, approaches and behaviors that are transforming the way the world looks at hiring.' If you think that the way you do things is better than others, educate the rest. That is a perfect way to differentiate yourself and become a leader as others adopt your method. Getting an influencer to be a partner with you is a winning approach. Nearly two out of every three consumers say that they trust influencer messages about a brand more than a company's advertising about their own brand.[13]

Change Whom You Compete With

If you had a flourishing fireworks business, whom would you think of as your competition? Maybe another fireworks manufacturer who has acquired a more state-of-the-art equipment? But what could change the competitive landscape? A sudden change of regulation could change your fortunes forever or technology that has been steadily improving in the lab could one day make your business redundant overnight.

A crowd of more than 100,000 Coachella 2017 concertgoers saw history in the making when 300 Intel® Shooting Star™ drones coloured the night sky. The dancing drones took the shape of a ferris wheel, then a rotating windmill, palm trees and other colourful 3D animated objects. This was competition of a different kind altogether.

Whom You Compete with can Change Overnight

When the Australian government banned firecrackers because of widespread fires caused by them, drones became a quick substitute. Drones were a ready option. At the start of 2020, drones were being used in China to replace firework displays.

As face-masks became mandatory during the pandemic, Prestige Ameritech ramped production up from 25,000 masks a day to 1 million masks a day. 95 per cent of surgical masks and 70 per cent of respirators used in the US are made overseas, and China is one of the biggest producers. A pandemic in the middle of a flu season means hospitals need many more masks. The main supplier cuts off the supply as demand shoots up with panic buying of masks by the public.[14]

Would anyone have bet their money on Prada, Gucci, Yves Saint Laurent and Balenciaga manufacturing face masks? But that's what they have done. A number of providers are 3D printing medical face masks as well.[15]

The $1.3 trillion automobile industry that employs 10 million people needs to adapt to the new realities of the post-pandemic scenario. High fixed costs mean that operating at lower capacity adds to losses. The top eight western carmakers lost $50 billion in the first quarter of 2020. WFH has reduced the need to commute. Investing in battery technology and growing the hybrid/electric vehicle segment is an opportunity for this industry to adapt. The leaders of these firms need to reskill the workforce or risk the irrelevance of this sector.[16]

The most telling data point was that the stock market voted Tesla as the most valuable automaker. The

Tesla market value of $183.7 billion went above Toyota's $178.78 billion. Not long back Tesla was looked at as a pipe dream.

You Peer Group Is Not Your Competition

In the analogue world, leaders looked to peers for competition. Benchmarking has been the norm. Some chose to lead and get the first-mover advantage. Others were more cautious. They reacted after watching how the first movers fared. But this strategy does not work in the digital world. When you think of the auto industry, competition could come from a search engine—Google. The Google Self-Driving Car Project, started in 2009 as Waymo, is one of the most iconic and tenured autonomous vehicle programmes. 'Anything that has wheels and moves along the surface of the earth is something that we, in the future, could imagine being driven by Waymo.'[17]

At CES 2020, Sony showed off their concept Electric Vehicle (EV). Would you ever put Sony in the category of a car maker?

Today, the competitors to a bank are not just the other banks but also Apple Pay, Google Wallet, Paytm, Alibaba, and even post offices.

Boeing is an American aerospace company that designs, manufactures, and sells airplanes, rotorcraft, rockets, satellites, telecommunications equipment, and missiles worldwide. If you were to think of the competition for Boeing, besides Airbus, who else would be a competitor for them? Each product line will have its own set of competitors with whom they have battled historically.

If wearing masks becomes mandatory for a while, would that threaten the business of hope/beauty? Should Lakme, L'Oreal, Maybelline, Estee Lauder, Revlon be worried if such a large percentage of the face is covered? Should they focus on eyeliners instead? Or would people wear lipstick and make-up just for themselves or to post on social media?

IMPLEMENTATION IDEAS

Map your current set of competitors. Replace two of them with Amazon and Google. How would that change the nature of competition you experience? How would it impact the functioning of every CXO and their teams? How would your talent strategy need to shift to respond to these changes? What is the time horizon for your strategy? Is it five years? Three years or six months?

Your Competitor Could Be a Digital Giant

Who you are racing depends on who you see as the competitor for cars and what you build. Automobile companies across the world are trying to think of the future of mobility. Depending on the question they ask, their competitive scenario will pan out. Is the future of automobiles about ownership? If so, then Uber and Lyft could be competitors. If you believe cars would become connected, then Samsung or Huawei would be the ones you look out for. Your competitors would change based on the dreams that you nurture.

1. The data that you have determines your competitor: Google is powerful because they know everything you have searched for. They have your address book. They know where you have gone with whom (they have pictures that you have saved on Google photos). They are listening to your voice commands at home. That lets a 'search engine and digital advertising' company think of building driverless cars or even flying cars. In 2009, Google launched its 'Moonshot project' to build a fully autonomous car (Waymo). Since 2009, its self-driving cars have logged 2.3 million driverless miles on test drives in California, Arizona, Texas and Washington. Waymo launched Waymo One, its commercial self-driving ride-hailing service for 400 residents of Phoenix, Arizona in December 2018. Waymo is not the first company to receive a public licence; self-driving startup Zoox got its clearance to join the programme seven months earlier in 2018.[18]

2. An Airbus 320, a vacuum cleaner and electric car are similar: Digital transformation begins by asking fundamental questions about the business strategy, the consumer and the talent that will be needed to implement the leader's vision. Once implemented, the culture of the organisation sustains the competitive advantage. If you are the head of an electric car-making company, it would seem normal that you look within the industry at other car manufacturers. In the UK market, Nissan launched 'Leaf' in 2010 and BMW, its 'i3s' model in 2012. In 2019, BMW announced that it was making an all-electric Mini, and Volkswagen plans to release an electric campervan, officially known as Microbus, in 2022. Volkswagen is also building Golf, the first volume model the car maker will launch, which is fully connected to the internet. The car is expected to have a hundred million lines of code, roughly as many as you would find in an

Airbus 320. Would you think of a vacuum cleaner making company as your competitor? Dyson announced its plans of launching their own EV by 2020. (Of course, the company went on to decide by early October 2019 that it would scrap the project as the 'fantastic electric car' it had developed was not 'commercially viable'.)[19]

Existing players like Airtel and Vodafone knew about the launch of Jio at least two years before. They were still caught in the legacy models and never anticipated that the unit of business will change from mobile calls to data. Changing the basis of competition and moving with lightning speed enabled Jio Infocomm to provide services to about 388 million customers. In April 2020, Facebook took a 9.9 per cent stake with a $5.7 billion investment in Jio. That would enable 400 million WhatsApp users in India to start using the service for ecommerce. Thirty million kirana stores can receive orders and offer quick delivery. That may provide an indigenous response to Amazon and Walmart's attempts at capturing the Indian market.[20]

IMPLEMENTATION IDEAS

Team Building Exercise for the Next Leadership Offsite: Let's Play 'What If'

For the next leadership team offsite, dedicate a day to mull over this question: what if one of these market shapers like Amazon, Google, Salesforce and so on decided to compete with you? What data would they have that could give them an advantage. How would they create a value-added product that would prompt customers to switch? Just when the leaders start sweating over these possibilities, tell them that your top talent just got job offers to join them. What would hold them back? Who will have the credibility and goodwill to make these people stay back? Do they know that this is the responsibility they have?

In case the leaders say that Amazon would never enter their business, remind them about Amazon's impressive list of competitors. They compete with eBay, Netflix, Time Warner Cable, Apple iTunes, Google Play Store, Best Buy, Family Dollar, Staples, Target, Walmart, Alibaba, JD.com, Oracle, salesforce.com, Accenture, and Citrix Systems, among others. Who would have thought that a bookseller or an ecommerce company would compete to win Oscars, Emmies and Golden Globe Awards?[21]

You have just learned that two of the biggest VCs are funding a startup that has gathered a lot of attention on social media. The founder has recently been quoted in mainstream media as saying that every inefficiency of the market leader is an opportunity for startups. They know that they are leveraging cutting-edge technology to rapidly wean away customers from you. The founder says, 'The market seems to favour the one who innovates and is able to tell a more compelling story. Smaller brands like us will leverage micro-influencers to gain credibility.'

You have also read somewhere that Harry's has carved out 4.3 per cent of America's $2.2 billion men's razor market from the likes of Gillette, whose share has fallen from 73 per cent to 53 per cent since 2009. The low-calorie ice cream Halo Top, created in 2012, was the top selling ice-cream pint in America five years later, ahead of Häagen-Dazs and Ben & Jerry's.

What would be your business' ability to create a 'moat' of competitive advantage?

Design is the Untapped Opportunity to Compete

The analogue world obsesses with tangible things, while the digital world creates competitive advantage based on intangible elements such as design, colour, aesthetics and music. A great design today is not about aesthetics. It is about how things work, say how a website works seamlessly across devices and countries and languages—which makes it a terrific experience.

Integrating design with the rest of the organisation is a three-step process.

a) In the first phase, companies view design narrowly, focusing on aesthetics and form: the colour, material and finish of products.
b) In the second phase, companies broaden their design emphasis to encompass end-to-end user experiences.
c) In the final phase, companies realise that design infuses everything they do; it transforms the entire company.

Design-driven transformation leads to a sevenfold increase in the market cap of Logitec as they moved from stage one to stage three.[22]

Design Makes the Organisation Boundaryless

Designers look at the customer journey across devices, countries and languages to generate insights. They do this across product lines and bring an outside-in view to the leadership team. When combined with the strategy team, design can anticipate shifts and trends that can have a significant impact on the survival of the organisation. Design is a strategic function in B2B as well as B2C businesses. Designers can help the business shape the customer journey as well as the employees' journey.

Jony Ive became the chief design officer of Apple in 2015. He joined Apple in September 1992, where he remained until his departure in November 2019. He was an industrial product and architectural designer who worked closely with Steve Jobs.

Ive designed, among other things, the iMac, Power Mac G4 Cube, iPod, iPhone, iPad, MacBook, and parts of the user interface of Apple's mobile operating system iOS. He also helped design Apple's major architectural projects, such as Apple Park and Apple Stores.

Apple's minimalistic approach towards design follows Jony's obsession with 'form follows function'. Pre-charging the phone (started by Apple) before shipping it is now standard practice for all smart phone manufacturers. Design has to satisfy not only functional, but also psychological and aesthetic criteria.

The electronic goods company Braun has been using designers since the 1960s. Their most celebrated designer Dieter Rams created the 'Ten Design Principles' that influences designers from B2B companies as much as B2C products.

In B2B businesses, monitoring the completion rates at every stage of the user journey, until the conversion, can be powerful design opportunities. Being able to simplify and speed up the experience at every stage drives growth opportunities.

Secondly, continuously monitoring the completion rates of crucial user journeys in the conversion funnel, such as signup, onboarding, and checkout flows is also important. It is also important to ensure design changes are improving completion rates against the baseline by chipping away at drop-off points.

Metrics like the cost of acquiring a customer and customer lifetime value must be standard data points that every employee must be equally concerned with.

IMPLEMENTATION IDEAS

Design Challenge: Map the customer onboarding process and identify every step and the time it takes for a new customer to complete it. Can they do it on their mobile phone as they wait for their coffee to be served in a restaurant? Study

What Is Good Design

1. Innovative
2. Useful
3. Aesthetic
4. Makes product understandable
5. Unobtrusive
6. Honest
7. Long lasting
8. Detailed
9. Environment-friendly
10. Minimal and simple

Source: Dieter Rams

the customer onboarding process across every product and service to simplify it. Now see if the process works equally well across every language and geography where you wish to have customers.

Do a similar exercise for the employee onboarding process and see if the time taken can be reduced without compromising on regulatory requirements.

Run a contest to ask new hires to design the onboarding process and see what steps (information) they found to be unnecessary.

From Multichannel to Omnichannel Experiences

Providing a seamless experience to audiences across digital and off-line channels can be challenging for multiple reasons.[23]

1. Disjointed data sitting in people's laptops (that crash and lead to disasters).
2. Functions gathering their own data, in their own formats making it impossible for anyone else to use.
3. Time taken to create content that is relevant and interesting.
4. Manual process of responding to marketing responses.

Consolidate data resources, unify measurement and reporting and automate marketing processes so that your entire marketing organisation has optimal audience visibility and can deliver experiences dynamically.

Design and data strategies are used across multiple channels to create a seamless user experience. When every customer touch point provides the same experience is when we can say that it is an 'omnichannel experience'. Having a multichannel experience is not good enough.

Today, data is the biggest source of competitive advantage. In the digital world, when the company gathers data of each transaction, it is possible for them to start categorising consumers in unique ways.

Netflix gathers data on each movie that a consumer has watched, the genre, the time, and even the ones people downloaded but have not watched. Each data point goes to make their recommendation engine better. Digital-first companies are 64 per cent more likely to have significantly exceeded their top 2018 business goals. 36 per cent of larger organisations are now using AI, particularly to enhance data analysis—50 per cent more than 2019.

Having so much data also means that these digital organisations need to respect customer privacy. This is one of the paradoxes leaders have to grapple with today. When the Cambridge Analytica scandal broke out, it was alleged that the data Facebook had gathered on people were used by Cambridge Analytica for their clients to sway the 2016 election outcomes in the US. Given that organisations have so much of information about a consumer, how they go about ensuring the privacy of the individual is respected will add to the consumers' trust and consequently, the bond they develop with the organisation.

Experiences Must Be 'Individualised'

Customisation: When you get a shirt stitched by a tailor, the tailor needs your measurements to ensure the right fit. Customisation involves getting the accurate measurements.

Some tailors sketch it out to show you what the pockets will look like. The more data you have about the customer, the more you can customise the offering. Additionally, knowing your ZIP or PIN code helps deliver the product to the customers' doorstep. It could also help in predicting the language in which you will transact. But there is a flipside—just because I stay in a certain country or state does not mean I speak a certain language. That is the limitation of data.

Knowing the customer beyond the data often involves human judgement and insight. When the service provider can understand the customer's context and tailors the offering, they move up the value chain to become a 'trusted advisor'.

Personalisation: Personalisation needs an understanding of the exceptions to the rule. The ability to make those exceptions creates a personalised experience. Personalisation is the ability of the service provider to know when to make an exception to the rule that governs the demographic you fall in to. The ability to add an additional keyboard of a different language enables personalisation. Transliteration keyboards make it easy for someone who does not know the script of the language to still write in that language.

Individualisation: Individualisation needs the product or service to evolve in real-time, with usage. Every time you use Google to look for information, the algorithm learns something about you that applies to everyone. And where there is an exception to the rule. The additional element is that every search done by a user also improves the Google algorithm in real time. Auto-correcting the common typos is an effort to improve the user experience (but it can also create hilarious errors).

Netflix allows family members to create separate viewing accounts for a single subscription. The home screen of every user is unique to that person. A family member sharing the account will have a different homepage that is unique to that individual. That enables them to serve separate movie recommendations for each member of the family. It enables individualisation. Netflix actually manages to individualise their offerings to suit the tastes of 200 million subscribers in 190 countries. The music app Spotify uses the same algorithm to individualise playlists.

IMPLEMENTATION IDEAS

1. Invite some high school students to go through and use your company website and identify all the words and phrases they do not understand. Ask them to identify all the places they found the navigation tedious. If these digital-born kids find it hard to understand something, then it is a warning sign.
2. Encourage people at all levels in the organisation to do simplification projects in another function of the business. Ask them to identify processes that seem annoying or pointless.

Design a Seven-star Experience

On a podcast with Reid Hoffman, CEO of Airbnb, Brian Chesky describes the brainstorming exercise they used to design experiences that make the product memorable.[24]

The simple design principle is when you get what you are paying for and what you expect, with no shortfall, it is a five-star experience. Then the guest could be asked what would turn a five-star experience to a six-star? When the host does something that is unexpected in a positive way and delights the guest, it qualifies as a six-star experience. The guest would go on to add things that would make it a six-star experience, the founders would challenge them further. 'No, tell me what would turn this six-star experience into a seven-star experience.'[25]

Taj Hotels has often left guests squealing with delight by thoughtful gestures like leaving a spectacle cleaning cloth for a guest. Their chefs delight the kids by creating dosas and pancakes in the shape of a bunny or a cat. Creating a delightful experience is an exercise in creativity rather than spending big bucks.

Customer experience is your customers' perception of how your company treats them. These perceptions affect their behaviour and build memories and feelings to drive their loyalty. If customers like you and continue to do so, they are going to do business with you for a long time and recommend you to others. B2B companies believe that the single most exciting opportunity for 2020 is customer experience (or CX) beating content marketing, video marketing and social!

Organisations do not hesitate to make investments in technology that improve the customer experience. But they are far more conservative when it comes to investing in ideas that improve the employee experience.

In the coming months, the Coronavirus pandemic will force many companies to reimagine their products, their communications strategies and how they sell. HR teams will have to learn to redesign the employee experience with people working remotely. They have to plan for situations where a returning wave of the pandemic may close parts of a country where their critical talent is located.

To Empower the User, Think Design

When a customer plans a trip to the Disney theme park, they can use their trip planning tool across devices.

The mobile app works pay tolls while approaching the park and chooses places to eat. It can also be used to pay for the purchases. The mobile app tells you how to find the attractions across the park and even the estimated waiting time. That empowers the customers to decide if they wish to wait or come back to the attraction later or save it for the next trip. The Disney Magic Band that can be worn like a watch doubles up as a room key in the hotel as well as a place to store photos clicked with your favourite Disney characters.

> **Four Key Digital Trends**
>
> Those companies that are succeeding are delivering first-class, personalised customer experiences (CX) built on a foundation of integrated marketing and CX technology.
>
> The importance of customer data, and the greater levels of urgency that are apparent when it comes to harnessing data for commercial gain.
>
> Companies are seeking greater control and ownership of their data, with a focus on compliance and concern about 'walled gardens'.
>
> AI has gained significant traction in the last year, but there are still significant barriers preventing organisations from reaping the benefits.
>
> Source: eConsultancy 2019 Digital Trends Report

Designers deal with questions about product or service usage. Was it easy to buy and easy to use? Was it easy to get support when one needed it? All of that needs specific designing skills. B2B software and even most HR tech software is still very primitive in its look and feel. Bringing in designers from B2C industries would be the first step.

IMPLEMENTATION IDEAS

Ask employees to suggest simple devices that they can build to calculate how long an employee or customer needs to wait. Employee experiences are shaped by an aggregation of 'micro-experiences' that happen even before the person joins the organisation.

Think of creative or funny signages that can make a customer smile when they step into your office. Ask employees to design a creative signboard to describe their role.

HR SaaS Systems Improve the Employee Experience

With 200 stores, V-Mart is one of the largest multi-brand value retailers with a sole focus on Tier 2 and Tier 3 cities in India. Their tagline is 'Price Less Fashion'.

In choosing the HR system, their CEO evaluated options ranging from large global ERP providers to SaaS based systems that are cloud-based.

Customers of the ERP system complained about lack of flexibility and delayed responses to requested features. ERP systems are notorious for low adoption by users.

The V-Mart CEO says he used only one criterion, 'The HR system must be for the employees and not the HR department.'

They wanted a system that had four attributes:

1. An agile system where additional functionality could be switched on as the business changes.
2. Implementation time should be less than six months.
3. An intuitive interface that can be used by employees without extensive training.
4. A mobile-first software that would work even with feature phones and low internet speed common to Tier 2 and Tier 3 cities.

Did the CEO get a HR system that met all the criterion, I asked Lalit Agarwal, founder of V-Mart. 'We chose PeopleStrong instead of a traditional ERP system. Those complex ERP systems would never be used by a store employee who uses a feature phone.'

Speed and simplicity are the cornerstones to providing great experiences. Technology helps with that. It is an enabler. Great employee experience stems from being treated with respect. Visible behaviour coupled with what that makes someone feel creates the experience.

When it happens consistently in the workplace, it becomes the culture. Culture is the soil that nurtures the garden of experiences for the customers and employees.

How can employers use technology to ensure that the experience of the remote worker or the freelancer is similar to the experience of in-office employees? This is a basic design principle. A principle of good design is that the experience must be the same for multiple user groups—experienced and novice. Or for suppliers and customers.[26]

Invest in the Human Experience?

Why do employees not use the HR system beyond the minimum needed to get by? Most organisations do not hesitate to invest in tech that improves the customer's experience, but things are different when it comes to investing in tech for employees. Work-related tech (for employees) is often clunky, tedious to use, and with horrendously poor user interfaces. Sometimes, it is a mishmash of technologies—a different service provider for payroll, a Learning Management System by someone else and an applicant tracking system that annoys every candidate. We often forget that the same employees expected to use the poor patchwork of HR tech at work are used to apps that have been designed by some of the best techies and designers in the world.

Employees who have never experienced a 'six-star or a seven-star experience' with their employer can never provide such a memorable experience to either the candidate or the customer.

Consumer wants a user manual?

Go back and fix your product design. Repeat. Rinse. Repeat.

What Do You Need: HRIS, HCM or HRMS?

1. Human Resource Information Systems (HRIS) are often used to manage employee policies and procedures. They offer information and reports for recruitment, training, compensation, workflows and reporting.

2. Human Capital Management (HCM) systems are usually more comprehensive and include most capabilities of an HRIS but add on talent management as well. HCM allows for greater planning, goal setting and succession planning.

3. Human Resource Management Systems (HRMS) contain elements of HRIS and may have some capabilities of an HCM solution plus provide payroll support. They combine many human resources functions, including benefits administration, payroll, recruiting and training, and performance management, goal setting etc. into one package.

Checklist for Selecting a HR Management System

1. Can it be used on a mobile? No? Look for another HRMS.
2. Can an employee use it without any training?
3. Is your data secure and encrypted?
4. Can it be implemented in 3-6 months? Will the HRMS align with all the existing systems to access data?
5. Does it cover every step of the employee life cycle?
6. Can the system expand with your business as you go across geographies and different types of business scenarios?
7. Is it easy to create modules, add functionalities and build custom dashboards/reports?
8. Is each module equally intuitively designed—e.g. recruitment, employee life cycle, learning, collaboration or payroll?
9. What is the after-sales support provided? Speak to other customers.
10. Can the system incorporate technological advances as they happen?

> **Why 'Essential Services' Workers are Low Paid**
>
> - Demand-Supply gap—There is no need for any specialised education or training. Abundant supply of labour unlike highly skilled jobs like surgeons that are in short supply. Think food delivery workers from Swiggy.
> - Hard to scale up productivity—It is hard to get one nurse to attend to more than one person at a time.
> - Poor bargaining power of the workers as compared to a large corporation that can afford litigation, PR etc. Uber or Ola drivers complain of lower earnings as more drivers have signed up.

Max Life Insurance had their payroll and performance data for 15,000 employees on the internal intranet because they thought it was more secure. Then in March 2020, the government of India announced a mandatory lockdown and all offices were shut. The payroll and performance data was inaccessible. Without that the employee payroll could not be processed.

PeopleStrong had forty-eight hours at the end of March amidst the lockdown to migrate all of that data to the cloud. It was only after the payroll was run flawlessly that the business could heave a sigh of relief.

Technology needs to be used as a tool to supplement business vision. Start by asking why you are using technology. Having that clarity within the sponsor team or the CEO/CHRO is a good sign. If the discussion is about features and costs, then the project is about cost saving and not employee experience. Ask yourself what you are trying to achieve. What do you want the technology to do?

David Rogers, author of *The Digital Transformation Playbook* says, 'Digital transformation is not fundamentally about changing your technology. It is about strategy, leadership and new ways of thinking.' He speaks of the five broad areas that leaders must focus on: customers, competition, data, innovation and value creation.

Investing in HR tech has become relatively simple. HR tech solutions like PeopleStrong, DarwinBox, ZingHR are popular choices to address talent acquisition, talent management, and human capital management needs. Before you choose any of them, ensure it is mobile and can be accessed by a distributed workforce in areas with poor connectivity. If employees with feature phones can do basic transactions, it makes adoption easier. Most of them offer AI-powered chatbots that can take away the need for humans to complete HR transactions.

Learning Experience Platforms (LXP) like Degreed and EdCast are replacing Learning Management Systems (LMS). They were developed as 'management' systems for learning focused on business rules, compliance, and catalogue management for courses. LXPs are all set to replace the $4 billion LMS systems because they make content discovery much easier. They offer learning pathways that help build the skill in a systematic layered way.[27]

Build Talent for the Digital World

The supply of talent is impacted by several factors. Let us consider some talent-related statistics from across the world:

Fifteen of the world's largest economies that make up 70 per cent of the world's GDP are facing a shortage of people in the working age. Twenty per cent of the world will be more than sixty-five years old by 2035. Two billion people will be sixty years and older by 2050, more than triple the number in 2000, according to the World Health Organisation.[28]

A shrinking workforce brings the burden of rising health-care costs, higher pension costs and diminishing fertility rates. Organisations are responding by raising the retirement age and delaying pensions. Add to this the fact that gig workers will make up half of the world's workforce. Millennials have started becoming managers of workplaces and Gen Z has started entering the job market. Politicians are increasingly under pressure to make up for jobs lost due to automation.

Kathleen Hessert is an expert on all matters Gen Z. She told me about a survey she did with 898 Gen Z students aged between thirteen and twenty-two.[29]

Gen Z was born in times of constant change and unlimited possibilities. Gen Z has one of the most diverse perspectives of the future there has ever been. They grew up with the highest tolerance for change and innovation of any generation. They are enthusiastic early adopters of chatbots and routinely ask Alexa for help with homework, to tell them jokes, spell-check and of course, for ordering pizza.

Seventy-eight per cent say smartphone is their #1 device and they spend two to five hours on it daily. The top social media platforms for Gen Z are Instagram, YouTube, Snapchat, Spotify and TikTok. The long hours spent every day on the internet and social media make them curious about engaging in different types of experiences in the real world. Games are gateways into online communities with their own cultures and layered identities.

Peers (people like them) have a stronger pull on Gen Z and actual friends carry the most weight when recommending brand products and services. They want brands to personalise marketing above all else. To have the greatest impact, brands have to enlist peers and friends. They carry more weightage than celebrities or marketing messages.

Adapt or Become Irrelevant

The $1.3 trillion automobile industry has dragged its feet on shifting to electric and hybrid vehicles. The pandemic has amplified the crisis that the industry faces in the short term and the threat of a decline in the long term. Ten million jobs are at stake given the structural challenges of the sector. High fixed costs mean swelling losses if production capacity is not fully utilised. Working from home is going to become more mainstream and that means less demand for cars to commute. The legacy business has been driven by the internal combustion engine which is fairly obsolete technology. But the industry has never worked to reskill the workforce in the legacy business or invested in battery technology.[30]

Mission—Not Majors

The African Leadership University is training future African leaders by moving away from more traditional university programmes; students select missions to pursue, rather than majors.

They run six-month courses in leadership and technical skills in areas like data science and operational management from low-cost setups such as co-working spaces. These leadership development experiences at scale are building ecosystems of entrepreneurship, innovation, and collaboration to prepare young people for employment and to become job creators.

They use income-sharing agreements to finance these courses. The students pay a share of their income to investors once they are employed. There is no upfront payment. They have campuses in Mauritius, Rwanda, and Kenya, and intend to expand to Johannesburg, Lagos, Cape Town and Casablanca.

Source: https://www.alueducation.com/campuses/alu-rwanda/

The Power Shift

Germany has been the hub of the automobile industry. It employs close to 835,000 people. It is grappling with dropping sales of cars across the globe. German auto production will be at a twenty-two-year low in 2019 and 2020.

Traditional car sales were dropping even before the pandemic. Meanwhile, Tesla wants to build a factory in Berlin, and Eurabus, a company in Berlin that makes battery-powered buses is bringing in the electric vehicle. Think of what that does to incumbents and their workforce. If they do not make the switch fast enough, they will be wiped out.

But there is the challenge of unemployment that will come with it. Electric vehicles are easier to assemble and require fewer workers and fewer parts. Their impact is forcing traditional car manufacturers like Daimler and Audi to announce job cuts. Suppliers like Continental and Bosch have also had to cut jobs. The combined effect is that tens of thousands of jobs had been cut by the start of 2020. The shift to electric vehicles could impact a shift of power from Germany to other countries in the global car business. That in turn could lead to an anti-immigrant sentiment that drives political power balances.[31]

IMPLEMENTATION IDEAS

The legacy business that has been the basis of economic prosperity, stability and employment will become uneconomical to continue because of the technological changes. What will it take to make India the manufacturing hub (because that provides employment to the largest number of people comparatively) of the world instead of China? If you are small and medium enterprise, what should be your strategy? And would it be different if you were a large manufacturing powerhouse?

Even before the crisis, Apple was trying to shift its portfolio from selling more devices to selling more services and accessories across those devices.[32]

Creative Careers—Untapped Opportunities

'There are 16,00,000 seats available in engineering colleges all across India. But in any given year, only 50 per cent of these are taken up. Every year, 80,000 students pay up to Rs 10,00,000 over four years to get an undergraduate degree in engineering. But only 60 per cent of these engineers find employment. Twenty per cent find employment in places where their engineering skills are not being used at all.

The average annual salary of a fresh engineering graduate is approximately Rs 240,000 to Rs 260,000. That means a payback period of three-four years for the money spent on education.

Yet, parents still continue to insist that their children take up conventional careers (medicine, engineering, law etc.). Many are not even aware of opportunities in non-conventional careers like animation etc.'

(In conversation with Anuj Kacker, President and Executive Director at Aptech Ltd.)

These forces all combine to shape the talent pool of the world. Education has to be recrafted with a much deeper partnership with employers who will shape the curriculum.

The employers must teach the curriculum along with regular faculty so as to give a perspective of theory and practice. A cross-industry consortium to fund research on areas that have applicability across sectors can be powerful ways to improve education and industry practices.

Most teachers and professors continue teaching in front of video conference cameras exactly the way they were teaching in the class. It was a 'live-telecast' of the class lecture making it a poor learning experience. Training everyone to adapt the materials and pedagogy to the new medium may make online classes far more effective in future.

Educational institutions face tuition shortfalls because of unpredictable enrollment and market-driven endowments are dwindling because of the stock market volatility. Families question whether it is worth paying expensive tuition fees if students will have to take classes online, from home. Online education is not the experience either the student or the families want. All of these are indications that the sector has to adapt itself to the new reality.

The 2019 Global Talent Competitiveness Index (GTCI) report reveals that Switzerland, Singapore and the United States continue to lead the world in talent competitiveness, while countries in Asia, Latin America and Africa are seeing a progressive erosion of their talent base. The report confirms that talent issues have become a mainstream concern for firms, nations and cities, with talent performance being seen as critical to growth and prosperity. The highest-ranking countries and cities tend to be the most open to entrepreneurial talent.

Google's Search Results

Google's search results reflect the changes that are foremost on our minds. The impact of social and physical isolation is certainly impacting what we looked for during these times.

It has changed our relationship with space and time and how we approach work or leisure. The way we consume content has changed so has the way that we express ourselves. The home has transformed itself into office, gym,

restaurant and entertainment centre all rolled into one. With travel not possible, people are looking for virtual safaris and concerts.[33]

The Impact of Three Dominant Feelings

1. Boredom: There is a higher need for novelty to fight boredom. Access to high-quality content on demand 24/7 means that they will be less engaged if the online course they are attending is poorly produced. The learning teams have to invest in upscaling anyone who is standing in front of a camera to engage with the audience. A much greater investment in improving people's communication across media would be needed.

2. Anxiety: Focus on health and discretionary spending is showing up more often in the searches. Investment in health insurance and helping people to manage their finances will be opportunities that will come up.

3. Uncertainty: People are anxious about their jobs and the future. Skill building as an industry will see a significant shift as people prepare to find jobs and opportunities across sectors and roles.

Make it easy for work to get done. Note that great employee experience is directly correlated with higher levels of customer satisfaction, innovation and profitability. Having access to information, simplified procedures, and technology are key outcomes that an effective HR tech can deliver.

IMPLEMENTATION IDEAS

1. What if all hiring is frozen for the next three years? How will you ensure that the current workforce is future-ready with skills that will need to keep your business relevant?
2. Think of an engineering college or business school where you have traditionally hired entry-level talent. What would you need to do to upskill the professors to become like an extended R&D facility for your organisation? How would you work with the professors of this institution so as to dramatically improve the quality of students graduating?

Leverage Employees

Your decision makers are just like you—time-starved. They do not have time to read elaborate journals especially when they are behind a paywall. If they find something which is interesting but will take more than three to four minutes to read, they will mark it and hope to read it later (which they never will). If you leverage your employees and have them create a powerful online presence, each employee can serve as a brand evangelist.

Why Do Apps Need to Be Updated So Often?

For games, app updates can be six-eight times a month. Businesses release updates four times a month to address security gaps and bug fixes.

The trigger for updates is often outside the control of the developer. Updates by the third-party systems which are frameworks used by the app often force updates. The library used by the app then needs to be updated.

As the audience for the app grows across different geographies, there could be legal requirements or peculiarities specific to a country that drive the updates. New hardware like different models of laptops with new features like face recognition and voice assistants etc. may need app updates.

New form factors* like Smart Watches need apps to be updated to work for these new kinds of screens and usages. Sometimes anniversaries and milestones demand celebration through app updates.

Dynamic pricing on e-commerce sites may also need to be kept in mind while planning updates.

If only humans stayed updated as often as these mobile apps, reskilling would be a non-issue!

I have run workshops for several organisations to teach their employees how to write blogs and content for social media. Most of my learning comes from getting more than a 100 employees in my team at Wipro to establish their online presence and create posts. They are authentic voices and

*Form factor is a hardware design aspect that defines and prescribes the size, shape, and other physical specifications of components, particularly in electronics. A form factor may represent a broad class of similarly sized components, or it may prescribe a specific standard.

connect with different networks. This is a powerful way to establish your social presence and are more effective than running ads. That is a very analogue approach to getting the word out.

Think Like an App—Not an Operating System

Remember the analogue world when computer companies used to release their Operating System (OS) upgrade every few years? The typical time lag between one version of the software and the next was an average of two years. They would be released only when everything was in working order. All customer feedback was aggregated and addressed in the next release.

Traditional ERP systems do just that, making them slower when it comes to responding to changes customers want. That is why nimbler HRMS platforms are replacing ERPs.

'Software is Eating the World'

For a traditional auto manufacturer, a problem with the braking system would mean an expensive product recall. If consumers complained about performance not being at par, the problem can only be addressed in the next model. But when Ford's F-150 model's brake performance was found to be better than Tesla's Model 3, Elon Musk simply updated the software code that the cars would automatically download and improved their performance immediately. This speed of response was impossible in the analogue world.

That is how mobile apps work. Software developers today release 'unfinished code' and constantly add new features after that—called the beta version of the code. The apps that you download today get updated every couple of weeks.

In the analogue world, innovations were done secretively and were brought out only when they were successful and complete. The digital world is in perpetual beta. Nothing is ever 'finished'.

Perpetual Beta, Even After Twenty Years

Paytm, the Indian e-commerce payment system and financial technology company, has stayed in perpetual beta. They view themselves as a twenty-year old startup.

At Paytm, a product is defined as anything a consumer—be it the end consumer, a merchant or a marketplace seller—interacts with. So 'Recharge' is considered a product. Paytm's implementation of Unified Payments Interface (UPI) is also categorised as a product. Paytm competes with wallet players such as MobiKwik, FreeCharge and PhonePe.

Paytm has launched bill-pay options. They are launching a partnership with Zoom where anyone can hold a ticketed event online. From insurance to brokerage and private wealth advisory, everything is a system of payments between buyers and sellers. That reminds me, why can't they be your bank? It turns out that is also part of their plans.

The culture at Paytm is described by its founder Vijay Shekhar Sharma as, 'No fear, no greed, no entitlement.'

That alone creates the mindset to thrive in an environment of constant shifts.

Making errors is fine: And the state of perpetual beta also implies that errors are a way of life. All digital giants have made gaffes.

Apple had launched Ping in 2010 as a social network for music. Ping was a failure. Apple went back and reimagined the product, then re-launched it as Apple Music.

Another time, Apple wanted its phone users to replace Google Maps with its own Apple Maps app during the release of iOS 6 in 2012. It bombed! In some cases, the map led users to wrong destinations that they complained about on social media.

Like any company in perpetual beta, Apple went back to fixing its maps. Its map has since been widely adopted even though it has not been able to surpass the acceptance of Google Maps.

Another case of a mammoth failure by a digital giant was Google Glass. The product was launched in a novel way—by giving the product to early adopters, and a whole slew of celebrities and letting them be advertisers, in a way. Safety and health concerns and aesthetically unappealing features, bad marketing, and little progress beyond its beta stage were some of the reasons that led to the product's colossal failure.

Walk Away from Your Past Successes

The lessons are very clear. The path ahead in the digital world is always unpredictable. Businesses have to stay in perpetual beta and constantly reimagine every variable in the business. IBM inventors received a record 9,100 patents in 2018, marking the company's twenty-sixth consecutive year of patent leadership in the US and crossing the 110,000-patent milestone. Nearly half of the patents granted to IBM in 2018 are pioneering advancements in AI, cloud computing, cybersecurity, blockchain and quantum computing. Not innovating is not an option. Staying still is not an option.[34]

When other retailers like J. Crew were filing for bankruptcy, Nike saw the global internet sales of its sporting goods rise by over a third in the three months leading upto February 2020. They learned from the COVID-19 experience in China and focused on moving their communication to reflect people being home. Instead of the usual social media posts, Nike resorted to promotional messages that have more in common with public service announcements than the creative flair usually associated with their marketing.

Nike's text-based ad reads: 'If you ever dreamed of playing for millions around the world, now is your chance. Play inside, play for the world.' Revenues from its Chinese online offering grew by triple digits in January and February 2020, year on year, as consumers shared workouts through WeChat and other social media. Nike's masterclass is being streamed more than 800,000 times a week on YouTube. They did not let their past success confine them to doing what has worked before.

It is never too late to walk away from your own successes. The best time to reinvent yourself is when you are most successful. Research shows that having stretch goals, is a great way to motivate people. Most workplaces tend to water down goals so that everyone gets the illusion of progress and development. Stretch goals motivate. Think about what motivates mountaineers around the world? Or Nobel laureates, who solve the unsolved mysteries of our world?[35]

IMPLEMENTATION IDEAS

In the post-pandemic world, how can you use the goal-setting process to motivate and inspire the workforce?

How can the lesson from Nike's digital pivot apply to your business?

What do you need to do to create new products and services to address the new opportunities in the post-pandemic world?

All HR Systems Reflect the Employers' Assumptions

The new design of the world of work must evolve in response to the changes that have happened in business models as well as the talent models. It is not about making do with adaptations from past HR systems. When the technical plumbing of the business is being changed, it is an opportunity to revisit all the business and talent processes.

1. *Remote only workplace assumptions:* From being co-located, to the remote only organisations and every firm in between, the assumptions will shape the leaders' choices. Installing productivity tracking software reflects the employer's assumptions about the commitment of the employees. It is an opportunity to ask why the employer hired such employees in the first place. What systems need to be put in place so that trust is implicit and explicit in the HR systems.
2. *GDPR rules for organisations:* Employees rarely have a choice in the data being gathered about them and the consequent decisions that they are subjected to. The problem is not in the data system but in

the way the data is being used. The information that is gathered about individuals to create inclusive policies (e.g. about the invisible disabilities or health conditions that the employee may have) can be used against them. Technology exists today that lets employers analyse emails for levels of engagement and possible employee attrition.

3. *The public data used by employers:* In 2013, Microsoft had spoken about using social media posts to identify mental health concerns.[36] The employers can use public health data to track employee behaviour and gather a lot more than what employees may wish to share. The problem is not in the data being gathered but to what use that data is being put. HR must define the assumptions and hypotheses behind any data being collected at an individual level.
4. *The contingent workforce model is your peek into the future:* Traditionally, the contingent workforce (by any name) has been the victim of discrimination and exploitation. Businesses like Uber and Ola (and many others) have positioned them as entrepreneurs who do it as a way of building 'flexibility in their work and income'. Talk to the cab drivers and they tell you that they are on a treadmill and without working long hours even when they are sleep deprived is the only way to make ends meet. They get no health benefits or opportunities for upskilling. The contingent workforce is an essential part of business models.
5. *Inclusion and diversity of talent (even for contingent workers):* Businesses have to go beyond a 'one time

use and throw' approach to contingent talent. Using CSR funds for investing in their insurance and health coverage is an easy step. Purchase departments in large organisations bully the individual service providers to lower their fee and do unpaid work. The contracts specify sixty to ninety payment terms. Even doing a day's work for a corporation can bind the freelancer to a non-compete clause. This exploitation must stop. Conferences and upskilling opportunities are often out of reach for freelancers. Sponsoring freelancers can be yet another usage of CSR funds. Freelancers can be a great way to employ opportunity-deprived talent.

6. *The business case for doing the right thing:* HR leaders will tell you that doing what is right can always be challenged by the CEO using the nuclear option of 'what is the business case' argument. It is easy to calculate the business case for things like hard skills which are measurable and can be counted. The investment in soft skills takes a back seat because it is difficult to measure and count the improvement from the investment. Investing in getting the organisation to understand issues of harassment, ethics and anti-corruption would never happen had it not been mandated by law. Making the workplace safe and hygienic has never mattered more to employees as many of them head back to the offices. There is no business case for doing the right thing. There is no business case for being truthful or fair.
7. *Don't leverage human tragedies to sell:* Katie Martell who calls herself 'unapologetic marketing truth-

> teller' says, 'Every industry event must move the industry forward. Provide actionable insight that help attendees solve their most pressing challenges. Challenge their status quo and give them new ways to approach old problems.'[37] Her documentary, *Pandermonium*, explores the collision of marketing, advertising and PR with social movements and the danger of brand pandering. Maintaining trust is one of the biggest challenges in the world of work. Whether it is trust between employer and employee or between the business and consumers or stakeholders, authenticity is the greatest trust builder.

You have to watch every company with no women leaders on their boards or leadership themes celebrate International Women's Day as a way to cash in on a marketing opportunity to sell their product. The reader smiles cynically and says they know exactly why those soppy messages are being aired to celebrate non-existent voices. Clue: The same three women who are in roles that are not taken seriously by the C-suite are made to appear in every Women's Day campaign. These are the same people who used to say, 'People are our most important assets.'

The pandemic was a jolt to help us question our assumptions about the world of work. HR and leaders must use it to question their assumptions about policies. Without that we see the same obsolete views about asking for ways to avoid doing anything that lowers shareholder returns even when it destroys the employees, the planet and the communities.

As the bestselling author Peter Shankman says, 'It is what you create outside of your selling, packaging and shipping that creates the brand value.' If you are the one telling people how amazing you are, people will just smirk. It is what people say about you when you are not in the room that matters. He shared some rules of building great customer experience that I will paraphrase:

1. When you make a mistake, own up. In a hyperconnected world you CANNOT lie and get away. It is also an opportunity to delight the customers by going above and beyond. That transforms the relationship from transactional to a human relationship.
2. Ask the customers if they give you the PERMISSION to send them more information and offers. Just because they had to share their email while buying something does not give you permission to bombard them with every flash sale you have. They don't care. Sending them text messages on their phone is worse. This trick worked when you only had a black and white TV. Drop it.
3. Invest in learning how to be a better communicator. Flouting grammar rules, misspelt words may grab attention. But they make the reader wonder why the company does not have great communicators who can simplify messages in a time starved world.
4. Try to help solve a problem—not sell. Stop chasing 'likes' and do things that make you likable. Being helpful (when I have nothing to sell) creates an experience that will build a relationship. Sales follow—not lead from the front. It is a different era, remember?

This is the era of HR. It is not about resources. It is all about human relationships.

References

1. Elon Musk's tweet was worth $14 billion. https://www.bbc.com/news/business-52504187
2. Sleep Less, Think Worse: The Effect of Sleep Deprivation on Working Memory. https://www.sciencedirect.com/science/article/abs/pii/S2211368116301875
3. Iconic brands go bankrupt too (twice in six years in this case) when they cannot adapt. https://www.bbc.com/news/business-46699290
4. Even the IT Industry seem to be any in adequately prepared to deal with the world's largest work from home transition done in the shortest possible time. https://www.businesstoday.in/current/corporate/post-coronavirus-75-percent-of-3-5-lakh-tcs-employees-permanently-work-from-home-up-from-20-percent/story/401981.html
5. Apple had to lower its guidance following the shakeup of its biggest supply chain—China. https://www.bloomberg.com/news/articles/2020-03-19/apple-s-supply-chain-woes-linger-even-as-china-recovers
6. Voice, quantum computing, Augmented Reality and Virtual Reality are some of the new opportunities that can be used to reimagine businesses. https://sloanreview.mit.edu/article/the-future-of-platforms/
7. Having a pizza company use driverless cars is certainly story-worthy. Dominos knows that it is not the tech but the human experience. https://techcrunch.com/2019/06/17/dominos-serves-up-self-driving-pizza-delivery-pilot-in-houston/
8. Your online reputation is your resume. What is the best way to protect your brand on social media? https://hbrascend.org/topics/can-protect-social-media-reputation/
9. Jack Phan's talk at the Adobe Experience Maker's Live is a must watch. https://www.adobe.com/events/experience-makers-live/2020/building-brand-equity-with-help-from-k-pop-stans.html
10. Sweden to End Twitter Experiment Letting Ordinary People Be Nation's Voice. https://www.nytimes.com/2018/09/16/world/europe/sweden-twitter-account.html
11. This is a quick read on what is social selling. But don't just stop at that try it out. https://blog.hootsuite.com/what-is-social-selling/
12. More and more new-age firms are setting up in-house creative teams. https://economictimes.indiatimes.com/industry/services/advertising/more-and-more-new-age-firms-are-setting-up-in-house-creative/articleshow/69179800.cms
13. Influencers play a powerful role in shaping the brand's relationship with its customers and consumers This applies to B2B customers as well as to B2C customers where it is commonplace. https://www.

convinceandconvert.com/influencer-marketing/influencer-marketing-statistics/
14. The perfect storm in a mask market. https://www.wired.com/story/surreal-frenzy-inside-us-biggest-mask-maker/
15. High fashion brands are now making face masks as well. https://www.theguardian.com/fashion/2020/mar/24/prada-the-latest-fashion-brand-to-make-medical-face-masks
16. The carmakers face of choice—they need to either adapt or face extinction. https://www.economist.com/leaders/2020/04/23/the-car-industry-faces-a-short-term-crisis-and-long-term-decline
17. Beyond the well-known names there at least forty other companies which are making autonomous vehicles. https://www.cbinsights.com/research/autonomous-driverless-vehicles-corporations-list/
18. Google parent company spins off self-driving car business. https://www.nytimes.com/2016/12/13/technology/google-parent-company-spins-off-waymo-self-driving-car-business.html
19. Dyson has scrapped its electric car project. https://www.bbc.com/news/business-50004184
20. Facebook and Jio combine forces. https://www.wsj.com/articles/facebook-takes-5-7-billion-stake-in-indias-jio-11587521592
21. Who are Amazon's main competitors? https://www.investopedia.com/ask/answers/120314/who-are-amazons-amzn-main-competitors.asp
22. The CEO of Logitec describes how the use of design-driven market transformation led to a seven fold increase in its market capitalisation. https://www.mckinsey.com/business-functions/mckinsey-design/our-insights/are-you-asking-enough-from-your-design-leaders
23. From gathering data across multiple channels—online and offline to creating personalized communication campaigns Adobe has set the standard for Omnichannel Marketing. https://www.adobe.com/in/experience-cloud/topics/omni-channel-marketing.html
24. This episode was one of my favourite. https://mastersofscale.com/brian-chesky-handcrafted/
25. Powerful exercise to trigger the imagination of your team on how to delight the employees or customers. https://uxdesign.cc/applying-airbnbs-11-star-framework-to-the-candidate-experience-3f0b9c4e68a3
26. Jakob Nielsen's ten usability heuristics is my favorite. But there are other options listed here. https://uxplanet.org/5-examples-of-brilliant-ux-design-8e847bf0bcc0
27. With the explosion of learning content, LXPs use AI to discover and recommend content. https://joshbersin.com/2019/03/learning-experience-platform-lxp-market-grows-up-now-too-big-to-ignore/
28. Many of the European Countries like Germany Sweden, Norway and

Monaco face the challenge of ageing populations. https://www.cnbc.com/2012/10/30/Countries-With-Aging-Populations.html

29. Kathleen Hessert is one the leading experts on Gen Z. She was kind enough to share her research with me.
30. The carmakers have to come together and figure out the future of automobiles in a world shaped by work-from-home and demand for clean tech. https://www.economist.com/leaders/2020/04/25/the-car-industry-faces-a-short-term-crisis-and-long-term-decline
31. Electric cars threaten the heart of Germany's economy. https://www.nytimes.com/2019/12/31/business/electric-cars-germany-economy.html
32. Apple sales rise even during the pandemic. https://www.wsj.com/articles/apple-sales-rise-slightly-showing-resilience-in-pandemic-11588280341
33. Search results give a peek inside our minds. Here is what people were searching for during the pandemic while they were isolated. https://www.thinkwithgoogle.com/consumer-insights/coronavirus-consumer-behavior-research/
34. Twenty-six years of patent leadership. https://www.research.ibm.com/patents/
35. The Paradox of Stretch Goals: Organisations in Pursuit of the Seemingly Impossible. https://journals.aom.org/doi/abs/10.5465/amr.2008.0038
36. Predicting depression via social media. https://www.microsoft.com/en-us/research/publication/predicting-depression-via-social-media/
37. https://medium.com/@katiemartell/why-oracle-modern-cx-2019-had-a-troll-temporarily-94ab425bab6a

5

A New Lens to View

The pyramid of Giza remained the tallest man-made structure in the world for over 3,800 years. The grave robbers looked for the same objects as the archaeologists. While the robbers went after the gold and precious items, the archaeologists discovered the wonders of a world long gone, by examining everyday objects. We need the mindset of an archaeologist, but we have to piece together the future. Solving this six billion piece jigsaw puzzle will need a new leadership model.

Digital Nomads are the hunter-gatherers of the world of work. They pack their laptop in a backpack and a few clothes into a suitcase as they cross borders. Everything is ambiguous, much like today's world of work.

Mobility Is Optional

With more than fifteen million confirmed cases across more than 200 countries, COVID-19 has changed the world of work more than electricity did.

It is still unclear when offices will run at full capacity again, or whether employees will need to work from a single location at all. According to McKinsey, the world will see 7.5 million fewer vehicles in 2020. Public transport utilisation has dropped between 70-90 per cent across the world. If offices do not expect employees to commute to the workplace, public transportation is not going to see an easy recovery.

Invisible Shifts

Some of the effects are less visible. As previously stated, the 202-year-old Brooks Brothers filed for bankruptcy in early July 2020. What made them pull down the shutters?

Offices started declaring casual Fridays. Wearing hoodies to work became the informal dress code to signal that you were cool and belonged to tech. This was the missed tsunami warning. Then the pandemic sealed their fate. People could work from anywhere in track pants and T-shirts and Brooks Brothers went bankrupt.

WFH changed to WFA

Work from Home was for many employers, corporate speak for an extra vacation day. It was done discreetly as a perk given to the boss' favourite. The boss would occasionally work from home, but it was not a universally understood acronym.

During the early days of the lockdown, WFH was meant to be a short-term measure. Then employers had to soon let employees WFA. Many employees had gone back to their hometown or village and this was inevitable. Work had become boundaryless. It could be done by anyone anywhere, in most cases. Hiring talent too became boundaryless.

Everyone now has access to the same information and is more digitally connected. The leader has to facilitate collaboration. Leaders can't micromanage anymore. Leaders have to focus on outcomes, not inputs. Leadership and management books have to be rewritten to deal with an entirely remote workforce operating from homes all over the world. B-schools have never taught their students how to deal with this world. Executive education is unprepared. People are making up their own truth as things unfold.

Generalists will find it attractive to be employed but their opportunities will be limited by the employer's vision ... Specialists can experience boundaryless opportunities

Casual, unstructured meetings and conversations with colleagues can be a barrier to efficiency. They are essential to drive innovation and create the emotional relationship with an organisation. WFA is convenient but will impact innovation because there is a value to spontaneous conversations that help people learn and riff off each other. One can piece together jazz concerts by recording individuals playing in their own homes and then stitch it together. But it would sound much like the music written by AI—devoid of soul. The notes are perfect, but it lacks the soul.

We Are All Digital Nomads

As work and talent become location free, the core of work experience is changing. We have all become Digital Nomads where the workplace has become invisible. Meanwhile, the parliament of Estonia created a 'digital nomad visa' that allows 'location-independent knowledge workers to live in Estonia for up to a year while working for employers or clients outside of the country, ushering in a new era of work—one where knowledge workers aren't tied to one desk or even one continent.'[1]

We may not be able to go to Estonia today, but we can be located in any part of India and be employed anywhere in the world. There is no need for a work visa. It turns out that being a Digital Nomad is more about having the right mindset than the visa. Our mindset works like an operating system.

Trend spotter Mary Meeker said in her 2018 report that 'freelance work is growing three times faster than the growth of the total workforce'. Work is also a source of our identity. Digital Nomads switch 'jobs' and their identity every few weeks or months. They move from highly skilled work to manual labour—any work that can be done from that location and pays enough. They do odd jobs to survive and thrive no matter what.

Here are some ways to build yourself a Digital Nomad mindset whether you are employed or are a freelancer.

1. **Stay flexible:** When medical devices (e.g. pacemakers) were built, to keep costs low, the software that was written for it was very limited. Cybercriminals soon learnt to exploit that. That created opportunities for doctors, who worked with cybersecurity experts and regulators, to create more secure medical devices. Collaborating is a great skill that opens up many possibilities.
2. **Become a creator:** Learn something with the intent of teaching it to others. Take a topic in your area of interest and deconstruct it to be able to teach others. Once you have done this a few times, move on to a subject that is adjacent to your area of expertise and try it out.
3. **Become a novice often:** Learning something from scratch is painful at first. But it is a confidence booster. You believe you can 'figure it out'. Books, podcasts, TED talks, Zoom webinars, discussions with other experts—there are many ways to feed your curiosity.

'We brought our office laptop home and continued as if nothing had changed.'

The Digital Nomads love thriving in ambiguity and learning on the fly. It helps them move beyond one role and one identity. Even if you are employed, a Digital Nomad's mindset is a fabulous advantage to have in the world of work.

Complex Equations

3. What do you think you are doing well?

4. If you were your own coach, what ideas would you have?

5. How can I help YOU?

6. What suggestions do you have for me to be a better manager?

Sign up for a weekly newsletter of visuals
https://abhijitbhaduri.substack.com

During the lockdown, I stepped out to buy some groceries from a small kirana shop run by Srinivas and his wife. In an effort to make small talk, I told Srinivas that he is in a business that remains unaffected even during a pandemic. After all, people still need to buy groceries. Srinivas shook his head and said, 'Business is down 50 per cent.'

He explained, 'The government is sending food to people every day during the lockdown. Most of these people are daily wage earners who are unable to go to work now. If food comes to their doorstep, why would they spend money and buy groceries from me? I don't know how long I can keep this shop going.'

The lockdown was sudden and forced people to take decisions that they would have otherwise made over weeks and months in the pre-pandemic days. When the police chase away squatters and illegal hawkers, who sell stuff on the pavement, most of them simply shift to a different location and continue with their business as usual. Most businesses did just that.

WFH simply meant picking up laptops and continuing work in exactly the same way as it was done in the office. Obsessed with not losing even an ounce of productivity, people did not pause to reflect on this change. They wanted the status quo to continue. What could've been the first building block of true digital transformation was lost. Besides hardware, software, connectivity and cyber security, leaders had to figure out how to hire, train and build bonds with someone whom they have only seen through a screen. The team leader of a Canadian firm told me, 'Online dating is crazy. But a virtual marriage is insane. That's how I am running my team. Human beings need to see each other to build trust.'

Offices were used to having a few members dial in to the meeting room where the decision makers were assembled. No one cared for the engagement of the people on call. In the past, people attended day-long classes and workshops by dialling in, but since the majority of the participants were physically present in the classroom they did not care about the minority who were joining in from remote locations.

Ever since we moved the office to our homes, videoconferencing has become essential to how meetings, hiring (and firing), appraisals and endless online classes and webinars are done. We have just assumed that everyone who knows how to run a slide deck can be asked to run a webinar. Employees deal with it by having the webinar run on the office laptop and the Netflix movie on their mobile.

The weekly meeting that used to take two hours when everyone was in the same room, was now moved to video.

At the end of the day, even socialising with colleagues is on video. Families juggle daily chores while responding to emails. Video meetings are often interrupted by family members walking past the screen causing embarrassing situations.

Teachers across the world have been told to offer classes online, so they are teaching the same way as they did when the students were in the classroom. The result is chaotic. There are complaints of parents joining the classes to evaluate the teacher's skills and calling them after class to give unsolicited advice. Evaluating the students is becoming tougher. Colleges face additional challenges. Many students are opting for a gap year and that may make the smaller colleges collapse because their funds will run out.

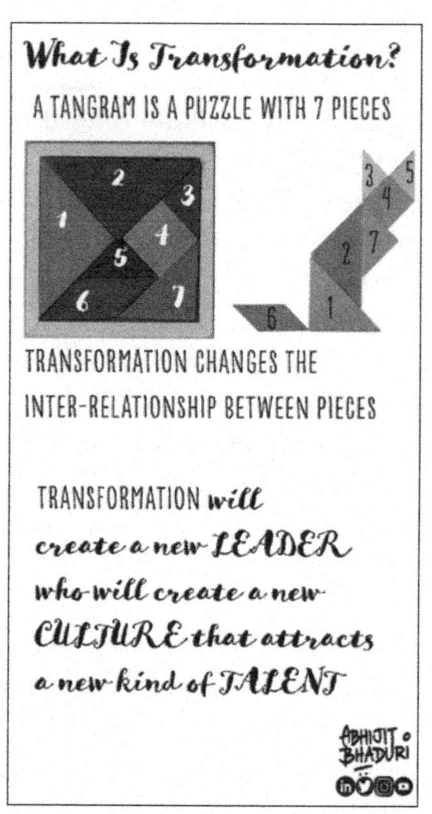

Maybe it will recraft the business model of educational institutes. Maybe students will not need to take student loans to get a degree most employers do not value.

Is College Irrelevant?

Google announced three new online certificate programmes in data analytics, project management and user experience because they can lead to 'high-growth, high-paying careers'. The courses are created and taught by Google employees, do not require a college degree, can be completed in three to six months and are offered through the online learning platform, Coursera. Google says it will consider all of its certificates as the equivalent of a four-year college degree for related roles at the company.[2]

A course that can be completed in three months and costs $50 gets you a head start towards a high paying career. Compare that to the cost of a four-year programme at Harvard. The total 2020-2021 cost of attending Harvard without financial aid is $49,653 for tuition and $72,391 for tuition, room, board, and fees combined. That is for one year. A four-year programme will cost approximately $300,000.[3]

Microsoft has launched an initiative to help 25 million people worldwide acquire the digital skills needed in a COVID-19 economy. They will bring in the LinkedIn learning programmes, the GitHub platform for projects and mentorship and create learning paths for changing the skill base of millions. Amazon's Machine Learning University courses are online. They are free and now available to anyone, not just employees.

The cost of education is prohibitive in most countries. The employability levels remain patchy and questionable. This is the perfect storm and an opportunity to lift millions out of poverty into middle class.

Is learning limited to employability? Skills have a shorter shelf life and need to be built with a short-term focus. It is probably more efficient to learn the hard skills online (any subject which has a single correct response). People will supplement these with discussion groups and experiments which will still need common infrastructure.

Colleges will be valuable if they focus on building curiosity and the love for learning. The Liberal Arts colleges will thrive. You need to be able to work with other people to build self-awareness and other-awareness, especially when it comes to learning about how to work with others to collaborate and innovate. Colleges will still be the petri-dish to ignite the ability to dream and work with other human beings. Learning about ethics, philosophy, design and all the cross functional disciplines will still need a peer group. But falling rates and leaps in immersive technology will create hybrid models. Education will be in the 'work-in-progress' category for a while.

Rediscover the Equilibrium

The work-worker-workplace equilibrium has to be found again. Making the workplace safe, vaccinated and hygienic is something we can no longer take for granted. From the seating arrangement to social distance in elevators and contactless security, checks are being set up everywhere. Airports, hospitals, restaurants, offices, supply chains and institutions are wondering how to prepare the place to be safe to do business. Post lockdown, when productivity was maintained, it was probably driven by anxiety and fear of job loss. Such a gain is not sustainable. Leaders are already worried about the fate of their innovation agenda. It may be too early to say WFA will replace going to an office.

Administrators are worried about getting people back in the office and being blamed for unexpected fallouts. One rule can no longer fit every worker. It is as if the work contract has to be rewritten for the new circumstances. HR teams are wondering if they need to create a post-pandemic version of HR. That may actually be an idea whose time has come.

Work From Home Story #1

The phone rings. It is past 7 p.m. in the evening. The boss is asking the employee to accept a video call connection. The employee reluctantly switches on the camera. The boss notices a beer mug next to the employee.

The boss points out that the visible beer can is not appropriate since this is an official call. The employee reminds the boss that it is after office hours and the unplanned video call was initiated by the boss.

System 1 and System 2

If you are asked to calculate 2x3, you won't need time to calculate the response (unless you are like me). But if you are told to calculate 435x7, it is likely to take more time and some brisk mental math. The first challenge is an example of System 1 thinking. System 2 needs more deliberate thinking and more time. It is tougher and not so pleasant. That is a peculiar contradiction of sorts.

We dislike predictability because our mind quickly figures out patterns. We love surprises because they break patterns. We need just the optimum level of difficulty and challenge.

As long as we can predict what the next step is, the brain moves to auto-pilot mode. When someone describes his or her job as 'dull' or 'having no challenge', you can bet there is nothing new in the work expected of them. System 1 thinking has no challenge. Learning anything new is painful and demands repetition because it draws on System 2 thinking until we get really good at it.

Psychologist Daniel Kahneman refers to this as System 1 thinking. System 1 thinking is fast, instinctive and emotional. In System 2 thinking, the decision is slow, effortful and logical. It accounts for only 2 per cent of our thinking.[4]

When we first learn to drive a car, we are using System 2. It is stressful and exhausting. The brain forms new connections between neurons. We have to remember many things about driving even as we look at everyone on the road rushing towards us. Once we have mastered the art of driving, we can listen to music and even talk to our co-passengers while we enjoy the sights and sounds around us.

Repetition helps us create new neural pathways that enable us to retrieve the new knowledge effortlessly. In laypersons' language we call this muscle memory when it is possible to do something without consciously thinking about it.

When we have no time to think things through we resort to System 1 thinking and that perpetuates the status quo.

Dealing with complexity or uncertainty, makes our brain use System 2 thinking. People describe the current scenario as VUCA which describes all the stress-inducing conditions, when the brain is on high alert trying to survive.

The pandemic threatened our survival. Our daily routines changed. The news reported deaths and the helplessness of experts. There was talk of job loss and businesses shutting down. People were working from home with the children and the elderly. Everyone was using System 2 thinking all the time. That led to fatigue and frayed tempers. Then there was Zoom fatigue and hygiene fatigue. Even before we had recovered from the first wave of the pandemic, there was a second wave and further job losses being predicted.[5]

Work From Home Story #2

The twenty-five-year-old girl tells her parents that she has a review meeting with her manager. 'He is very short-tempered and shouts a lot during the meetings.'

As expected, the boss gets upset during the review and uses a profanity. The girl switches off the speaker but her father has heard the boss curse. A visibly upset father asks, 'Is this the kind of language your colleagues use? Why don't you lodge a formal complaint with HR?'

Free Ivy League classes—any takers?

If you did not get a chance to attend an Ivy League college, you could do it for free during the pandemic. Several colleges offered hundreds of free courses.

People were quick to sign up, but a much smaller percentage actually completed the course. Nevertheless, getting Ivy League education has never been easier. They can get the content but not the experience of going to that college. Is that a compromise?

It was a challenging period for colleges, as the pandemic had destroyed all enrollment projections for the academic year starting in the next few months. It was unclear how many students would be able to (or would wish to) travel for the start of the next academic year. Students did not know if college hostels would be functional, and whether families could afford tuition payments amid rapidly deteriorating economic conditions.

Study From Home Story #1

The schoolteacher is teaching her class on video. She notices that the students are deeply engaged in the lecture.

She is blissfully unaware of the students actively exchanging messages on WhatsApp where they are trading cruel jokes about her and a few are trading salacious clips they have downloaded from an adult site.

Educators have always sneered at online classes as being inferior to attending in-person lectures. Now that may become the default method. Who will train millions of teachers on how to teach while on camera?

'Online Class Is Not the Real Thing'

Aditya (not his real name) had secured admission to Harvard Business School and was all set to join classes in August 2020. Then he learned that Harvard University had advised students not to return to campus after spring break in mid-March 2020. 'I don't want to pay $200,000 to learn through videos. Online class is not the real thing.'

Students worldwide had to cope with abrupt loss of campus life, animated debates in classes, extracurriculars, traditions like convocation and all the other things that made up the college experience. Educational institutions struggled with loss of revenue and funds to invest in salaries and research. Keeping the lights on for a smaller group of students made it financially unviable. Business schools are saddled with tuition fee losses if the number of applicants fall or seek deferred admission. Those which have limited financial reserves will collapse. But getting students to the campus may risk spreading the virus and impacting the professors who are often in the age group that is vulnerable. Without the network that an on-campus experience creates and without the prospect of on-campus job offers, students may rethink their choices. That creates a downward spiral that will take years to rebuild.

System 2 Thinking to Reimagine Work

In India, I learned to drive on the left side of the road. When I first started driving a car in the US, I had to reorient myself. It was a strange feeling to drive on what I had always known to be 'the wrong side'. However, that was the rule in the new country. While getting into the car in the US, I would open the door to the passenger side, because my brain would be on autopilot unless I made a conscious effort to learn and relearn. Even after a few months of driving on the 'right side', I would find myself fumbling at the roundabouts, trying to remember that I needed to go anti-clockwise instead. Unlearning is extremely hard.

Work must be omnichannel: The lockdown forced organisations to let their employees work from home. Many businesses were caught unprepared for this digital transformation on steroids. While senior leaders have been used to working from home, it was not a privilege that was shared with everybody. The untested assumption was that people will not work hard if they work from home.

When the lockdown happened, most businesses were gobsmacked trying to figure out what work from home would look like. Overnight desktops, laptops and portable 4G hotspots were bought for everyone. Hard to believe we never thought of this. VPNs were used to secure data.

Each role had to be reimagined and adapted to how it would operate in a digital environment. Comedians have learned to do their routine minus the studio audience.

Lack of high net speed connections and software that kept transactions secure were the first set of problems businesses had to solve. The bigger problem was that work was shifted lock, stock and barrel to the home. What skills would the learning and development team need to be effective in the new omnichannel environment where a certain percentage of roles may never need to work in a co-located space again? What skills would make managers effective in running remote teams and still keep productivity high?

New skills to learn: Team managers had never been skilled in managing project delivery when the entire team was remote. Video conferencing became the new toy that everyone discovered during the lockdown.

Every minute was allocated to a meeting or else devoted to mandatory online classes. 'It is business as usual,' the employees were told. It was business as usual only for the digital giants who were becoming even more powerful and growing at a steady rate. The rest of the businesses should have hunkered down and reimagined the work-worker-workplace equilibrium.

A lily pad is growing in a pond, doubling in size every day. On the twentieth day, the pond is fully covered. When was it half covered? System 1 thinking tells you that half of twenty is ten. But the correct response needs you to pause and think and put aside your System 1 response. You say the pond was half covered on the nineteenth day, right?

Let us not redesign the new world of work with System 1 thinking.

The Greatest Skill Gap Worldwide

It is not to say that people have not managed working with teams that are geographically dispersed. All multinationals have had employees operate from different countries. They would periodically get the global teams together for conferences in different regions.

Every function would have its regional meetings. The country heads of Asia would meet regularly every quarter for their reviews. The functional teams would do the same. As part of the HR team at PepsiCo, every HR director would take turns to host the quarterly meetings. The HR team in each country got a chance to socialise and learn from others. There are functional meetings, country meetings, regional meetings and global meetings.

When the work-worker-workplaces equilibrium changes, we have to reimagine leadership, talent and culture.

But when the entire team is remote, they are not necessarily working in the same country or even the same continent. Add to this visa restrictions that many countries put up, and talent will go boundaryless. But managing a boundaryless population is going to become the greatest skill gap.

Reimagine Work and Learning

Kavi Arasu, an expert in organisational effectiveness and learning design says, 'Instead of reimagining work in this new setting, we simply assume that the same work is happening in a different location—the home.'

'Speaking to a Zoom camera does not turn it into a webinar. Familiarity with PowerPoint is not the same as facilitating learning. Dumping endless hours of meaningless (but mandatory) webinars onto the employee is not going to get them upskilled. Learning has to be reimagined for this new medium. The classroom has moved,' says Kavi.

Unbundling of Work

Li Jin is a partner at Andreessen Horowitz, focused on early-stage consumer investments. In particular, she's interested in marketplaces and technology that enables people to turn passions into professions.

She talks about the 'unbundling of work'. She says that people no longer have to go through an organisation to reach the buyer of their services. From teachers, podcasters, live streamers of video games, authors ... they can all take their work directly to consumers and monetise their talent.

There are marketplaces for all kinds of skills—from dumpling shoppers to fitness geeks and Math nerds—to enable monetisation independent of an intermediary. You are your own organisation.

Joshua Karthik Rallapati is the CEO and product designer for getpepped.com, a site that aims to help creators reach their audience and monetise their services. 'Use it to build a first or second income' is their motto. Getpepped.com is a marketplace for anything that can be sold as a video or audio download or played live to a paying audience. Joshua's brother, the celeb photographer Joseph Radhik offers a week-long course on photography. It is an opportunity for your audience to buy into your experience. The digital platforms offer reach, opportunity for impact and help you build your personal brand, independent of the organisation.

Imagine if you were the fourth wicket-keeper or the tenth wicket keeper for the Indian cricket team. Someone had to be very lucky to get a chance to be chosen consistently. The IPL effectively becomes a talent market for cricketers—

including retired players who can be experts who provide insights and show patterns that are invisible to the audience. The individual player is valued through the auction. The value accrues directly to the individual.

The Learner Has Millions of Choices

An employee attending an online course at home is not the same as the employee attending a training programme in the office. Binge watching slickly produced serials and movies has refined our standards. Viewers are used to stopping a Hollywood blockbuster if it is not engaging in the first few minutes. Sandhya, an employee of an audit firm says, 'The office meeting or online course has to be better than the Netflix movie I could watch instead.' She simply switches on a movie on her mobile while the employer-recommended online class plays on her office laptop. Learning from an online class needs the course material to be structured differently.

Employees are anxious about their future. That needs to be addressed by the head of the business. Learning is a social experience. Online courses must provide that. That is a big puzzle that has not yet been solved. Breakout rooms and webinars on Zoom are about as effective as the happy hours/dinners that companies celebrate on Zoom. They remind me of children cooking with make-believe kitchen sets. Parents also indulge them by pretending the 'dinner' was awesome. We are in that phase of online learning. So let us keep the System 2 thinking on.

Communicating through Video—A New Competency

Most online classes are excruciatingly boring because they have the speaker continue for long stretches without involving participants. This can be done through polls, parallel chats, drawings, videos, quizzes built in every few minutes. It is hard for the speaker to see the facial expressions of the learner, which would be essential to build engagement.

How long would you watch an ad about devices, apps and software? Twenty seconds, maybe thirty? A seven MINUTE ad that speaks about how everything that needed you to be co-located can be done by using the right devices, apps and software is a fantastic example of storytelling done right. Look up 'The whole working-from-home thing—Apple' on YouTube. The human elements prevail so sharply that even though Apple products feature in every scene, they do not come in the way of your experience.

If the video experience in online learning is not at par with a TED talk, the participants will switch off faster than you think. Google offers a video builder with built-in templates and formats that can allow you to make multiple versions of the content. It is easy to use—try it out.[6]

L&D teams must teach managers how to conduct reviews and give feedback on video, teach online classes, and even tell them how long a virtual meeting can go on before fatigue sets in. It will help people learn that every meeting does not have to be done through video.

Leveraging Audio—The Untapped Opportunity

India is the world's third largest podcast listening market. The number of listeners is going to rise from four crore in 2018 to 17.61 crore in 2023. India's music, radio and podcasts market was worth Rs 5,753 crore in 2018 and could double by 2023.[7]

According to a16z,* new technologies like Apple AirPods, connected cars, and smart speakers have made it much easier for consumers to listen to audio content. That creates revenue models for audio content creators. There are now over 700,000 free podcasts available and thousands more launching each week. One-third of Americans now listen to podcasts monthly and a quarter listen weekly.[8]

Try It Out

1. Use audio clips to create instructions that can guide a newbie as they get started. Try it for your onboarding programme. Museums have been doing it to tell stories and build interest in the exhibits.
2. Podcasts can be a powerful learning medium. Use them instead of sending readings. Discussions with experts can get people excited enough to explore a topic on their own.
3. Use podcasts with consumers to tell your brand story.
4. Instead of sending a presentation about your organisation, create an audio version of the business and engage listeners.

---

*Founded in 2009 by Marc Andreessen and Ben Horowitz, Andreessen Horowitz (known as 'a16z') is a venture capital firm in Silicon Valley. The numeronym is the first and last letter of the firm with the character count in-between.

5. Twitter has introduced audio tweets. Here are some creative ways you can use the function (you can find many more creative uses):
   a. Share brand stories by consumers
   b. Share a short announcement about an event
   c. Share a news item and include what it means to your industry/organisation or profession
   d. Wish someone on their birthday with an audio tweet
   e. Run an audio quiz

Learning by Simply Being There

In a college, students learn not just from the class lectures but also through heated debates with intellectually superior peers. The informal interactions with alumni and faculty are a crucial part of the learning experience.

In the same way, people learn about the work-worker-workplace equilibrium by observing their peers and leaders. Learning is a social process.[9]

Without being co-located, they will miss out on learning by observing the behavioural and emotional responses that others have to a situation. Leadership is a contact sport, they say. That may need some rethinking and adaptation. People will need to reflect and reimagine work, learning and socialising in the new setting. We have not had time to think it through. It is a new world of work.

Creating a New Language

When adults try to learn a new language, they try to translate every word from a language they think in. One of the tips experts share is that we need to start by labelling everything around us. Language learners are always embarrassed about their mistakes, especially when they make it in front of native speakers. Experts say, 'Native speakers are like doting parents: any attempt from you to communicate in their language is objective proof that you are a gifted genius. They'll appreciate your effort and even help you.'[10]

The organisations have a chance to create hybrid opportunities. Creating a more human organisation to address the world of work is a task that leaders have to undertake.

Our assumptions about work have changed. It does not have to be done in the office or in the workplace. Neither is there a distinction between home and office nor a different point of time clearly marked for work or leisure. This ambiguity causes stress. People do not know how to behave and often freeze. The leader can use this ambiguity to join the exploration to create the workplace that people desire without compromising on business needs. Helping them think of skills rather than jobs, gets employees prepared for the future.

Leadership models were insulated from the outside world and are driven by the leader as the all-powerful figure leading the organisation. This is the age when employees and customers own the brand. Employee activism is forcing leaders to take positions on sensitive issues like politics, race and transgender rights—all issues the previous generations of leaders swerved away from. The leader's success in the new world of work lies in leading through inspiration and influence rather than by brute force and power. This is the time for the employees and leaders to dream together and then join hands to turn those dreams into reality.

New Roles in HR

If you have been to a hospital recently you would've noticed the bewildering array of specialisations that many of them offer. Options to consult an Orthodontist, Maxillofacial surgeon, Periodontics, Prosthodontics etc. were not commonly found in hospitals. Specialisation shows the evolution. There may be a need to create new roles in HR. Here are a few I would start with right away:[11]

1. **Talent Sherpas:** They will be experts in employer branding and will have a powerful presence in all the talent communities. They will be the evangelists for an organisation's culture and will be able to craft a winning proposition for the candidate as well as the organisation. The Talent Sherpas will have a way of understanding the skills and learning capabilities of people and can suggest roles that help the candidate to realise their potential. They know the internal candidates just as well and can help develop and retain the internal talent pool.

2. **Onboarding Experience Designer:** Organisations hire people. Yet there are not enough people who know how to onboard a new hire. And by that I don't mean giving them office space and a laptop. Onboarding happens when a new hire feels mentally integrated and contributes to the role as was expected when he or she was hired. Designing an onboarding experience is like being an instructional designer. It is about sharing the tips and nudging the new hire to navigate through the culture while making new connections and getting buy-in on the expectations of key stakeholders. Definitely a task for a designer.

3. **Motivational Insights Analysts:** Many more employees are motivated by work passion than career ambition. Yet we know that motivation is a deeply personal process. Two people doing the same job could be motivated by two different needs. These analysts will be able to shape the

role, the total rewards system and the feedback process in a manner that makes it meaningful to the employee. It is surprising that we have left the important business of motivating employees to people who usually have no special training in this field. And yet we expect people to stay motivated.

4. Employment Contract Designer: More and more professionals are becoming available through apps. Working models are changing. The pay-per-use model is giving rise to terms like 1099 workers (in the US) which refer to those workers who are offering their services to companies (like the Uber drivers) as contrasted with W2 workers who are permanent employees on the rolls of the employer and who get benefits like paid time off etc. Every country has different employment laws and as new employment formats evolve, so will the levels of complexity. The employment contracts are going to get more complex and will need someone who knows employment law and works with Talent Sherpas and Motivation Analysts to create employment contracts that are in line with the evolving models of work.

5. Learning Curators and Hackers: Changing business models and regulatory environments need people who can pick up just the right amount of knowledge in time, to translate it to the task at hand. Learning curators will be able to quickly understand the knowledge and skill gaps that are barriers to performance. The curators will be able to create byte-size modules of information and hack the best way to learn complex information and skills. This will need skills of personalisation of the content because people have differing learning styles.

6. Weak Signal Receivers and Sense Makers: In a world where speed is everything, the ability to pick up early signals makes all the difference. Many of these signals are bubbling up in conversations on social media. Senior leaders often complain of feeling overwhelmed by the amount of information they have to consume and make sense of before they react to it. Having someone who can listen to those signals and cull out only what is relevant for the leader to react to is imperative. Very often this means connecting apparently unconnected pieces of information. This needs someone who understands the strategy of the firm and uses that to filter the signals from the noise.

7. Technology and Data Ethicist: As employers start collecting more and more data about the employees, it is important to have someone who represents the ethical framework for data usage in the organisation. Think about it like the equivalent of someone governing the General Data Protection Regulation (GDPR) framework for the firm. Should the firm use face-recognition technology to mark attendance of remote workers? Should the company push keystroke logging software without informing the employees?

New Possibilities

Traditionally, organisations have worked based on one rule that every employee of the organisation had to follow. Then came the era of five or six sets of rules that applied to five or six types of employment contracts that were offered by an organisation. What if each individual employee had their own unique contract based on all the possible variables they could choose from. Today, several startups and digital disruptors have very few employees. Will these organisations create new models of performance management and rewards? Will they grow their own talent by hacking new ways of learning at a rapid pace or will they buy out talent on a pay-per-use model? The possibilities are immense.

As new business models appear, it will trigger the creation of new roles in HR. For the workplace norms to evolve, we need to build new specialisations in HR.

References

1. Estonia's visa for Digital Nomads could become the prototype for firms. https://sifted.eu/articles/digital-nomad-visa-estonia/
2. Google's new courses offer three high paying opportunities. https://www.cnbc.com/2020/07/13/google-announces-certificates-in-data-project-management-and-ux.html
3. Cost of Harvard education. https://www.harvard.edu/about-harvard/harvard-glance
4. Thinking fast and slow is a must read book to understand how various kinds of biases and heuristics tends to challenge a rational decision making process. https://www.nytimes.com/2011/11/27/books/review/thinking-fast-and-slow-by-daniel-kahneman-book-review.html
5. Even before the first wave of coronavirus has been handled, a second wave is predicted. https://edition.cnn.com/2020/05/02/health/coronavirus-second-wave-fall-season/index.html
6. YouTube video builder. https://create.withgoogle.com/tools/youtube-video-builder
7. Podcasts are growing in India. https://www.newindianexpress.com/entertainment/hindi/2020/jun/28/lend-me-your-ears-how-podcasts-bring-voice-amid-quarantine-2161409.html
8. 'A Podcast About Podcasts' by a16z is a must listen. https://a16z.com/2019/05/23/podcast-ecosystem-investing-2019/
9. Albert Bandura theory of social learning stresses how we learn from the emotional reactions of others around us. https://www.instructionaldesign.org/theories/social-learning/
10. 'Don't worry about making mistakes', and many other tips on how to learn a new language. https://blog.ted.com/how-to-learn-a-new-language-7-secrets-from-ted-translators/
11. '6 HR roles for the future' was written in 2016 but I have updated the roles. https://www.peoplematters.in/article/leadership/6-hr-roles-future-12904

6

The Convergence

Trends and Insights

During the border skirmishes between India and China, people suggested that India should boycott Chinese products. Chinese apps were blocked. Chinese restaurants faced hostility. No one focused on the Chinese companies like Alibaba and Tencent that have invested in startups like Paytm, BigBasket, Snapdeal, Zomato, Byju's, Dream11, Hike, Ola and Swiggy. Are these 'Indian' startups? These are not questions that can be answered in a binary manner. In a hyperconnected world, the answers lie entangled like noodles with socio-economic-political-historical factors. It is the time of convergence.

The British Broadcasting Corporation (BBC) says, '... the drivers, cooks, migrants, students, and many blue-

and white-collar workers watching and sharing videos have driven up India's average mobile data consumption ten times in two years, to more than 10 GB per user per month, roughly the same as in the USA.'[1]

Before we get carried away with that, we have to remember that India still has 300 million mobile subscribers trapped in the 2G era. Their feature phones do not let them access the basic uses of internet. Maybe they will leapfrog straight to 5G. More than 450 million smart phone users (about one-third of the population), armed with the cheapest mobile data plans in the world, are hooked on to watching videos.

Do Organisations have Nationalities?

Video sharing app TikTok lets users post short clips that are less than a minute, usually set to music or a film dialogue. There was Musical.ly, which was a lip sync app that became a rage. The Chinese giant ByteDance bought Musical.ly and added some features and TikTok was born. Overall, it has been downloaded more than two billion times. Its user base is young, with 41 per cent of them between sixteen and twenty-four years. Chinese apps always generate fears that the company may share user data (location, user profile, sexual preferences and much more) with the government, whether intentionally through data requests or unintentionally through surveillance software.

The bigger the organisation, the more important it is to build trust with stakeholders, not just within the country of origin but also in the other geographies. Tension and skirmishes at the Indo-China border resulted in India banning several Chinese apps. Citizens, especially those who did not like the taste of Chinese cuisine anyway, drowning in a rush of patriotism did their bit by boycotting Chinese restaurants. But we often forget that in an interconnected world, venture capital is the lifeline of startups. Money rarely carries a passport. Yet, economics may be the casualty when socio-political issues get intertwined with business.

Is Colgate, an Indian company or is it an American company operating in many countries including India? Is Jaguar Land Rover an Indian company or British? What is the nationality of Wipro or Cognizant? Can businesses have the equivalent of a passport? In a hyperconnected world, issues of ownership get fuzzy. Everything has converged. It is not about nationality, it is about trust.

Trust—Not Nationality

TikTok had appointed Kevin Mayer (hired from Disney) as CEO. Digital firms have servers and users in different countries, each with its own set of laws and regulations.

Their product or service generates data and insights that go far beyond the product or service the firm offers. Trust building activities like hiring (and losing) an American CEO or setting up a legal entity on US soil will not solve the trust issue. The millions of data points of 2 billion users already exists on the Chinese servers. Add to that the data that exists about each of us in the largely online world that we have been forced to live in because of the pandemic, the problem is more complex than ever before. The data can be hacked by a rogue state, the dark web, or even a company discreetly funded by an enemy state. There is no getting away from having to build trust between countries if we have to move ahead.

Insights from Search Trends

What people search for can provide insight into what is weighing on the minds of the population. Google trends provide handy insights that have implications for employers and employees alike. Google's annual trends and insights report is called What is India Searching For. By analysing millions of daily search results, the report released in April 2020 shows trends that surface based on half a billion Indians hooked to mobile devices.[2]

TREND 1

Search is a constant companion—always on

While India is holding back on discretionary spending, that does not stop them from searching for 'the best' (for instance, 'the best way to study', 'the best way to lose weight') as they build their consideration set before they actually buy something. People spent almost four-and-a-half hours per day on their smartphone as the COVID-19 disruption continued especially on VOIP chats and social networks. With no access to organised retail, consumers searched for options that were hyper-local. People want to see a range of possibilities even if they are out of reach right now. It is often sobering to learn of who or what the consumer thinks of as a substitute for your product or service. The consumer wants the best and the most accessible in a hassle-free manner. Tip: do not assume that the customers who wanted your product before the lockdown, still want it at the same price.

IMPLEMENTATION CHALLENGE

Starting a Conversation with Your Customers and Employees

- Talk to your employees to identify the concerns and challenges they have. This may be the quickest market survey that you could do.
- Is your product or service available where your customer is? Does your brand show up in a search? What keywords would the customer look for while searching for your product or service?

TREND 2

Authentic, transparent and visual (preferably video)

Online video accounts for more than 70 per cent of India's total data usage. Videos empower the customers and

GOOGLE SEARCHES ON 500M SMARTPHONES
WHAT MATTERS TO INDIANS NOW?

TREND 1: 'NEAR ME'

- AVAILABLE CLOSE-BY
- TRANSPARENT INFO
- BRAND MUST BE OMNICHANNEL

TREND 2: KNOW MORE

70% DATA USAGE IS FOR ONLINE VIDEO EDUCATION TO HOBBIES

LUDO KING - MOST DOWNLOADED

SOURCE: GOOGLE, WHAT IS INDIA SEARCHING FOR

employees to verify information. It also means that the brand must continuously work to build trust. Not surprisingly, immunity and home-remedies feature prominently. The report says, 'From everyday learning to advanced skillsets, e-learning has been clocking hundreds of millions of views everyday over the past couple of years and will likely sustain for a longer time.' There is a 270 per cent growth in searches where people are looking for simple solutions. For example, people search for 'easy dinner recipes', 'easy to draw' or 'easy home decoration'. There will be a huge demand for people who can simplify complex ideas or people who can help others build their skill through simple videos.

IMPLEMENTATION CHALLENGE

Reimagine How You Communicate with Customers and Employees

- Health and safety are going to continue to be important to the customer and employees. How will you constantly communicate that your supply chain is guaranteed to be virus-free and safe? Communicating trust will become a top requirement of every leader.
- Find out about two YouTube and Instagram stars who have your employees hooked. Ask these social media users and mavens to create content that you will use to upscale employees. Ask the influencers to teach your leaders how to communicate through mobile videos.
- Help your employees build skills and businesses that can serve them well if they need to work from home

or in case they are ever unemployed in the future. If any of their family members wish to supplement their income, help them build the skills they will need.

TREND 3

Making online payments the default norm

India is home to the second largest unbanked population in the world. COVID-19 made bill payments impossible through cash and cheques due to the fear of spreading the virus. Making it easy for the product or service to be paid online attracts the second billion consumers as they go online. Searches about UPI from non-metros grew faster at 79 per cent compared to metros at 28 per cent. UPI transactions exceeded those of debit and credit cards in both value and volume. More than 10 million merchants now accept UPI payments.

After a two-week project was delivered, a client sent me an email saying that if I wanted my payment in thirty days, I would have to agree to be paid only 60 per cent of my fee. I would get 80 per cent of my invoiced fee if I agreed to get paid after 120 days. To get 100 per cent of my agreed fee, I would have to wait for 180 days!! Ask any freelancer and they will tell you how the large buyers routinely 'lose invoices' to delay payments to the small and medium businesses.

IMPLEMENTATION CHALLENGE

Reimagine Your Payment Systems—To Pay and Get Paid

- Several organisations use the same payment terms for every supplier. They pay them after sixty or ninety days. These terms are common for an individual freelancer as well as a Fortune 500 company listed as a vendor.

- Ask ex-employees to rate the ease of getting their final settlements and dues. Do an analysis of how long it takes for an employee to get the business expenses reimbursed.
- Reimagine how consumers can adopt and build trust with your payment systems across categories.

TREND 4

Instant gratification

In a time-starved world being able to get something on demand is becoming the baseline for most consumers. They do not like to wait for the long introductory scenes and credits while binge-watching serials. Netflix allows them to skip the credits and offers to start the next episode five seconds after each one ends.

People are looking for organisations and employers who can provide on-demand, commitment-free products and services. Freelancers and gig workers are an example of an on-demand, commitment-free talent pool. Talent pools like this allow for instant gratification and are likely to prove extremely convenient to employers. Since trust is going to be such an important necessity, ensuring the health and safety of the freelancers and gig workers (read 'essential services') will become important to sustain businesses.

> As Indians look for both escape as well as entertainment amidst social distancing norms, the surge in interest for mobile app downloads as well as streaming platforms clearly indicates the step-up change in the on-demand services universe.
>
> Source: ThinkWithGoogle.com April 2020

IMPLEMENTATION CHALLENGE

Build Instant Gratification

- By giving the power back to customers to either start or stop a service they consumed, and simplifying the fulfilment of their needs, brands have a clear opportunity to reimagine the relationship with their consumers.
- Identify opportunities where employees can experience instant gratification. For example: Micro learning courses, where employees watch videos of no more than two to three minutes and take a short three-question quiz to receive a piece of a completion certificate (much like pieces of a jigsaw puzzle). Share information on how they are doing relative to their peer group.

TREND 5

To have a personalised interaction with the brand or employer

There was a 120 per cent surge in search interest in branded and unbranded customer service related queries in March 2020 alone as compared to previous months.

Graphical User Interface (GUI) uses graphics to improve the user experience. Conversational User Interface (CUI) uses emotions and natural language.

Using AI- and ML-powered chatbots in recruitment shows an improved candidate experience and lower recruiter time spent on answering repetitive queries. These are the two big advantages that users cite. Fifty-two per cent users

USING
A
CONVERSATIONAL
CHATBOT IN HR
1. IMPROVES THE
CANDIDATE'S
EXPERIENCE
2. SAVES THE
RECRUITER'S
TIME
USEFUL TO PROVIDE
24X7 SUPPORT WHILE
HIRING LARGE NUMBERS
USE FOR SIMPLE,
REPETITIVE LOW
VALUE TASKS
KEEPS CANDIDATES ENGAGED
SOURCE: TLNT.COM
ABHIJIT
BHADURI

deploy their chatbot at the application stage. Almost 21 per cent use their chatbots to further their recruitment marketing.

The central government of India launched a WhatsApp chatbot, 'MyGov Corona Helpdesk', to address queries regarding the COVID-19 outbreak. The chatbot was developed by Haptik, a conversational AI platform to provide timely updates and help citizens find answers to their queries about COVID-19. According to Haptik, within a month more than 55 million messages had been sent by over 20 million users.

IMPLEMENTATION CHALLENGE

Personalised and Humanised Conversations

- Identify areas where your marketing communication can be personalised by using digital tech.
- By analysing performance data and various data points about the individual employee, create a personalised career track that will help the employee build skills for the roles they aspire to.

Building the Mindset and the 'Heart-Set'

One of the most powerful ways in which organisations can drive the change would be the use of video and audio in employee related communication.

1. *'With me' videos:* There is an interesting genre of videos on YouTube which are called 'with me' videos. These videos show someone studying for hours together in front of the

video. That is meant to inspire you to study along with the person whose video you are watching. If that person studies for three hours, the viewer is expected to do the same at their end.

Popular media talks about the increasing 'with me' videos as a way for isolated people to meet their social needs. There is another powerful reason that people miss—the social aspect of learning. In college I learnt much from my conversations with the smart and creative students that I was surrounded by.

During the lockdown there was a 600 per cent rise in 'with me' videos. YouTube said that since March 15, there was a 590 per cent increase of average global daily uploads that had 'at home' in the title compared to the rest of the year. Instagram Lives went up by 60 per cent in video views during the lockdown.[3]

Joining other team members for even fifteen minutes every day, to learn something together, can be one of the most inspiring ways in which leaders can be role models. Learning together with the team leader has the added advantage of people ideating about how to implement what they are learning. It is a great way of institutionalising learning, in the flow of work. When the motivation of one team member drops, the others step in.

2. *Constraints drive innovation:* In her book, *Creativity from Constraints: The Psychology of Breakthrough*, Patricia Stokes argues that 'highly creative individuals are comfortable being highly variable'. According to Stokes, the transition from master to creator comes when the expert imposes novel constraints on their domains. The ability to innovate and apply ideas to solve a problem needs 'creative confidence'.

Why Do You Need a Designer for a Voice Assistant's Personality?

Amazon's voice assistant Alexa has a team that designs her personality. The job description for a Voice Personality Designer on platforms such as LinkedIn says the team needs someone who can 'craft successful conversational voice interactions and compelling spoken prompts. Collaborate on a team that writes jokes, songs and stories, as well as guides the complex, developing relationship between the user and Alexa'.

For instance, when Alexa answers a consumer's question, should it sound like an expert or someone more relatable? Should the voice be that of a man, a woman or a child? What should the accent be? Then there is the matter of choosing the dialect for the voice assistant, as also its tone of voice. How should it respond when the listener asks, 'What is the temperature?' Should it merely rattle out the response factually in a serious tone? Or should it do so in a playful or naughty manner? Every tone has an impact on the listener.

Every listener's setting is different. How much should technology address such details if it has to become a part of one's life?

Kelley brothers have the bragging rights to tell us a thing or two about ideas, creativity, design and more. IDEO founder and Stanford d.school creator David Kelley and his brother Tom Kelley, IDEO partner and the author of the bestselling *The Art of Innovation*, tell us how to believe in our own ability to be creative. Successful innovations arise out of a blend of three drivers. People must find it desirable, the business must find it viable to produce and distribute using their business model and the technology used must make the idea feasible.[4]

3. *Teach your team to be 'experience designers':* If you had to redesign your experience of getting a cup of coffee, how would you do it? No, don't start by brainstorming. Think like a detective trying to solve a wicked problem which has no single correct answer. Become an insight detective. Try to understand what is driving people to make those choices. Start by understanding why people are getting their coffee and drinking it the way they are. Observe what they do every day and what is common to the days when they do not follow the routine. Sit in coffee shops and be a silent observer. Interview as many people as possible to find out why they did what you saw them do. What are their rituals around coffee drinking? How long do they actually spend while drinking coffee? Do not hesitate to ask people even the most obvious questions.

The CEO of HubSpot suggests that building a product-market fit may appeal to the more logic and analytics driven person. Can the ability to understand emotions lead to building an 'experience-market fit' as a way to replicate competitive advantage? Instead of tracking metrics like purchases, uptime, usage, etc. track the experience of the product rather than just the feature functionality. Experiences that trigger emotions such as surprise, joy, anticipation, thrill, etc. can create powerful emotional bonds. This works just as well for customer experiences as it does while designing employee experiences.

The payments software company Square measures something it calls 'the perfect swipe'. This is a blended metric that captures measures like time to complete transaction, percentage of successful swipes and the time it takes for a receipt to arrive after the purchase is made. This is a far better reflection of what the end user experiences during the transaction.[5]

4. *Post COVID-19 frugality as a social shift:* With a record number of people becoming unemployed and fresh entrants to the workforce being unable to find internships or jobs, there is uncertainty. Consumers are likely to buy small units of goods like sachets. Instead of buying something, renting a product and taking up monthly subscriptions will see greater adoption. The trend is likely to be further strengthened by the need to be environmentally conscious.

The resale market is growing twenty-one times faster than retail since 2016. Millennials and Gen Z are adopting second hand goods two-and-a-half times faster than other age groups according to thredUP (the world's largest online thrift store where you can buy and sell high-quality second hand clothes). Fifty-six million women bought second hand products in 2018, up from 44 million in 2017. thredUP describes their business model in four steps:

- Make it easy to sell from home, attracting millions to participate in resale for the first time.

- thredUP's algorithm uses millions of historical data points to instantly determine what something is worth.
- thredUP automates processing of up to 100,000 one-of-a-kind items a day. The photographs of clothes are categorised and tagged automatically, making them easy to sell.
- Mobile apps make it convenient to buy.

5. *The next billion does not speak English:* Sharechat, India's first vernacular platform serves as a digital window to the next billion users. They allow 35 million users to create content in fourteen Indian languages. Sharechat is the next billion's answer to Facebook. Sharechat's broadcast chat feature allows users on mobile phones to broadcast conversations and commentary about any topic they like. They can tag their content to make it easy for others to find. Bengali has over 250 million speakers, Punjabi has over 100 million speakers, Telugu has over 74 million speakers and Tamil has 70 million speakers. These are all markets hungry to speak to someone in the language in which they think and feel the emotions that they cannot do in any other language.

- The Indian government has also been a proactive presence in this area. Its BharatNet initiative has managed to bring more than 1,25,000 panchayats online through an optical fibre.
- Globally, India now has the cheapest average 4G rate at $0.26 for one gigabyte.
- Google has partnered with Tata Trusts and they are working to improve digital literacy among women from villages and are training them on how

to employ technology for business and education. Google powers 400-plus railway stations with free Wi-Fi that changes access to information for even the poorest. Google is investing $10 billion in India to enable 'affordable access and information for every Indian in their own language', build new products and services that are deeply relevant to India's unique needs, empower local businesses who want to go digital, leverage technology and AI for social good in sectors like health, education and agriculture.

- YouTube has become a global archive. Close to 200 million active users from rural India are accessing the internet on their mobile.

Traffic Jams Mean Lots of High Paying Jobs

India, China and Nigeria are together expected to account for 35 per cent of the projected growth in the world's urban population until 2050; of these three, absolute growth in urban population is projected to be the highest in India. According to the research institute, Oxford Economics, all top ten fastest-growing cities by GDP between now and 2035 will be in India.[6]

PwC identifies urbanisation as one of the five megatrends that impact business. Close to 1.5 million people migrate to cities every week. In a country like India, it puts pressure on the urban infrastructure that makes living and commuting for work challenging, to put it mildly.

If you want to see where the jobs are, look for places where the rush hour traffic is maddening. The TomTom Traffic Index compares 416 cities across fifty-seven countries on six continents, to rank urban congestion worldwide. The worst traffic congestion in the world was in Bengaluru. The other nine cities on the list are: Manila, Bogota, Mumbai, Pune, Moscow, Lima, New Delhi, Istanbul and Jakarta.[7]

1. *Invest in building digital skills*: As the youngest country in the world, India is going to see tremendous opportunity for the next five decades but its track record in employment and employability remains stretched to its limits. A partnership between the government and some of the market shapers like Apple, Google, Netflix and Adobe is advisable to build digital skills by creating memorable learning experiences.

2. *Invest in developing soft skills:* There are also other shifts that impact talent pools. Less than 2 per cent of farmers' children want to be farmers. While 18 per cent of the boys wanted to join the army or the police, 12 per cent wanted to be engineers. Young girls preferred teaching (25 per cent) or working as a doctor or a nurse (18 per cent). About 13 per cent of boys and 9 per cent of surveyed girls also said that 'any government job' is preferable. The sector itself is an unattractive option for talent.[8]

Every year thousands of engineers abandon four years of education to apply for an MBA. Only 3 per cent of engineering graduates get a salary of Rs 8–10 lakhs per annum.[9] Career opportunities in areas beyond the traditional—medicine, law and engineering—are unknown. There are new fields opening up that combine adjacent fields to create new opportunities. Entry level jobs that are done today by engineers and graduates will soon be automated. The opportunities that will come up will need strong engineering skills with an ability to communicate and collaborate with people. Soft skill development has been non-existent in India. We need to invest heavily in this area.

Trends in Pay

Dr Fermin Diez of Singapore Management University talks about the trends in pay. Everything is changing to prepare for a world where more than one third of the workforce will be freelancers and gig workers.

Salary surveys used to be the way compensation and benefits (C&B for short) got their benchmarks. Jobs and job families got compared across different businesses with weightages for multiple factors. Pay practices are now getting focused on skills. Skill surveys are being done instead of salary surveys. LinkedIn could soon be the source for not just the resume but also the salary information. Blockchain will protect the authenticity of the information.

The reasons to get a bump in pay have also changed. Productivity and unique skills remain strong reasons for extra pay. As the workforce begins to work from anywhere, pay will soon move to a location based model to reflect the cost of living of the location where the person is based. The pay model of the Digital Nomad will become the model for everyone. Eventually mobile phones will record the locations where the person has worked during the pay period and payment will be made accordingly. This will have special implications not only for expatriate pay but also for local employees who may choose to work out of locations beyond the metros. Gender equity becomes a big driver to bump up salary and create a fair workplace.

TRENDS IN PAY

DR FERMIN DIEZ

MORE THAN 1/3 WILL BE FREELANCERS

ESPECIALLY FOR EXPATS

PAY MORE FOR:

- LOCATION
- PRODUCTIVITY
- SKILLS
- WAGE GAPS
- GENDER EQUITY

CANDIDATE'S PREVIOUS PAY INFORMATION FROM

- LINKED IN
- SKILL SURVEYS
- BLOCKCHAIN

Even the way people get paid is changing. Expatriates are often choosing to get paid in crypto-currency. Besides the pay for performance, it gives the chance of an upside as the currency fluctuates. That is no different from getting a stock option where there is the possibility of a huge upside if the stock does well.

Case: GE Digital

One company that has been at the heart of the convergence is GE Digital. In in 2011, GE opened a software centre in San Ramon, California, 38 kilometres east of San Francisco. The then CEO Jeff Immelt wanted GE to be a 'top 10 software company' by 2020. In February 2017, the Immelt projected GE Digital as the poster child of its entry into the digital world. That plan went into a spin. In October 2017, John Flannery replaced Immelt as the head of GE. Very soon Larry Culp replaced Flannery in October 2018. Each change in GE's leadership forced GE Digital to shift its focus.

In December 2018, Larry Culp launched GE Digital as a $1.2 billion industrial Internet of Things (IoT) software company. The company is today a GE wholly-owned, independently run business with a renewed new brand and identity.

On 1 July 2019 Pat Byrne joined GE Digital as the Chief Executive Officer reporting to Larry Culp, the CEO of GE. In a recent blog post marking his first year at the company, Byrne confirmed, 'GE Digital is now a growing business.' But the path to growth has not been straightforward.

In the years from 2017 to 2019, the digital business saw many active pivots. It started off trying to build an industrial platform during Jeff Immelt's leadership. At the time, the focus was on having customers develop their own solutions on the platform which was called 'Predix'. The Predix platform was marketed across many industrial sectors without a clear industrial focus.

Despite some high-profile customers, the platform failed to gain traction that the company had hoped. Industrial customers highly value deep domain expertise from their solution providers—something pure software players still find challenging today.

GE also learned that the customer cares more about the applications and not the platform on which the applications were run. Think about it like using Facebook. The consumer is indifferent to the platform on which Facebook is run—Android or iOS, the consumer does not care.

That was the trigger to pivot the business towards growth. From a platform-led strategy, GE Digital pivoted to an app-led strategy, focusing on accelerating customer time to value where it had the strongest product/market fit.

The second pivot came when the company had to decide which customers they wanted to serve. The 'new' GE Digital's primary focus is to provide industrial software and services in four key markets where they have the strongest domain expertise:

- Electric Utilities & Telecommunication
- Power generation (gas, steam, and related plant operations and service support);
- Oil & Gas industry and related adjacent markets; and
- Select manufacturing applications and digital transformation projects.

While the Predix platform remains a key part of GE Digital's delivery model for many of its products, the focus today is on delivering value for customers via key applications.

Purpose, Lean Leadership, and Talent

In 2015, GE Digital positioned itself as a 'hero brand' that would usher in the next Industrial Revolution. It was a flamboyant, marketing driven business which was trying hard to be like the startups in Silicon Valley. This style seemed to go against the grain of an industrial company that celebrated 125 years in 2017.

Today, the new GE Digital CEO Pat Byrne argues that GE Digital should be seen more as a 'Sage Brand', driven by a clear purpose that puts customer needs at the core of its operations. That purpose: 'transforming how industry solves its toughest challenges, by putting industrial data to work'.

'Industrial companies prioritize keeping their people safe,' says Byrne. 'Our software helps them do that by reducing risk and maintenance costs. At the same time, we are helping many customers to achieve their long-term strategic goals—such as enabling more renewable energy on the grid. It's not just digital transformation, it's business process transformation.'

At the heart of GE Digital's own transformation is a new focus on lean management.

'People often think of lean as applicable for manufacturing businesses, but GE Digital is seeing just as much opportunity in software and services,' says Byrne.

'Within GE Digital, our lean strategy is helping us to transform in a way that reduces waste and puts customer value first. We focus on daily management, standardising work, and disciplined problem solving, all in service of delivering great value to our customers.'

This is also transforming GE Digital's talent strategy. The focus is on finding people who take pride in helping the customer win – and that starts at the top. GE Digital's new leadership team all have deep experience in using lean to operate businesses and functions, and this culture is being extended through the entire organisation.

GE Digital is back to the drawing board as a Dreamer. It has seen its pivots and is now executing against its strategy. The leadership team is building the talent pool and strategy that will take it to the Unicorn stage. Under this new approach—and despite the tumult of the global pandemic, it is already seeing success. Will it succeed for the long term? Time will tell.

In Conclusion

The biggest shift for HR teams today that I see, is moving away from top-down approaches to policy and process adherence to engaging with employees to create dynamic workplace cultures and engaging employee experiences. HR leaders tend to think of innovation as being the domain of the R&D team. We know that employee expectations of work, and its place in their lives, is changing.

When you think of a policy as work in progress, we get to use the mindset of an innovator.

References

1. Reliance Jio offered data at a throwaway price and made the net accessible to everyone. https://www.bbc.com/news/world-asia-india-47537201
2. Google's annual research on what the trends are included the impact of COVID-19 on the search results. https://www.thinkwithgoogle.com/intl/en-apac/country/india/what-india-searching-insights-brands/
3. The increase in screen time during lockdown. https://gadgets.ndtv.com/apps/features/coronavirus-lockdown-streaming-youtube-netflix-instagram-cooking-fitness-education-videos-2237179
4. *Creative Confidence: Unleashing the Creative Potential Within Us All*, is a book I would absolutely recommend. Here is a review that will motivate you to get started. https://timesofindia.indiatimes.com/blogs/just-like-that/creative-confidence/
5. Experience Disrupters: A New Breed of Growth Leaders. https://blog.hubspot.com/marketing/experience-disruptors-a-new-breed-of-growth-leaders
6. India will see urbanisation but needs to invest in planning for the influx. The ten fastest-growing cities in the world are all in India. https://www.weforum.org/agenda/2018/12/all-of-the-world-s-top-10-cities-with-the-fastest-growing-economies-will-be-in-india/
7. The TomTom index makes you wonder if a hyperconnected world needs this. https://www.tomtom.com/en_gb/traffic-index/ranking/
8. Rural youth prefer not to be farmers: Survey. https://www.developmentnews.in/rural-youth-prefer-not-farmers-survey/
9. Engineering jobs is a challenge. https://timesofindia.indiatimes.com/home/education/news/only-3-engineer-graduates-get-high-quality-tech-jobs-in-india-report/articleshow/76998063.cms

7

Blurred Lines

The biggest impact of the post-pandemic shift is that many lines that divided and organised the world into little boxes and categories have been blurred. Nothing seems to be binary any more. More options have emerged. That means we have to rethink and reimagine the world of work.

Some years back I was invited to Xavier Labour Relations Institute (XLRI), Jamshedpur, my alma mater. I was excited to take this trip down memory lane and relive the good times I had had as a student. As the cab turned a familiar corner, I caught a glimpse of the XLRI Boys Hostel. But everything around seemed to have changed. There was a new academic block in place of the cricket field, tennis court and basketball court we used as students. The boundary wall of the campus had been extended and a brand new international guest house, auditorium and houses had been built.

There was a part of me that was craving to see the old building. This was a glitzier, better-looking version, but I was grappling with a sense of loss. A loss of the familiar world that I had expected. New courses had been introduced, new affiliations had been formed and yet I was the only one there stuck in the past. The older professors had all retired. I experienced what Rip Van Winkle must have felt after sleeping for two decades.

A lot of us will experience the same feeling when we walk into what used to be the old office. A lot of lines have blurred. Gender has moved from being binary to being not just physical or emotional but also fluid. UK Facebook users can now choose from one of seventy-one gender options, including asexual, polygender and two-spirit person.

Our Relationship with Time and Space Has Changed

The pandemic has changed several business models for good. Every business that was dependent on human proximity has changed. Leaders have to learn how to navigate the work-worker-workplace equilibrium across blurred lines. The biggest sporting event reluctantly vacated the dates that were blocked four years back. Many athletes lost their place on the victory podium because the day they had been training for, for years, had changed by a year. Every time the coach asks them to prepare for 2021 Olympics, a voice is bound to ask, 'How can you be so sure?'

The Premier League, the richest soccer league in the world, with massive worldwide viewership, was suspended on 13 March 2020, after Arsenal manager Mikel Arteta tested positive. After an uncertainty of a hundred days, the League returned. Only 110 people—including players, referees and coaches—will be allowed in the red zone around the field of play, and everyone will be required to have a negative COVID-19 test in the previous five days as part of a medical passport that will see a barcode scanned before they can enter.

No matter which field you pick, the equilibrium between work-worker-workplace has changed. Until the rules of the new equilibrium get established, there will be no agreement on what exactly is the 'new normal'.

Sports-Sportsperson-Sports Arenas

The 2020 Tokyo Olympic Games were expected to attract around 10,000 athletes and 500,000 international visitors. Japan had invested billions to build competition venues and expanded hotel capacity. Japanese businessmen were expecting a record turnover in 2020 thanks to the visitors. What they are confronting instead is financial ruin. In recent memory the Olympics have always been held in a leap year. The 2021 Olympics in Japan has changed that paradigm. If social distancing norms have to be maintained in stadiums, sports has to be redesigned. Imagine having to sanitise the gymnasium equipment after each participant has used it.

The careers of many sportspersons have changed. They practise for a lifetime to be able to peak at their performance during the event. If the Olympics have been postponed, so has the list of super heroes in every sport. Many people who would have won medals and become part of sporting history, will now be replaced by some other names. Some sports will lose the best players because the sport involves proximity with many others. From football to rugby, the lives of players have changed.

If the Olympics are held in 2021, will the stadiums be packed with people, to show their support and not let the virus defeat the sporting spirit? Or will the stadiums be redesigned to respect humanity's new norms of distance and time? Will this mean that millions of fans and athletes will turn to e-sports instead? Will the sceptics now classify it as a sport and not as a simple competition? Or has the line blurred?

Time and Space Will Change At Work

Partners have complained that the loved one spends more time in office than at home. Death by overwork ('karoshi') describes the culture of Japan where employees dying, either from stress-related ailments (heart attacks, strokes) or by taking their own lives because of the pressures of the job are looked at with awe and sadness. In the 2015-16 financial year, the government registered a record 1,456 karoshi cases. Workers' rights groups claim that the actual figures could be many times higher due to underreporting.[1]

Stay-at-home mothers have wondered if they would have been celebrated more had they worked in an office instead. Radio stations cheered up commuters suffering from Monday morning blues. They cheered the end of work on Friday evening. All that has changed forever.

The employer's scrutiny will be intensified whenever people return to the office. They operative word is 'whenever'. Just as the bombing of the Twin Towers changed the experience of air travel forever, the pandemic will change the experience of work. Touchless scanners and thermal cameras will measure temperatures and scan key cards. Business cards will be politely refused. Every employee will get large areas marked out for themselves. The employer is likely to ask more invasive questions about your health and where you went for your vacation or weekend trip. That in turn may get other colleagues worried. If someone uses a disinfectant to wipe their desk, a colleague may protest about being allergic to disinfectants.

The divisiveness is just a flicker away. Do I have the choice to wear a mask? Can my employer send me home if colleagues throw a fit over someone not wearing a mask? Is that discretionary behaviour or mandatory? Colleagues will get aggressive about what other colleagues are doing or not doing that is putting everybody at risk. Travelling for work or otherwise is off the table. So are conferences. If you are at home, you may be expected to give the employer permission to track your keystrokes and take snapshots of your screen to check how often you are aimlessly surfing without reason.

This was not a change that was voluntary. The future of the office will look completely different and so will our relationship with work and colleagues.

YouTube as the Digital Archive of the World

Indian Musical Experience, a contemporary museum of music created in Bengaluru by the Brigade Group, is an attempt to blend technology with the traditional method of learning from a guru.

The nine internationally-designed exhibit galleries explore various facets of Indian music—genres, history and artistes—through storyboard panels, artefacts and computer interactives. During the lockdown, they invited artistes to do live chats on Facebook to educate people about forgotten storytelling traditions.

The 'Sound Garden' segment at the museum provides hands-on experience of the principles of sound frequency, vibration and resonance. Will fears of contracting the disease make visitors shun a visit to the museum or a concert, especially for interactive exhibits that were the star attraction in pre-pandemic days?

Music is being accessed in India across multiple channels:

1. ISRO's Edusat is used in rural schools with no broadband. TV broadcast, two-way access to internet video conferencing, web-based instructions and commercial satellite TV bring music into rural classrooms!
2. Websites and learning platforms like AcharyaNet, SMA, Sharda, Surdemy and Pratibha Music make it easy to learn music.
3. Audio and video streaming platforms like YouTube, Vimeo and Spotify have millions hooked already.
4. Facebook has a network of 2.7 billion active users and localised music groups put out content regularly.

The lockdown is turning many YouTubers into creators. It is an opportunity to rethink the future of everything from sports to museums. From work to leisure.

Work and Leisure: Time, Space and Identity

1. *The blurring of time markers:* On 1 July 2018, South Korea reduced its maximum working week from sixty-eight hours to fifty-two hours in a bid to boost the country's productivity, improve living standards, create more jobs and hopefully reverse the declining birth rate. From 1 January 2020, businesses with 50 to 299 employees were also mandated to comply with the fifty-two-hour work week.

France delighted employees with a law that established the workers' 'right to disconnect'. It requires companies with more than fifty employees to establish hours when staff should not send or answer e-mails. It aims to ensure employees are fairly paid for work, and prevent burnout. CEOs of other nationalities saw this as a severe setback to productivity. Mentors advised their proteges to continue working at home after office hours, but press the 'send' button only when it was legal.

Pre-pandemic, CEOs worked an average of 62.5 hours a week. Unless you were Elon Musk who claimed to have brought his work week from 120 hours to eighty hours per week. On an average, the CEOs monitored for a study by Harvard Business Review worked 9.7 hours per weekday, which totalled just 48.5 hours per work week. But they also worked 79 per cent of weekend days at an average of 3.9 hours daily, and 70 per cent of vacation days with an average of 2.4 hours on those days.[2]

More time at work was compensated by the hour, in case of unionised employees (if they were white-collar employees) and mainly blue-collar workers. In the US, those expected to work longer hours without extra compensation are called 'exempt' employees. For an employee to be considered exempt, they must 'use discretion and independent judgement, at least 50 per cent of the time and must earn more than $455 per week'.[3]

Time and motion studies have been used to drive productivity norms in factories and offices. In case of blue-collar work, it was literally a case of 'time is money' but overtime is more money! That no longer will be the source of differentiation in a post-pandemic world.

Performance management systems and compensation norms have been created for generations to reward more physical presence in the office. Office politics has been shaped by crafty people who could convince others that they were putting in more time than their peers. Promotions only reinforced the belief that it was quantity of work (or quantity of time spent) that assured others that you were indispensable.

Work and socialising that was done after office hours and on weekends (think golf with the boss or customers) built careers. Interrupting family dinner time with office calls has always been secretly admired and rewarded. Having a life beyond office time was viewed as 'low commitment' or worse still, 'no engagement'.

Meetings became a symbol of collaboration. When people shifted work to home, the meetings were replaced by video-conferences. The time allocated to the meeting remained unchanged. A two-hour meeting, scheduled to be held at a workspace continued to be held on video for the same duration without any consideration for its diminishing effectiveness.

During the pandemic when work was formally required to be done at home it made people realise that working from home may actually be far more demanding than being co-located with others. Slow internet speed and lack of access to printers etc. lowered productivity. The bosses believed that if the employees were no longer commuting for work, time that would have been spent travelling to the office and back could be legitimately added to the daily work schedule.

But when we moved our work from the office building to our home, the line between weekends, weekdays and long weekends was blurred. The line between work, coffee breaks, domestic chores and managing homework for schoolgoing children had to be fitted in the same twenty-four hours. Education has moved online and we assume that every parent has smartphones and laptops to spare for the kid. And the money to pay for data and the space to study while the parents work in another room. Teachers in private schools in India are struggling to teach online with parents sitting through their classes and then bombarding them with feedback on how to teach better and hold the attention of the kid. These phone calls come at all odd times. And yes, most teachers are not being paid.

A working mother told me that her six-year-old complained that even though her mother was at home, she had no time to read her stories because the door to her 'office' was always shut.

When offices reopen, the traffic on the road may be thinner than earlier, but screening people before being allowed in to the workplace will be more cumbersome, with thermal scanners and apps designed to track movement in the workplace between colleagues. Confidential information can no longer be whispered into someone's ears. Hanging around in crowded bars with colleagues after office hours may no longer be as commonplace until the fear recedes.

Here are some suggestions to build time boundaries:

a) Divide your day into fixed start and end times.
b) Take time off during the day. If a twenty-minute nap in the afternoon or a walk can refresh you, block that time in your calendar.
c) Take a day off and do something that energises you. Tell your colleagues that you will not take office calls.

2. Workspace is blurred

'Once we can get a majority of people vaccinated, then it's probably back in the office.'

Netflix cofounder and co-CEO Reed Hastings

Human beings have always equated the ability to waste precious resources as a proxy for importance and power. Expanding the personal space is a way of establishing one's relative status in society. The king stayed in a palace or castle with abundance of space. The royal family would construct a mausoleum in the middle of a garden.

Office spaces are often monuments built to pander to oversized egos. The corner office has been the most coveted space in the building given to the CEO or the C-suite. In India, many high-ranking government officials had their egos massaged by being given offices which were wastefully large, to compensate for salaries that were lower than those in the corporate sectors.

One would expect that digital market shapers would not need offices, but they are the ones building wastefully large workspaces. In 2013, when Yahoo! withdrew its WFH policy, there was an uproar. Marissa Mayer, its CEO said in-person meetings boosted the quality of decisions and ideas. IBM directed 5,000 at-home employees to start coming into offices in 2017.

An organisation like Google was admired for its campus, which had everything from swimming pools and nap pods in the office. Gourmet food was cooked by chefs in multiple cafeterias to cater to the taste buds of the geeks. Critics claimed that it was all a conspiracy to ensure that the employees would hate to go back home and continue working to keep Google stock rising. Google and its parent company, Alphabet, will allow its employees to continue working from home until at least June 2021.

Apple's campus built like a spaceship cost them $5 billion and covered 2.8 million sq. ft. Two years back, Facebook moved into its 430,000 sq. ft., Frank–Gehry-designed headquarters. It is now adding another 1.75 million sq. ft. to include a grocery store, a pharmacy and 1,500 housing units. Amazon is sweeping up office space in Seattle.

The tallest building in San Francisco has mindfulness areas on every floor inspired by Vietnamese Zen Master Thich Nhat Hanh. It is the headquarters of Salesforce.

Steve Jobs designed offices at Pixar such that computer scientists, animators and editors were in separate buildings. Separating these groups, each with its own culture and approach to problem-solving, discouraged them from sharing ideas and solutions. He then moved everyone into a single building that was designed to encourage 'casual collisions'. Most problems are getting so complex that they need interdisciplinary teams to work together. That is just what digital leaders are creating. Reed Hastings, co-CEO of Netflix says that in his business WFH is a bad idea. The world will probably settle down to a hybrid model where even after a vaccine is found, more people will choose the freedom to work from anywhere periodically.

The new word in office design is ABW or Activity-Based Workplace design. Workspace no longer signals hierarchy, but is based on the nature of work. Innovation needs frequent work to be done in short bursts by interdisciplinary teams, which enable divergent perspectives. Then there is a phase when different ideas have to be combined and synthesised. These need isolated work spaces where people can be left undisturbed. This part of the job can still be done at home. Offices must have huddle rooms for brainstorming. They also need private spaces for phone conversations, and some 'unassigned' spaces for guests.[4]

> 'Companies rarely promote people into leadership roles who haven't been consistently seen and measured. It's a familiarity thing, and it's a trust thing. We're not saying that the people who get promoted are stars during every 'crucible' moment at the office, but at least they're present and accounted for. And their presence says: Work is my top priority. I'm committed to this company. I want to lead. And I can.'
>
> —Jack Welch (2007)

In the post-pandemic world of social distancing, some conventions about space as a proxy for power will get challenged. Even the lowest category of employees will need to be given more space. Contact-tracing tools are being devised so that employers can pinpoint which employees may have been exposed to the virus, without needing to shut down entire floors of an office or individual manufacturing plants. Office photocopiers and pantries will see more refusals for tea and snacks—a ritual common in offices across India.

In several countries, despotic leaders have used the pandemic as an excuse to identify and round up leaders of the opposition and minorities. They have used social media to whip up sentiments that further their political agenda. It is not hard to assume that some organisations will use health-related apprehensions to gather more data about employees, install surveillance equipment and justify it in the name of public safety. That could mean some employers could keep the union leaders away under the pretext of health-related concerns. Or they could eliminate jobs being done by older workers since they are more vulnerable to the virus. Will that happen?

Hubstaff is an activity monitor that gives managers a snapshot of what an employee is doing. Broken down into ten-minute increments, the system tallies what percentage of time the worker has been typing or moving the computer mouse. That percentage acts as a productivity score.[5]

It is equally likely that legislators and employers may need to implement unusual measures to get workplaces restarted. But it is also worrisome to think how despotic employers could use the health and safety concerns to violate the right to privacy and remove troublemakers without compensation.

Social Trends

500 MN INTERNET USERS IN INDIA --> MORE THAN US + MEXICO + CANADA

PROUD TO BE INDIAN

LOCAL HEROS, KABADDI, REGIONAL LANGUAGE CONTENT IS COOL

CONFIDENT WOMEN

USING DIGITAL TOOLS LIKE YOUTUBE TO LEARN, BE ENTREPRENEURS & MAKE THEIR OWN DECISIONS

BALANCE INDIVIDUAL IDENTITY PLUS FAMILY & COMMUNITY

ABHIJIT BHADURI

SAME SAME BUT DIFFERENT REPORT, THINK WITH GOOGLE APAC, AUGUST 2020

Facial recognition technology is being introduced in several airports across the world including in some airports like Delhi and Bengaluru in India. That could make boarding cards, passports etc. unnecessary to identify authorised passengers, as scared travellers reluctantly try to get over their fear of the disease. Touchless entry into the airport can be reassuring and could be just what will help the travel industry revive itself.

It may even be possible for governments to feed images produced from a DNA sample into mass surveillance and facial recognition systems to tighten its ability to track dissidents and protesters as well as criminals.

Here are some suggestions to mark your space:

a) Using the same space makes your mind see it as a workplace.
b) Avoid working out of your bed especially if you watch TV while you are in bed. It blurs the lines.
c) Choose a virtual office background for your zoom calls. It protects your privacy. Your colleagues or clients cannot look inside your home unless you invite them in by removing the virtual background.

Blurred Lines in HR Systems

Performance management generates a lot of heat but rarely sheds light. Goals are set at the beginning of the year. Yet when they are evaluated, most people feel underappreciated because they did many more things that seem to have been ignored. Then there is the bell-curve. Managers dreaded having to explain to their team that even though they did well, someone did better. Blaming it on HR provides an easy escape route. This is one system where the employer tries to show that the appraisal is an objective process and the employee is convinced it is all about *showing the boss that you are working hard.* Leaving five minutes after the boss leaves or sending an email late at night have been age-old methods used to curry favour.

Face time has two components: the expected face time and the extracurricular face time. Expected facetime is simply being seen at work during regular business hours. This leads to people thinking of you as reliable and committed even though they have no idea what you may be working on.

Extracurricular face time is being seen at work outside of normal business hours—arriving before most employees, staying late or coming in to work on the weekend.[6]

Now there is analytics. The timing of the first email sent in the morning to the Wi-Fi hotspot, who gets the most emails, to the new business contact added before going home are all data points being collected. Employers are parsing those interactions to learn who is influential, which teams are most productive and who is a flight risk. Microsoft tallies data on the frequency of chats, emails and meetings between its staff and clients using its own Office 365 services to measure employee productivity, management efficacy and work-life balance. Bunch.ai analyses the tone of Slack channels to gauge team chemistry and morale.[7]

Even if the post-pandemic world comes back to seeing more employees in the workplace, the managers have to be trained to get over their natural instinct to only trust people they see hanging around the office. This is one of the first areas to address. Performance management when the workforce is remote is the next big area for building skills.

Workforce analytics, performance analytics etc. are in the same realm as the use of psychometric assessments used for hiring or promotions. The employee often has little control over the competence of the person administering or interpreting the data. Some psychometric instruments like Myers-Briggs Type Indicator (MBTI) are widely used but a few experts like Adam Grant say it is meaningless. To quote Grant's tweet, 'The MBTI is astrology for nerds. Say it with me again: personality types are a myth, traits are on a continuum, and the major dimensions include extravert-introvert, agreeable-disagreeable, reactive-stable, open-traditional, conscientious-spontaneous.'[8]

Case: Crompton Greaves Consumer*

Crompton Greaves Consumer is a $600 million Indian consumer company with 1,500 employees that is known for its excellent quality consumer electronics.

From 2016, the company started shifting its strategic orientation from being B2B-centric to a consumer-centric approach. That meant having to re-orient the customer-facing functions such as sales and service. It meant holding them accountable for better quality and speed of response. Even the marketing team needed a different way to communicate directly with the consumer. The mindset is the operating system that defines our behaviour. While the employees had to change their day-to-day responsiveness, the leaders had to create a culture that emphasised and rewarded a new set of behaviour.

*In conversation with Satyajit Mohanty, CHRO of Crompton

Satyajit Mohanty, the CHRO for Crompton said, 'We started shifting our strategic orientation to a more consumer-centric organisation more than four years back. Like most organisations on a culture transformation journey, we went about debating and defining standard behaviours, training people on the same, including them in the performance and career development systems and so on. It was even more critical to drive this mindset into customer-facing functions such as sales and service teams. A lot of emphasis was put into defining standard market-working patterns for sales force, training them for desired behaviour while visiting retail outlets, and strong communication by leadership at all levels.

'However, over time, we observed that at ground level, the needle on the desired behaviours was not moving as we thought. Obviously, there was some progress on this, but we had underestimated what it took to change the mindset. We leveraged the latest research in the field of psychology and behavioural economics—the behaviour change models advocated by renowned scientists such as Richard Thaler, Daniel Kahneman, and Chip and Dan Heath.

'We realised many things:

a) The desired behaviour norms had to be individualised. The challenges and strengths for each person differ. So one size does not fit all.
b) When the business is doing well, the leaders have to explain the rationale of the change to the team first before they even think of adapting the new behaviours.
c) Ask why people are not demonstrating the desired behaviour. The reasons could be the perceived

"criticality" (or lack of it) of the change. Sometimes it is the work processes design that becomes the barrier. Make the behaviour change easy and remove all barriers that cause friction in adopting the new behaviour. Peer support helps the change.

'Based on those, we created a three-step model that was specific to *each* employee. Behaviour change is specific to each person. This was our key insight.

a. Define one key target behaviour to be changed. Align the leaders on what that critical behaviour could be. When we started, the sales leaders didn't agree on which behaviour change would have the highest impact. That also involved understanding the current habits of each employee and an "incremental" objective for each.
b. We stepped into the shoes of the employees. That made us empathise with them about processes that needed to change. For example, not having to come back to the office in the evening to file reports let them visit dealers who were far away from our sales offices.
c. We implemented a system where each employee could see the progress being made, and every small movement was noticed and appreciated.

'While this is still work in progress, we feel confident about this being a breakthrough approach.'

Human connections and CONVERSATIONS trigger creativity. Create white spaces DURING the work day to read, reflect and learn.

Decision-making Criteria are Blurred

Human resources leaders and chief executives might spend sleepless nights trying to find out who really needs to be in the office and who is likely to be a hazard for others. Organisations like Facebook and Amazon have deferred return to office for a long time. But then these are the world's most digitised workplaces. Most businesses estimate that at best only 30-50 per cent of employees will need to be in office. A survey by LinkedIn showed that not everyone was eager to return to the office. While 38 per cent of Gen X said they would willingly return to the workplace as soon as they were allowed, one in three Gen Z (29 per cent) and millennials (32 per cent) said they would continue working remotely until they felt safer about being around others, said the LinkedIn Workforce Confidence Index. One hypothesis is that the digitally-savvy are comfortable working remotely while the older employees miss meeting colleagues face to face.[9]

This is leading companies to decide what kind of data they need to collect about the employees—not just what they do in the office and who they are in proximity with; they may also need to track where the people have spent time outside of the office. We have seen that when it comes to privacy versus safety, people are happy to give up privacy. Many employers will need to track information about employees which in normal circumstances, they would not have. The pandemic, of course, creates the justification to seek all kinds of data points.

Employers are debating whether to bring people back in batches or shifts. There is a possibility that even white-collar workers may have to be staggered in shifts to be able to adhere to social distancing norms. In some cases where the equipment cannot be taken home, employers may need to reimagine how the desks will have to be organised in the office spaces. Some are colour-coding the desks to designate which ones can be used. Coffee machines and cafeterias in offices are not open to the few employees that are in office.

When I go to a nation-wide chain of eyewear, my footwear gets sanitised, and sanitiser is liberally applied on my hands as the security guard records my temperature. When I step into the store, I notice that all employees are wearing gloves and masks. That reassures me but I am a little distressed when the store manager wants to record my mobile number. He notices my hesitation and tells me it is a directive from the government. I protest and tell him that the mobile data can be linked to purchase patterns and health data etc. It is not something I would want. But the store manager shrugs and says, 'It is a mandate from the government.' I relent.

Any decision where there is discretionary decision-making being applied, is a sticky area. Is a certain function more important than the others? If the junior employees are called back to work, the employer could be accused of putting them in harm's way. If the seniors are called back, the rest of them would wonder if that is a sign that the seniors need to huddle together to plan layoffs. Without building trust through dialogue, getting everybody to work is not going to make the organisation more productive.

IMPLEMENTATION CHALLENGE

What norms of personal data collection will be useful to assure people that the information will be used only for ensuring that the workplace is safe?

What can be done to ensure that minorities and all the workers will not be discriminated against, as the employees collect data through intrusive questions and surveillance technology like cameras and key stroke logging software?

Will the use of masks trigger the development and implementation of improved face recognition technology in the workplace?

In the Crisis Lies the Opportunity

Being able to certify that the supply chain is entirely safe can create the largest business opportunity ever in the face of the pandemic. From sourcing the ingredients to production in the factory and that finally the last mile of delivery in the hand of the consumer, each step has an opportunity to build trust.

Employers who can guarantee that they value the health and safety of every employee, every vendor and even the gig workers who they rely on for essential services will attract the best talent.

From hands-free door openers that can be 3D-printed, to basic ventilators, the COVID-19 pandemic has ushered in a new era of urgent innovation.

Wipro Infrastructure Engineering (WIN) developed a sanitising walkway with the support of Defence Research & Development Organisation (DRDO), called ClearWalk—a sanitisation walkway, in a bid to help to fight COVID-19. The sanitisation walkway is an enclosure which has been fitted with specially designed spray nozzles creating fine water particles to give maximum coverage to the person walking through. Each module can be set up and installed within six to eight hours.

The same team also developed MediKart—a robot equipped with the monitor that can carry medicines and other necessities to patients, so that the exposure of the virus to health workers is minimal. It is fitted with a camera which allows the health practitioner to observe the patient remotely.

Pharmaceutical companies are working with regulators to share information more effectively and undo requirements that slow progress. Supercomputing systems are being combined with simpler clinical trial methods to speed up drug discovery. Telemedicine like online education has exploded worldwide. Drones are being used to deliver products to remote areas. The whole world has woken up to the possibility of getting eliminated by the virus. While drug discovery is a process that takes decades, the pandemic has made every country come together to speed up innovation in this area. Health apps have been built that can be used to diagnose multiple health markers, detect symptoms and deliver medical advice.

Bengaluru-based startup Razorpay has partnered with furniture company Featherlite, to allow people to rent office furniture to help them work from home. Paytm has partnered with Reliance General Insurance to create a COVID-19 insurance plan. Customers can purchase the plan in just a few minutes, on the Paytm app.

The pandemic has prompted a wave of innovation that will improve our quality of life.

IMPLEMENTATION CHALLENGE

What can be done in the supply chain to ensure that each step is safe until it reaches the hand of the consumer?

What changes in the physical layout and workplace norms will allow for projects that thrive on active collaboration to remain unaffected by social distancing norms and the use of video technology?

Blurred Lines in Talent

The sources of talent will no longer only lie in the English-speaking world. As previously stated, India, China and Nigeria are together expected to account for 35 per cent of the projected growth in the world's urban population until 2050.

Even if these populations are not as educated and skilled as what employers expect, they will soon present the only choice in a greying world. Talent will no longer be ready and employable. The willingness of the candidate will be the only thing that talent-starved greying economies will look for.

Millions of employees have returned to their hometown and villages from the cities of India during the pandemic. If employers and the infrastructure allowed for these people to continue working from their hometowns and villages, the cities would see less congestion. But now, it is essential for these people to find employment that pays reasonably close to what they earned in the metros. Businesses could use this as an opportunity to jumpstart their operations while creating options for the smaller cities.

India needs to create almost a million new jobs a month. There are also other shifts that impact talent pools. As previously stated, less than 2 per cent of farmer's children want to be farmers.[10]

Every society has beliefs about race, religion, gender etc. These also spill over to the workplace and determine workforce composition. Is a nurse in a hospital male? Is the tabla player accompanying the singer a woman? Is the surgeon or the psychiatrist male? Should women be hired to lead an all-male sales team? Can a transgender person be the CEO of an organisation? The answer that comes up first in our head determines whom we find acceptable in certain roles. While we try to use algorithms to remove hiring biases, it does not take away the human factor that makes it easy or difficult for such a person to succeed even after being hired.

Employers will have to think about talent continuity, every time they plan for the scenarios that could possibly threaten business continuity. The skills needed at all levels within the organisation, and those that are necessary to bring the product or service to the customer have to be carefully considered, each time when the business plans are revisited. If critical talent is unable or unwilling to return to the workplace—especially in mission critical roles—the management must have a plan to tackle the situation.

HR must make talent maps of available skills, capabilities and experience in the workforce. Then identify availability categories—full-time, hourly, contract and gig workers. Then create a network of trusted partners to share, borrow or 'rent' talent from each other. Think about it like the compensation planning clubs that businesses have where they share benchmarking data and pay practices. The lines between full time workers, remote talent, on-site workers, essential workers, mission critical skills have got blurred. Building those new definitions can be a start.

Sometimes an external event throws open the floodgates of opportunity. The ban on TikTok came as a huge opportunity for video-sharing platform Roposo. They were adding 500,000 users *an hour* as soon as TikTok got banned. In thirty days, the customer base would double to become 100 million. The Bangalore based Chingari got over 17.5 million users in three weeks against 3.5 million on the day of the ban. Having a hockey stick growth in customers can turn into a nightmare if the product is glitchy and the features are not slick enough.

Leaders have always known that it is not enough to simply focus on efficiency. An innovative competitor can blow away the market overnight. The difference between successful companies and those that died during a crisis lies in the leaders' ability to focus on innovation as much as cost efficiency. Both are necessary.

Safi Bahcall, author of *Loonshots,* describes these as phase transitions. Water turning to ice is a phase transition, when the nature of the substance changes radically. It is important to focus on efficiency and innovation at the same time but it is hard to find teams that do both equally well. The startups and unicorns focus on innovation but lose track of efficiency. The culture of incumbents rewards efficiency and the culture preventing innovation from servicing in time. To turn this crisis into an opportunity for growth, the talent strategy must blow the line between people who love to innovate and the people who build efficiency.

Tech is Brahma, Vishnu and Shiva

Technology is the Brahma, Vishnu and Shiva of the world of work, workers and workplaces. Brahma, the creator of the universe, is showing up as technology and creating new kinds of work that need new skills that workers need to use in workplaces that have not existed before. Digital marketers, drone pilots and app developers have all popped up in the past decade because of new technology. Facebook has more users than the population of China or India.

Technology (like robotics and AI) acts like Vishnu, the nurturer, to augment human capabilities in the way humans are working in the new workplace. Robot-assisted surgery allows doctors to perform complex procedures with minimal invasion. Algorithms are helping auditors identify credit card fraud. Drones are being used to identify leaks in oil pipelines that go through the desert. One person manages 25,000 servers in a Facebook Data Center.[11]

Shiva is the destroyer. Technology is playing that role in destroying centuries-old traditions that defined what work and workers were. Stenos and typists who were commonplace in offices at one time, have disappeared. Even the once prestigious role of an executive assistant has disappeared. When someone is in their fifties and loses a job, they often have to take up jobs that are more physically strenuous and pay far less. Look around and see how much the workplace has changed.

As businesses limp back from the COVID-19 challenge, it may be worth crafting a new business model supported by a new talent strategy and a new set of norms to govern this new workplace. It may look like the workplace we left behind. It is not. Any resemblance with the past is an illusion.

Going to Office Will Be Like Going for a Movie

When it comes to watching movies, the default setting has been that the viewers go to a multiplex a few times a year. The pandemic has already changed that equation in favour of the digital world. People have discovered the possibility of watching the latest releases on Netflix, Amazon Prime or any of the other platforms like Hotstar, Voot, Alt Balaji etc. ... the choices are too many to list.

During the lockdown, several movie producers decided not to wait for the multiplexes to open and instead released their movies online. Pre-pandemic, in the weeks before the movie's release, a lot of marketing money was spent on creating hype to ensure that people were going to line up to go to the theatre.

If for whatever reason the movie was not released on that particular day, the producers had to spend the marketing budget all over again to create the hype. Releasing it online seemed to be the smartest way to pivot the business

during the pandemic. Releasing a movie online for a few days or weeks could give the movie producers the revenues they need in a shorter window.

Multiplex owners began bleeding during the lockdown because of the rentals and real estate costs they had to incur to keep the multiplex going while audiences were watching movies at home. Even after the lockdown was lifted, theatres are only likely to be partly full, given the paranoia, apprehension and social distancing norms. Eventually it may be a sign that it will be an 'and' world. Much like the shift happening with ebooks. The paperback will not disappear but digital versions will see a faster rate of adoption.

Not surprisingly, in the pandemic, digital businesses grew and thrived. Apple reported a 1 per cent revenue increase in the quarter ending March 2020, to $58.3 billion. Amazon had to hire additional people to keep up with the demand. Their sales jumped 6 per cent, to a record $75.5 billion. Google and Facebook grew. Disney+ signed on more than 60 million subscribers in the first eight months of

2020—a goal that they were supposed to reach in five years. Netflix became bigger than Disney because the theme parks that were Disney's cash cow remained shut. Retail, travel, hospitality, automobiles and all brick and mortar businesses struggled. Schools and colleges scrambled to get their teachers to speak to cameras, leaving them feeling awkward.

After the financial crisis in 2008, the five biggest banks—J.P. Morgan Chase, Bank of America, Citigroup, Wells Fargo and Goldman Sachs got even bigger. The demonetisation move put digital payments on the fast track. During the pandemic, as consumers avoided exchanging paper currency to avoid transmitting the virus, digital payments gathered momentum.

After the COVID-19 crisis, the degree of digital transformation done in business will determine who will stay in business, while shattering the competition. The ones who could sell were also the ones who had invested in HR technology that enabled the employees to continue working remotely. The businesses that invest in employees and customers equally will thrive.

Going to the office may become much like going for a movie to a multiplex. For most people it will be an occasional journey they will undertake.

The real shakeout will happen in leadership teams, talent strategies and workplace culture. It will need to be built again—this time with a focus on experience design, not processes. This new workplace culture will keep the customer or the employee at the centre and build across functions and departmental siloes. The usual approach of prioritising customer experiences over employee experiences will fade away as we build a new world of work.

References

1. In India, where there is no universal national limit for maximum working hours, workers do not have a guaranteed minimum amount of annual leave. https://www.bbc.com/worklife/article/20180504-which-country-works-the-longest-hours
2. As the CEO, you were expected to devote your life to the office. https://www.cnbc.com/2018/12/10/elon-musk-says-working-120-hours-in-a-week-was-a-show-of-leadership.html
3. What makes a role 'exempt' in an organisation? What is it exempted from? https://www.hr.ucsb.edu/what-exempt-employee-or-position
4. The biggest tech giants are all building the biggest workplaces. https://abhijitbhaduri.com/2017/10/12/digital-giants-building-offices/
5. There is a danger that employees may be giving up their privacy to comply with the employer's need to track productivity. https://www.wsj.com/articles/the-new-ways-your-boss-is-spying-on-you-11563528604
6. Why showing your face at work matters. https://sloanreview.mit.edu/article/why-showing-your-face-at-work-matters/
7. Microsoft is one employer who gets insights based on the usage of its software suite. https://www.wsj.com/articles/the-new-ways-your-boss-is-spying-on-you-11563528604
8. Adam Grant has long since said that MBTI has no scientific validity. https://twitter.com/adammgrant/status/986255991548280832
9. Could it be that the digital natives are more comfortable with remote work. https://www.outlookindia.com/newsscroll/indian-gen-z-millennials-will-wait-to-return-to-work-linkedin/1881284
10. Rural youth prefer not to be farmers: Survey. http://img.asercentre.org/docs/ASER%202018/Release%20Material/aserreport2018.pdf
11. Automate and abstract: Lessons from Facebook on engineering for scale. https://architecht.io/lessons-from-facebook-on-engineering-for-scale-f5716f0afc7a

8

Empty Maps

Many cultures drew world maps long before the modern age. Obviously, none of them really knew the whole of the world. No Afro-Asian culture knew about America, and no American culture knew about Afro-Asia. But unfamiliar areas were simply left out, or filled with imaginary monsters and wonders. These maps had no empty spaces. They gave the impression of a familiarity with the entire world.

—Yuval Noah Harari in
Sapiens: A Brief History of Humankind

An Undiscovered Continent

A Chinese app TikTok that offers memes and lip sync options becomes popular among American Gen Z (and several older folks who see this as a passport to qualify as 'young'). The app is seen as a stress buster during the pandemic. India bans the app (plus almost sixty other apps) during its military brushes with the Chinese at the border. The fear is that the app collects lots of data about the users and censors/pushes content that may shape radicalisation and political dissent in the population. The app does not show content about Tiananmen Square or Hong Kong protests. Meanwhile, the growing tension between the US and China gets sharper. TikTok stores American user data in Singapore and Virginia and gets an American CEO. They suggest that American private equity firms buy off the share of the Chinese investors. The US contemplates asking Apple and Google to delist TikTok from the app stores. Microsoft offers to buy TikTok's American business. The US government wants a share of the sale price ... These are all empty maps.

A case of pneumonia caused by unknown factors, detected in Wuhan, China was first reported to the WHO country office in China on 31 December 2019. It was a disease which didn't have a name and it did not even catch anyone's attention. The new decade was welcomed in. Experts debated on 1 January 2020 how this would be decade for dreams and hopes. By 30 January 2020, a public health emergency of international concern was declared, but the disease still did not have a name. On 11 February 2020, WHO announced a name for the new Coronavirus disease: COVID-19.[1]

By the next day, the death toll in China had reached 1,113 and the total number of confirmed cases rose to 44,653. There were 393 cases outside of China, in twenty-four countries. In the next ninety days, the virus had spread to at least 177 countries, killing more than 280,000 and infecting more than four million.

Officials announced that the Summer Olympics in Tokyo would be postponed by a year. Only three previous Games had been cancelled, all because of war: in 1916, 1940 and 1944.

India's prime minister ordered all 1.3 billion people in the country to stay inside their homes for three weeks starting 25 March 2020—the biggest and most severe action undertaken anywhere to stop the spread of the Coronavirus. But the virus continues its death and devastation, shutting down civilian life and shuttering businesses. Its socio-economic-political impact is worse than the havoc wreaked by the Great Depression.

There is no time to do the tests that are done over a prolonged period when a vaccine is launched. There is a race by Big Pharma to produce the vaccine. There is an institute in India that manufactures 70 per cent of the world's known vaccines. They will make 400 million vaccines available to India. Who should get vaccinated first? Someone suggests the defence personnel be the first ones. If the vaccine has a side effect, that could have devastating repercussions on the country's defence. What would you do? We need to approach this issue with the humility that empty maps demand.

These Are Empty Maps

Human beings have been drawing maps of the world long before they knew about every landmass. These maps had no empty spaces. The maps conveyed a false impression of complete knowledge. Something changed during the fifteenth and sixteenth centuries. Europeans began to draw world maps with lots of empty spaces—a clear admission of ignorance of large parts of the world.

These empty maps triggered human curiosity and inspired explorers. New lands and new knowledge began to be discovered at a scale and speed that had never been seen before. So what happened in our collective history to allow this to happen? It was the acceptance of the limits of our knowledge.[2]

Our view of time shapes our response: It is often said that the pandemic fast-tracked the changes that were already underway. When people started working from home it was done out of no choice. Employers and employees viewed it as a stopgap arrangement that would end in a few days or at best a few weeks. It was like holding our breath underwater for a bit when we go swimming. When we go diving, we know that we will need more oxygen than what our lungs can hold. What we are going through is like learning to live underwater.

Once we realised that this was not going to be a short-term arrangement, we attempted to recreate what we were familiar with. Meetings that were held in conference rooms simply moved online. Conferences asked speakers to record their talks and played them in sequence. A boring speaker sitting in a poorly lit room with patchy sound and densely packed illegible slides and poor content became a familiar figure. Maybe virtual conferences can create a whole new format based on research and testing hypotheses.

Despite evidence suggesting that this was not something anyone had seen for centuries, leaders pushed their employees to believe it was 'business as usual'. It was a reflection of the leaders' inability to recognise a tsunami, leave alone a subtle signal from the market. The closest reference that was studied was the flu epidemic of 1918 even though the world of work had changed many times over since then. It is like studying how doctors treated patients before antibiotics were discovered. We need people who can redraw the maps. These would be new products and services that would emerge as new business models. The new equilibrium of work, worker and workplaces would be found through new models of leadership, talent and culture.

Online erases old signals of power: Take for instance the levelling power of the Zoom call. The screen size is uniform for all participants. There is no other visual cue to find out who the real decision maker is. In an office, a candidate or a vendor could draw that conclusion from the size of the office or know instinctively that the person sitting at the head of the table was the most powerful person in the room. Video calls have democratised the meetings. The virtual backgrounds look the same for most people. The Zoom meeting is the great quashing of hierarchies. Unless you look at the amount of air time the boss takes in the meeting. That is one habit that has spilled over from the meeting rooms to the Zoom screen.

The boss frequently forgets that listening is the key to being more powerful. Want to look for a leader who will struggle in the new world of work? Measure the air time he (usually found more in males) takes in meetings.

WORK: Anytime, Anywhere, Anyone, Anything ...

Before the pandemic, the only option to work was in the office. If you were senior enough or the boss wanted to make up for not giving you a raise, you could get to work from home but that remained a secret between you and the boss. If the rest of the organisation ever got to know that you were singled out for this special treatment, there would be a rebellion on hand. Work was meant to be done in the workplace—the office. Then the early days of the pandemic made work from home as the default choice. We learned about a new three letter acronym WFH.

The virus created multiple kinds of responses from businesses. Those who were able to pivot and make sure the business could be run any time, from anywhere, by anyone and could respond to make anything were the ones that survived and even thrived.

Companies that helped people handle tasks surrounding death and dying online—from hosting videoconference memorials to preparing documents—have been growing in recent years, thanks in part to changing attitudes toward mortality among millennials.

Retail has been hard hit by the virus. J. Crew filed for bankruptcy on 3 May 2020 and four days later Neiman Marcus did the same. On 15 May 2020, the 118-year-old chain, J.C. Penney filed for bankruptcy in the US. The chain had more than 800 stores and nearly 85,000 employees.[3]

Case Study: Air Travel

The second order impact of a 50 per cent drop in air travel in 2020 has resulted in Rolls Royce engines cutting back 9,000 jobs. GE Aviation has seen its revenues drop to half. 100,000 flights per day have dropped to a trickle creating mayhem in the $1.3 trillion travel industry. The 10 million people who man the shops at the airports, the cooks who prepare in-flight meals amongst others, are impacted. The 2.7 million airlines workers and 1.2 million employees making aircrafts face an uncertain future. There are more pilots on the ground than in the sky.

Source: Economist.com, Aug 1, 2020

Industry giants Boeing and Airbus SE had built orders for more than 13,000 jets but with the collapse of the industry they have had to deal with hundreds of orders being cancelled as several airlines faced bankruptcy. British Airways followed Qantas and Lufthansa in retiring the Boeing 747 in July 2020. Boeing and Airbus are expected to lose $300 billion.[4]

Responding to Weak Signals

The challenge for a market shaper is to have the agility to respond to weak signals. Separating weak signals from noise is one the biggest skills leadership teams have to demonstrate. Move too soon and the firm is running distracted. React too late and the business collapses before anyone can make alternative arrangements.

A Century-old Marriage Is Breaking Up

For a century, theatre owners and studios have had a symbiotic relationship. A new movie release in the theatre is marketed aggressively for a few weeks. If the movie release is delayed for some reason, the marketing budget is wasted. The same amount of marketing money has to be spent when the movie is ready for release again in the theatre. So the studio must get the movie to the audience after they build up hype. The movie then appears in digital platforms months after the theatre release.

With theatre attendance being low, NBC Universal Studios decided to bypass theatres and release *Trolls World Tour* digitally. And made $100 million in three weeks through digital sales. This is a structural shift that changes the relationship between studios and theatre owners.

Audiences are signing up for digital platforms where they can watch movies at home. Historically, theatres kept a larger percentage of the profits. So a digital release is more profitable for the studios. Disney has its own channel Disney+ and Warner Brothers have HBO Max to release the best of their films.[5]

In India, it is estimated that theatres will lose Rs 80-90 crore every month that they remain shut. A release on Netflix offers great returns. Small-budget movies made for Rs 25-30 crore may find digital sales an attractive alternative.[6]

No surprise then, that Bollywood was quick to follow suit. The Amitabh Bachchan starrer *Gulabo Sitabo* was the first big movie from Bollywood that skipped the cinema theatre release and announced its premier on Amazon Prime.

INOX, a theatre chain expressed its disbelief by saying, 'INOX would like to express extreme displeasure and disappointment on an announcement made by a production house today, to release their movie directly on an OTT platform by skipping the theatrical window run. The decision of the production house to deviate from the globally prevalent content windowing practice is alarming and disconcerting.'[7]

This was not an exception. Sony Pictures Networks Production announced that the biopic *Shakuntala Devi: Human Computer*, starring Vidya Balan, would have a 'world premiere' on Amazon Prime. Irrfan Khan and Radhika Madan's *Angrezi Medium* had already premiered on Disney+Hotstar. Kannada, Malayalam, Telugu, Tamil movies followed. The convenience of digital releases is undeniable and may herald a structural shift in the world of entertainment. A new business model has emerged during the pandemic. It is here to stay.

Shifts in Consumer Needs

The pandemic made people think hard about their lifestyle and choices. The result has been a far more frugal consumer who is apprehensive about the future. As the world gets into a recession, consumers are going to make a fresh set of choices about brands they engage with. Conspicuous consumption is going to be replaced with more thoughtful engagement.

Plant-Based Meat

The pandemic has upended the $213 billion US meat industry, forcing industry giants including Tyson Foods Inc., JBS USA Holdings Inc., Smithfield Foods Inc. and Cargill Inc. to temporarily close plants.

At the same time plant-based meat makers like Beyond Meat, Impossible Foods, and other traditional food companies are all betting on the rise of meatless alternatives that could permanently change food habits of people.

Consumers are driven to try out alternative options because of compulsion. It may be too early to say if this shift to plant-based meat is simply a forced choice or if it will become the preferred option even when animal meat returns to the shelves.

Simplification and minimalism: The pre-pandemic consumer used brands that augmented their sense of self. The post-pandemic consumer will work with brands that are sustainable. Marie Kondo made consumers aware that there was beauty in minimalism. The same philosophy will translate to people simplifying their life. The lockdown made people realise that spending time at home was not an inferior option. Simplification is in.

'Planned obsolescence' no more: Manufacturers of products found that new markets could be created if only they stepped away from the 'built to last' philosophy. Saying that repairs cost more than replacement products, to pushing for aesthetic upgrades that frame older product versions as less stylish—there are a million ways to drive sales.

The 'Phoebus cartel' in the 1920s, brought together representatives from top light bulb manufacturers worldwide, such as Germany's Osram, the United Kingdom's Associated Electrical Industries, and General Electric (GE) in the US (via a British subsidiary), and colluded to artificially reduce bulbs' lifetimes to 1,000 hours. That may explain why not using carbon filament in bulbs makes bulbs burn out faster and drives up revenue.[8]

Rethink innovation, marketing and finance: Philip Kotler, the marketing guru, describes the power of this troika. Innovation produces attractive new products. Marketing supplies the tools to reach consumers and motivates them to buy. Payment systems encourage low-income consumers to buy on credit. Since some weaker companies and brands will most likely vanish, consumers will have to find reliable and satisfying replacement brands.[9]

British vacuum cleaner giant Dyson designed a ventilator in ten days and automobile giant Ford produced 2400,000 protective face shields in less than three weeks.[10]

These are great examples of adopting a perpetual beta mindset of creating a good enough solution with speed and then iterating to improve it with the help of consumers and users. The crisis seems to have created a boundaryless workplace like nothing else has.

In India, a Kochi-based firm called Asset Homes offered to convert trains that were idling during the lockdown to hsopitals. This was an innovative solution to utilise idle capacity and also supplement the hospital space needed, especially for rural areas. The math was simple.

'We have 12,617 trains with twenty-three to thirty coaches in our country. We can easily convert them into "mobile hospitals" with facilities like consultation rooms, medical store, ICU and pantry. Each train can accommodate at least 1,000 beds. Using the 7,500-plus railway stations, the patients can be admitted to the trains,' the firm's managing director reportedly wrote in the offer.[11]

During these Extraordinary Times, Prioritise Building Trust

Trust is a complex human emotion. Imagine a friend who shares a problem with you. You offer a solution right away and your friend is likely to assume you have not given it enough thought. If you take very long, the person will feel you have not given the matter enough importance. Your response has to be offered after a brief pause to assure the other person that you have given it enough thought.

When a shop prices a product at Rs 499 and we offer a Rs 500 currency note, we like it when the shopkeeper offers to return a rupee. Conversely when a restaurant bill comes up to an odd amount (after adding GST and other taxes) say Rs 507.23, offering the credit card is an easy option to pay the exact amount or to round it up. What if the Rs 507.23 had to be spilt between three friends. In that case, generosity helps even though it does not make a material difference to anyone to round it up or down. By loosening up in your transactions with the people in your life, you're showing that intangible things like friendship and feelings take precedence over the transaction. Focusing on the relationship builds trust.

This is also evidence that efficiency and precision offered by digital payment apps like Venmo, Square Cash, Zelle, Google Pay or Paytm have streamlined our lives. But they lower trust between friends especially if you pay the precise mathematical number that your calculator shows up.[12]

To build trust, consumer-facing companies have been far more proactive in engaging with influencers than B2B businesses. The post-pandemic world where face-to-face interactions are going to be dropping dramatically may require a fresh view of how to work with influencers.

Building trust through influencers: B2B influencers can craft trust-based relationships with the customer. They know how to communicate in a manner which is engaging, and their large online following is proof that the community trusts their recommendations. They can be far more effective in building brand awareness and engagement that results in inbound-leads through the communities they nurture online. By taking the brand engagement online, a B2B influencer can single-handedly take your brand to geographies and audiences that would be expensive to reach through a traditional sales team. They turn your business digital and boundaryless.[13]

Advertising done by the business is very often the most visible face of the brand. Changing the communication at a time of crisis is one of the fastest ways in which brands can build trust. Apple, Facebook, Ford, Uber and Walmart changed their communication to encourage people to stay at home. And found ways to connect the message with the core of their brand. Building trust during a crisis is more important than other times.

Facebook and Google dominate the digital ad market, and brands are reluctant to turn off the tech companies' powerful advertising tools. Facebook has been coming under pressure to regulate hate speech and divisive content.

It gets 70 per cent of its money from the ads placed by small and medium-sized businesses. The top hundred brands spent roughly $4.2 billion on Facebook ads last year, representing around 6 per cent of the company's nearly $70 billion earnings from ad revenues, from 8 million advertisers in 2019. The advertisers need Facebook more than Facebook needs them.[14]

Then came the 'Stop Hate for Profit' campaign that drew in the bigger players as well. Walt Disney, Unilever, Starbucks, Ford, Verizon and many small marketers stopped advertising on the platform in July 2020. Disney was planning to spend more than $200 million on ads in the first half of 2020. While that is a large sum of money, it is unlikely to impact Facebook enough to take action since smaller enterprises across countries will continue to use Facebook, because it is the cheapest way to reach their audience.

Market shapers can never be economically impacted to do the right thing. It is only an ethical leadership team that can make that shift. Facebook will have to wait for Mark Zuckerberg to have that realisation. The market shapers can hide behind obscure regulation and pressurise lawmakers through lobbying firms to look the other way. Regulators are hopelessly unaware of the possibilities and dilemmas of Big Tech to be able to rein them in. That can only be done by community boycotts or by Big Tech itself.

For businesses, that often means abandoning their plans and connecting with the consumers to become relevant in their lives. Ninjacart, an India-based fresh produce supply chain startup, is offering subsidised rates on provisioned fruits and vegetables to old-age homes, orphanages, and lower economic areas in India.[15]

Sensemaking Builds Trust

What are some ways in which leaders can get the employees to make sense of the complex scenario that is unfolding across sectors, driving different changes—some temporary and some that are likely to drive permanent structural changes in the business models? Being able to simplify and connect the dots is what sensemakers do. They create a narrative that people can hold on to. They are storytellers who can give people hope during a crisis.

Some ideas to get started as a Sense Maker

- *Data plus stories drive action:* Computer scientist, activist, and artist Joy Buolamwini, revealed the potential harms and biases of facial recognition software. Amazon, IBM and Microsoft said they will pause or halt police use of their facial recognition technology. By combining powerful storytelling with data, sense makers can build trust and drive action.

- *Use sense makers to upskill people:* Help your employees and customers share common experiences. It will help them form new connections as they deal with social isolation. Adobe's sound engineer Jason Levine—or 'Adobe Jesus' to his acolytes—is among Adobe's elite software trainers, whose job title is 'principal worldwide evangelist.' The charismatic Levine has been commanding the attention of thousands for the last seventeen years. His typical online tutorial gets tens of thousands of unique views from all over the world. What if your L&D team were challenged to create something similar?

He turns software training from a serious task to one that is part entertainment and part conversation with a friendly instructor who happens to be an expert. The audience loves it. Sensemaking and training when combined is an addictive combination.

IMPLEMENTATION CHALLENGE

- How can your brand become a powerful source of information about trends and information that impacts your sector and the lives of customers? Dettol Indonesia created a video to show people how to wash their hands properly.
- Encourage your employees to create 'with me' videos. YouTube is full of 'study with me', 'cook with me' videos. Let employees showcase their skills.

It would be a missed opportunity to treat the post-COVID workplace as the old workplace but with everyone wearing masks and sitting apart. It is an opportunity to rethink the employer-employee contract. The relationship between all segments and stakeholders of the ecosystem will need to be established again. It is a new language that will have to be learnt.

Vulnerability Builds Trust

When leaders share their vulnerability, they build trust. This is the first time in the world of work when the leader is as uncertain about the future as the employee. This democratisation of information, or the lack of it, is creating a new contract between the employer and the employee. When leaders admit they are vulnerable, they are building trust. 'I don't know' is a new phrase the leader has to get used to. It takes a courageous and self-assured leader to admit that it is their own judgement and not precedents they are relying on.

How to Choose Your Workplace Tech

Businesses have to invest in HR technology that creates seamless working no matter where the employee chooses to work from. What should you look for?

1. *A globally distributed workforce:* Build your workplace technology by assuming that every employee works out of a different time zone or country. What would you need to do to ensure that they can be hired, onboarded, managed, appraised and rewarded without a hitch? What will it take to ensure that their skills are at the cutting edge?
2. *Pay-per-use:* Invest in scalable HR SaaS based software that can be implemented in a few weeks. No one trained 2.7 billion people on how to use Facebook. Your HR software should be just as intuitive to use. Instead of investing in bloated ERP systems that take an army of consultants to implement, businesses are using pay-per-use workplace software. Technology not only makes it easy to collaborate, it creates a delightful employee experience.
3. *Continuous skilling*: Skill-building at scale needs to be done much more efficiently with technology. When Indus Towers decided to train 5,000 employees across ten branch offices, they had a complex business problem on hand. Indus Towers had to improve the uptime of 170,000 sites that provided the common infrastructure for major telecom and wireless operators. The learning solution created by PeopleStrong was mobile-based, bite-sized and contextual. The analysis of the training's effectiveness

for the workforce could be completed in a day instead of forty-five to sixty days that a manual process took. Eighty-three per cent of the field engineers saw an improvement in the assessment scores compared to the previous years. This resulted in a 58 per cent improvement in performance. Investment in HR tech certainly paid off for Indus Towers.[16]

During the financial crisis, organisations turned to the Chief Financial Officers (CFOs) to lead the operations. This is the time for the CHRO to lead organisations into the new world of work. This is the time to learn the new language that the world of work is switching to. It is time to build your vocabulary.

Pay-Per-Use Sales Need Different Skills

When the way of doing work changes, the old skills are replaced by a new set of skills. The people who were skilled in the previous methods of doing work were not necessarily the ones who would be able to learn the new skills and build a new mindset to succeed in the new paradigm.

The B2B buyer is now getting digitally savvy. In the post-pandemic era, with restrictions on travel and requirements for social distancing, sales will no longer be about influencing, convincing and persuading. Remote selling through videos and digital channels are replacing face-to-face meetings and sales made over a drink at the bar.

The focus is now on connecting, collaborating and shaping solutions. Business tech solutions are becoming subscription-based because of SaaS products. Cloud products are becoming consumption-based. The consumers

realise value only when customer success teams work with users to shape solutions. Value-creation is by listening, empathising, sharing perspectives and facilitating agreements between decision-makers. Customer success teams at companies like Oracle and Salesforce are being led by women, perhaps because they are stronger than men at listening and empathising with the customer.[17]

Could You Build a 'Digital Twin' of Your Business?

A digital twin is quite simply a clone that receives a continuous stream of data, information and updates from the real machine or system. According to Gartner, the world's leading research and advisory company, 'A crazy variety of some 21 billion connected "things" are at this moment collecting data and performing all sorts of tasks. The majority are consumer devices, from smart speakers to watches to door locks. The rest serve business: medical devices, engine sensors, industrial robots, HVAC controllers

… almost every enterprise now relies on IoT devices in one form or another.'[18]

These billions of sensors that are available in the world make it possible to get this stream of data. A digital twin makes it possible to experiment with problems and even predict breakdowns by analysing data. Digital twin versions of jet engines, locomotives and gas turbines are tracking wear and tear on the machinery, maximising operational efficiency and predicting when these machines will need maintenance—often before they break down.

Tesla has a digital twin for every vehicle they manufacture.[19] Data is constantly being transmitted back and forth from the car to the factory. If a driver has a rattle in a door it can be fixed by downloading software to adjust the hydraulics of that particular door. Tesla regularly downloads software updates to their customer's cars based on the data they are constantly receiving from each VIN.[20]

A Thought Experiment

In the world of talent management, digital twins raise interesting possibilities and challenges. Apple could bring back the digital twin of Steve Jobs to do the launch of the next product.

What if the organisation wants to create digital twins of their top performers and have them take all the decisions? If your top performer has been asked to leave because of charges of embezzlement or harassment, does the employer still have the right to continue using his or her digital twin?

Digital Twins Are Already Around

Surgeons are creating digital twins of the heart before they perform surgery. Accenture has created a digital twin of AnPost—Ireland's postal service. By creating twins of vehicles, routes and sorting centres, they can create more efficient routes and different processes. Singapore has built a digital twin of the city and is using it to create plans for an emergency response and make changes to the traffic flow and resources before implementing it. Kaeser Kompressoren started selling air-as-a-service where the customer is only charged for the time the compressor is used.[21]

Futurist Cathy Hackl says, 'Many people will live in smart cities and in time, humans will live in a smart world. Every lamppost, house, and street sign will have a digital twin in the metaverse. In that metaverse, each person will have a digital twin who will be linked to themselves.'[22]

When people create their digital twins, will they share diseases and mental conditions too? Who owns your DNA, and who can bring you back in a digital or physical form in the future? Is that a decision for the individual or their legal heirs? What if convicted criminals want to create their digital twins before they are hanged? Should that be allowed?

Workers: Automation, Jobs and Skills

As news of the lockdown came through on the television channels, people hurriedly packed their belongings and decided to migrate back to their home towns to be with their families. Those who could afford air travel were lucky.

Migrant labour crowded into the trains and buses that were leaving the cities, in a bid to return to their villages. Then there were millions who started to walk hundreds of kilometres to be with their loved ones rather than stay in the city where they had come to earn a living. Employers who run small- and medium-scale enterprises watched their talent pool dry up before their eyes.

In most countries, migrants are viewed as the cause for all problems. People blame them for everything, from unemployment to crime. Ironically it is the migrants that are at the forefront of the pandemic battle. In Australia 53 per cent of the doctors are migrants while 29 per cent doctors in America are migrants. Some 40 per cent of medical and life scientists in America are foreign-born. Half the big American tech firms were founded by a first or second-generation immigrant.

Emotions in the Workplace

We expect job candidates to be 'passionate', yet we dislike any display of emotions at work. It has been considered unprofessional. Maybe it had everything to do with the nature of work. The industrial revolution was built on the ideals of standardisation, uniformity and regularity. Not surprisingly, there was no place for emotions at workplace. The new workplace designs have to be spaces that nurture creativity, inspire and energise. They have to build space for emotions.

When employees come back to the workplace, we have to keep in mind that this is not the workplace that we left when we hardly said a goodbye as we picked up a laptop and went home. During the lockdown, the world changed and made humans understand their mortality and helplessness.

From the billionaire to the migrant labour walking back home, three feelings were universally experienced—uncertainty, mortality and loneliness. We were uncertain about our jobs, our future and worried if we would die alone, unloved and isolated from our loved ones. Imaginary scenarios of being left without any income and with a mountain of unsettled debts crossed every human's mind.

'You are going to have to grow up faster than some generations.'

Barack Obama
to the graduating class of 2020

The Golden Moment for Entrepreneurs?

Across colleges and business schools all over the world, the graduating class is worried about the future. Internships are being cancelled. If some people are lucky to get the internship, it is being moved online. Students around the world are blaming the timing of their entering the workforce in a year where the world of work seems to have hit a dry patch. Across India, the lockdown has forced several educational institutes to put their placement processes on hold. Even students who have received offers from companies are not sure if their appointment letters will be honoured.[23]

Companies like TCS, Google, Wipro and Capgemini, made the news because they were honouring the job offers made at the campus. Some like SAP, Morgan Stanley, Salesforce, Palo Alto Networks, PayPal, Citigroup, JP Morgan, Bank of America and Booz Allen Hamilton took a ninety-day no lay-off pledge.[24]

In the US, the same pattern was impacting internships and job seekers. Employment platform Yello found that 64 per cent of student internships that were cancelled did not provide any form of alternative offer. Eleven per cent of students said that they have been offered a postponed internship; 7 per cent said they were guaranteed a final round interview next year; and 6 per cent a full-time offer next year.[25]

This could simply be a golden moment for entrepreneurs. And for freelancers to build their portfolio of work when the playing field is not so crowded. The way to do this would be to change the lens with which to view careers.

Reframing Careers

One thing is for sure, predictable and well-paying employment may become a thing of the past. Careers, jobs and employment may need to reframed. One such method would be to think of the money to be earned and dividing it among multiple 'employers'. Job work may become the default option for most people.

Instead of looking for one employer, what if the person thought of distributing the employment between multiple employers. That is just what every freelancer does—generate an income by working for multiple employers. This may

be the perfect time to think of becoming an entrepreneur or freelancer.

A startup that built a robot that could make a custom-made pizza, raised $375 million before going bust. Imagine what you could do if you had a solution for a problem that the world was grappling with.

Assessing the Learning Health

The 800-year-old Cambridge University became the first British university to move all student lectures online for the entire upcoming academic year starting in October 2020 and ending in the summer of 2021.

Byju's is an educational technology edtech platform that made its app completely free during the pandemic. The founder-CEO Byju Raveendran describes the pandemic as an inflection point in education that is impacting 1.5 billion students worldwide. 'Earlier, students used to spend two to three days per week on our platform. As a result of the lockdown, they are using the platform on a daily basis and spending an average of 100 minutes per day. In the last month alone, we saw over 6 million new students learning from our app.'[26]

In the analogue world, training departments of companies have often competed with each other to announce how many 'man-days' of training per employee have been achieved during the year. Measuring number of training days is a weak attempt by organisations to look at skill-building with the same lens as sales. You could visualise a board outside the office that says, 'Trespassers will be trained'. Training centres are evaluated on the basis of asset utilisation. The pandemic brought back the same mindset. In a May 2020 news report, Air Asia India's head of people and culture stated that its employees had clocked 2.43 lakh hours of learning in total during the lockdown.[27]

When work shifts, it immediately triggers a skill gap in the workforce. We have seen the awkwardness with which teachers in schools, professors in colleges and leaders in organisations use video conferences to simply 'perform' in front of a camera. The design of the experience of learning impacts how quickly the workforce can be upskilled.

According to Nishchae Suri, President—Asia Pacific, Middle East & Africa for EdCast, 'Owing to the pandemic there has been a surge in the adoption of digital learning. However, organisations across the board are struggling with designing learning experiences that are unified, curated, personalised and engaging. According to the EdCast LHI Study 2020, 91 per cent organisations do not consistently personalise learner journeys to accommodate individual goals, preferences and styles of learners. The mantra for engaging the modern day learner is 'Just in Time', 'Just Enough', 'Just for Me'. Jardine Matheson (a diversified Asian-based group with 464,000 employees) has not only deployed the EdCast Learning Experience Platform (LXP) but also integrated the platform with Microsoft Teams to give its employees access to valuable learning and insights directly in the flow of work. Learning is the New Working!' EdCast suggests measuring the Learning Health Index on eight parameters.[28]

1. The agility of the learning function and how future focussed it is
2. Ability to develop and test new products and track competitive scenarios
3. Policies and processes that govern the learning team
4. L&D portfolio
5. Learner experience
6. The culture of learning in the organisation
7. Tools and technology used
8. The competence of the learning and development team

Global Warming Solved through a Burger? Impossible

The opportunity to solve a problem that was considered impossible is what attracted the attention of Pat Brown. He was a tenured professor at Stanford University working on various kinds of biomedical problems including the AIDS virus, gut microbiome etc. He had built the Public Library of Sciences in 2001 to make scientific journals available for free that were otherwise behind a paywall.

Then he discovered the problem that would leave him flabbergasted. The carbon emission that comes from the livestock and agricultural land that gets used for the meat producing industry is more than what is produced globally by every car, truck, aircraft and ship combined. 'You cannot nag people into changing their diet,' says Pat Brown. He set out to create a product which meat lovers would prefer because it would give them the same sensory pleasure, nutrition and convenience as animal-based meat.

In 2009, Pat raised $9 million from Vinod Khosla to start Impossible Foods that would create plant-based 'meat' that would look, taste and smell the same as animal-based meat. By 2011, he decided to leave his tenured professorship at Stanford and pursue this extremely risky venture because he was deeply committed to that mission. It is said that sometime around 2012 or 2013, Google offered approximately $200-$300 million to acquire the company which Pat Brown rejected.

In 2016, the 'impossible burger' was launched. David Cheng, the celebrity chef, who loves meat so much that he refuses to list any vegetarian dishes on his menu, raved about the taste of the burger on social media. Millions of impossible burgers are now sold across fast food chains like Applebee and across 7,000 outlets of Burger King. The meat lobby is furious and wants lawmakers to state that anything listed as meat must be made from an animal. The meat lobby has made every effort to discredit impossible burgers as 'not healthy', made from GMO and so on.

Consumers believe that if it looks like meat, smells like meat and tastes like meat, it does not matter whether it is made from a plant or an animal. Consumers always win, because they are the ones who fund every enterprise.

Work: Which of these Tasks Will You Do?

Machines and outsourcing will take away some tasks. We know that every job is made up of a set of tasks. If bulk of the jobs follow the three criteria that is used to determine automation, the job is likely to be lost to a machine. On the other hand, jobs that are highly dependent on understanding human emotions are likely to have an extended runway (at least for the moment).

1. Rule-based tasks

This uncertainty will certainly lead to some of the employees deciding to invest in automation rather than to depend on the human labour pool. When deciding to automate, 'rule-based work' will be the first that will get done by machines. Anything which is a rule-based, unchanging task that has a high volume of repetitive transactions makes it a prime choice for automation. Better image recognition technology combined with rules that are dictated by algorithms are doing many things once done by people.

These rule-based tasks will get done by machines, algorithms and platforms. The calculator is the most commonplace example of a machine that we use to do basic calculations. The physical device has now been replaced by software which is now available on every phone and laptop. The more complex calculations get done through spreadsheets which allow customisation. For example, Excel enables the user to write simple macros or programs that can speed up tasks.

Chat bots are getting better at using natural language processing to answer simple questions. They are being used by many human resources professionals to answer routine queries. PeopleStrong's chatbot Zippi was customised to respond to routine queries employees have about HR policies. (See the Max Healthcare Case Study below for details).

ICICI Bank, India's second-largest private sector bank has deployed software robotics in over 200 business processes across various functions of the company. At ICICI Bank, software robots have reduced the response time to customers by up to 60 per cent and increased accuracy to 100 per cent, thereby sharply improving the bank's productivity and efficiency. ICICI Bank uses an AI-based chatbot, named iPal that interacted with more than 3.1 million customers in a few months, answering about 6 million queries, with a 90 per cent accuracy rate.[29]

In rule-based tasks, the task gets taken away from the human and is done by software. The companies that sell such software and services are some of the biggest employers. Accenture, IBM, TCS, Cognizant, Infosys, Capgemini, DXC, NTT, HCL and Wipro are the top ten IT service companies in the world. Many firms in this space also do very high-end complex tasks that are described in the second category.[30]

Case Study: Max Healthcare

India's leading providers of comprehensive, seamless and integrated world class healthcare services, Max Healthcare, has fourteen hospitals and provides treatment across twenty-nine specialties. Max Healthcare employs over 2300+ doctors with international level expertise.

The overall Human Capital Management solution included the following modules—Recruit, Onboarding,

Leave & Attendance, Transfer, Confirmation, Payroll, CTC Reimbursements, Exit process. The automated chatbot Zippi contributed heavily to the overall employee experience.

A number of these transactions have been historically done by the HR team. The rule-based, unchanging task with a high volume of repetitive transactions makes it a prime choice for automation.

2. Cognitively complex tasks

Many of the tasks that require an extremely high degree of technical knowledge or multidisciplinary approach can be classified as cognitively complex. These tasks cannot be done by machines and often attract a handful of people across the world who are qualified to do these. Cognitively complex tasks are usually handled by the top 1 per cent of the global talent pool in the field. Machines may augment these tasks but eventually it needs a human to do these.

Google's search algorithm is an example of a cognitively complex task. Fields that require depth of knowledge gained by research and reading are in this category. Second-order specialist functions in every field have examples of cognitively complex tasks. Someone who has studied compensation or incentive design in the area of compensation and benefits has learnt a cognitively complex task. Within the HR function of an organisation, the compensation and benefits function is a specialist function. Someone who specialises in incentive design is a super-specialist within the speciality.

A surgeon may specialise in orthopaedic surgery. A surgeon who performs surgery for sports injuries to the spine is working in a second-order specialisation. Such super-specialisation is demanding and every patient needs a unique individualised response. By dealing with lots of these unique scenarios, the surgeon can find patterns that allows him or her to apply their learning to other patients or apply it in a different setting altogether. Dealing with sports injuries to the spine can give the surgeon a unique specialisation for helping others with spinal injuries during war or in manufacturing factories. Once the person has built depth, applications across other areas can broaden the opportunities for the specialist.

Too narrow a specialisation can be as limiting as having skills that are not differentiated enough. Building some degree of depth and specialisation is a signal that the skill needs to be used in different settings or industries to become valuable. That holds true for specialists as well as super-specialists.

3. Emotionally complex tasks

A perfect example of such a role would be that of a hostage negotiator. They need to operate under conditions of extreme stress where one false move can get a terrorist to blow up a building full of people. They have deep understanding of their own emotions and are able to manage them exceptionally well. In addition, they are also very good at understanding the emotions of others and can tailor their responses to elicit a certain kind of response.

Emotionally complex tasks are the counterpart of the cognitively complex tasks described above. These are supremely specialised skills that only a very tiny percentage of humans find hard to handle. These are hard to automate.

Jobs which are extremely stressful with a low margin of error cause an extraordinary degree of stress.

An air traffic controller's job needs someone with nerves of steel to manage multiple variables with a very short window of time done several times a day, every day. It needs someone who has an extraordinary ability to control her responses no matter what the provocation is. Emotionally complex jobs are not for most people because of the extraordinary level of self-control needed to deal with almost every interaction.

Most jobs that involve dealing with the fragile emotions of people who have been hurt or abused are all roles that need people with extraordinary human skills. The same can be said for roles that involve interacting with people who have severe degrees of disabilities. Teachers who teach children in special education or those who work with people dealing with autism or other cerebral developmental challenges need to have the mental strength and resilience to work with people where they see very little progress every day. Yet these jobs are extremely meaningful.

Undercover agents who need to assume a different identity and live under the radar in an enemy country, are those who are performing emotionally complex roles. Navy Seals and commandos generate a sense of awe among us because their job descriptions are impossible to predict. Every assignment/mission is different in its own way. Their jobs will be the last to be automated, if at all.

4. High Human-Touch tasks

While a lot of the content that is taught in schools is now available for free through various edtech sites, people still crave to be taught by a human. The average completion rate for the MOOC ranges anywhere from 5 to 15 per cent.[31]

As technology makes it easy for content to be transferred to the students through online classes, the value of a teacher who can inspire and motivate the students has never been higher. Many of us have made career choices based on our feelings for the teacher who inspired us with their worldview. It is equally true that many of us changed our career tracks based on our feelings for a teacher we disliked.

The experience of education is what people crave for. Being able to discuss and debate what the professor has taught with friends, over a cup of coffee, the sports and theatre facilities, living in the dorm, are part of what creates memories.

The best professors, coaches and designers know how to inspire, motivate and encourage people. Roles that require working with emotions are hard to describe in tangible, numerical and measurable terms. These are precisely the roles that require very high human touch and skills. In an organisation, very often the support functions like Learning, Marketing, Design etc. fall in this category. These are hard to automate.

What are some examples of jobs that are emotionally complex? Most people squirm when they have to tell someone that the job they've done is not up to the mark. They open up the conversation with something appreciative and then gulp before they sugar-coat the harsh message and quickly end up with something massively positive. And then there are people who do not care about leaving someone bruised and debilitated with their feedback. Any interaction with them feels like having sandpaper rubbed all over a bruise. But luckily for us there is a third category of people, who use their words and non-verbal ability to communicate so well that it inspires people to improve. It is no wonder that people managers roles need to be assigned to those who enjoy doing these interactions every day.

Customer service roles, public relations, marketing, HR, sales and any role where success is dependent on the ability to understand, convince and negotiate with others and senior leadership roles in organisations are examples of high human touch. These are all jobs where two people with the same skill will achieve completely different outcomes. In many of these jobs every couple of years there comes a time which demands a response where there is no precedent. When the firm they are working for gets embroiled in some controversy, the high-touch job can get morphed into an emotionally complex task. When the context changes, a high human-touch role could become as demanding as an emotionally complex role.

The pandemic threw us all into a huge space of uncertainty. HR leaders had to navigate this uncertain scenario where the rules had not been formed and all the employees were working in a new context. The entire organisation was going through its business uncertainty and everyone seemed to be on the edge all the time.

5. Creators, influencers and creative visionaries

In 2019, I launched a podcast called 'Dreamers & Unicorns'. The premise was to draw attention to the world of work. My belief was that formal employment in a firm was going to diminish drastically to match the rise of freelancers.

The businesses could draw on a skilled talent pool of specialists without having to bear the heightened cost of salaries, benefits and increments etc. The popularity of the podcast took the production team and PeopleStrong (the title sponsor) by surprise. Within days of its launch, it was trending at the top of the charts.

The guests spoke about how they continuously reinvent their crafts (and their creative identity) and the rise of the creative class. As machines start doing more and more of the transactions, the work that depends on human creativity will become more important.

New formats, new platforms for stories

Digital media has evolved rapidly in the era of social media. Every platform has its share of successful storytellers. It has spawned millions of creators and new formats of storytelling. Stand-up comedy, poetry on Instagram, live streaming of shows by ordinary people have all emerged as commercially viable formats. Storytelling formats have changed to short form (three-minute movies) and are being made for YouTube.

Books are heard. Poetry is seen. Audible, the audiobook retailer and publisher, saw its revenue in the UK rise by 38 per cent in 2018: the year before, the company posted a 47 per cent sales increase. Research suggests that, in the UK, audiobook sales will overtake sales of ebooks in 2020.

Creative visionaries like Canadian-Punjabi poet Rupi Kaur, has nearly four million followers on Instagram. She has completely by-passed publishers and connects directly with her readers. She serves her poetry in visual form.

It is called 'Instapoetry'. She breaks the stereotype of a struggling poet and has earned millions. Her 2014 book, *Milk and Honey*, has sold over 2.5 million copies in twenty-five languages and spent seventy-seven weeks on the *New York Times* best-seller list.

What is a fair compensation to pay for a single photo to be posted on your social media handle? If you are Kim Kardashian, you should expect between $300,000 to $500,000 for a single Instagram post. For longer-term endorsements, Kardashian typically signs multimillion-dollar deals. Her attorney says she recently agreed to a $6 million annual deal with a wearable-consumer-goods company.

Most others who work with influencers don't have to break a bank to amplify the brand message.[32]

Facebook influencer pricing: $25 per 1,000 followers

Instagram Influencer pricing: $10 per 1,000 followers

Snapchat Influencer pricing: $10 per 1,000 followers

YouTube Influencer pricing: $20 per 1,000 followers

Even a traditional retailer like Marks and Spencer is moving more of its marketing budget from traditional media to digital, as the pandemic forces its clothing and home division to become a 'pureplay' online business. This was triggered by a 70 per cent drop in volume in the first half of 2020.[33]

In 2017, online behemoth Amazon reported that in the United States over 1,000 independent authors—publishing on the Kindle platform—made more than $100,000 in royalties.[34]

In a world that is spoilt for choice, influencers build trust especially for B2B brands. 'The main benefit is that influencers humanise a brand and capture the personality behind the logo. Additionally, influencers raise brand awareness and engagement by giving companies access to an audience they may not otherwise have through a trusted and credible source.'

Market shapers like Amazon, Alibaba, Apple, Facebook, Google, Netflix etc. wield influence over a larger number of people (consumers) than the heads of many states. Alibaba has more customers than the number of citizens in Russia. Facebook controls information for more than 2.6 billion people (as of March 2020). That is more than the population of India and the entire African continent put together.[35]

We may be entering a phase where the economic power of a few companies combined with the data they own about people may give them more power than the government. Political enemies use this information, espionage, assassinations, cyber-attacks and proxies to weaken the enemy. With more and more businesses moving online it is reasonable to expect that organisations will become far more attractive targets for hackers and organised crime. A competitor spreading disinformation through a combination of facts and fake news could undermine the trust the consumer has in the product quality or the hygiene standards of the organisation. Business leaders are ill-prepared to handle the new media. As they move more of their business online, it is imperative to understand how fake news and social media could build or damage the brand overnight.

The British government has set up a task force to handle this information around COVID-19.[36]

In the post-pandemic scenario, businesses now have to learn to communicate with a set of consumers and customers whose worldview has been reshaped. Take the simple example of displaying the privacy notice to customers. Giving them too much information about privacy could make them anxious.[37]

Bullet-proof glass is meant to protect us, but being aware that we are sitting in a car with bullet-proof glass makes us aware of the danger we would have otherwise ignored. Having a skilled writer convey the right amount of information without setting off alarm bells is important. In a world where trust is vital, businesses will depend more heavily on skilled communicators. The privacy policy has to be 'reasonable' and must explain things adequately, but not made super-salient. It requires someone who is extremely good at understanding complex human emotions (how else would you know what is reasonable?) and express it in just the right set of words.[38]

Your Uniqueness is a Feature of the Passion Economy

Some writers describe this as the 'Passion Economy'. While traditional organisations always frown upon someone who does not fit in, digital platforms like Substack and Podia are built for monetising uniqueness. These platforms allow creative individuals to engage with their audience directly and monetise the engagement. This creates an opportunity for ongoing monetisation that has never been possible before. These platforms offer digital products and services and encourage direct interaction between the creator and their audience at scale.[39]

Many digital platforms of the gig economy make the service provider anonymous and substitutable, these creative platforms thrive on individuality. They view individuality as a feature, not a bug.

Their SaaS tools enable service or product providers to run their own business. You need only a hundred fans to pay you $1,000 a year, argues Li Jin. She talks about the $10 billion self-improvement industry; adult learning/continuing education is a $55 billion industry in the US alone. NYU Professor Scott Galloway's two-week online course 'Strategy Sprint' teaches the basics of brand strategy for $500.[40]

On Twitter, @JoshuaKarthikR says, 'College was about picking the institution, not the teacher. And now the 'passion economy' is about picking the teacher/instructor directly, not caring for the institution/ platform at all.'

He goes on to ask, 'But which instructor do you pick? Someone

- with experience in my field
- with success in my field
- that I'd like to be more like
- that I like'

The ability for the best creators in fields ranging from teaching to photography, the opportunity to connect directly through digital platforms will be the big opportunity for the bright creative and digitally savvy youth who do not find jobs. They will soon discover that their passion for comedy, writing, broadcasting, teaching, interior decoration can be monetised directly once their craft reaches a certain number of people.

IGTV is striking a deal with 200 approved, English-speaking creator partners, including Adam Waheed and Lele Pons, plus a handful of major advertiser partners like Ikea, Puma, and Sephora. Instagram will share an 'industry standard' 55 per cent cut with creators for the content they create.

While there are stories of computer programs that can draw, compose music and write storylines well enough to fool anyone into believing that these are done by humans, creative visionaries will always have a space in the world of work.

Topping the LinkedIn 2020 list of most in-demand soft skills are creativity, collaboration, persuasion and emotional intelligence—all skills that demonstrate how we work with others and bring new ideas to the table. It is no surprise that creativity remains the number one soft skill that employers look for in their star employees.[41]

Tech that drives efficiency enough to make workers irrelevant can also help build skills for the future. When employers have the choice to shut down a factory to drive efficiency, must they also think of investing in the reskilling of the population that would be made redundant?

The New Continent Has Been Discovered

For thousands of years, not only the greatest thinkers and scholars but also the infallible scriptures had known only Europe, Africa and Asia. Could they all have been wrong? The world of work is that new continent that has just been discovered.

References

1. The Coronavirus timeline shows the tsunami of change. https://www.who.int/emergencies/diseases/novel-coronavirus-2019/events-as-they-happen
2. *Sapiens: A Brief History of Humankind*, Yuval Noah Harari
3. J.C. Penney, 118-Year-Old department store, files for bankruptcy. https://www.nytimes.com/2020/05/15/business/jc-penney-bankruptcy-coronavirus.html
4. An analysis of the $103 trillion air travel industry. https://www.economist.com/business/2020/08/01/air-travels-sudden-collapse-will-reshape-a-trillion-dollar-industry
5. Trolls are eating up the movie theaters in US. https://www.theverge.com/2020/4/29/21239703/trolls-world-tour-amc-digital-streaming-theaters-nbcuniversal-disney-warnerbros
6. Multiplexes face an uncertain future. https://www.livemint.com/news/india/hollywood-shows-the-way-takes-top-movies-to-viewers-homes-11588999975867.html

7. Multiplex INOX was visibly alarmed. https://www.ndtv.com/entertainment/multiplex-inox-disappointed-and-alarmed-by-amitabh-bachchan-film-gulabo-sitabos-digital-release-2229088
8. The electric bulb could last much longer, but it won't. https://www.bbc.com/future/article/20160612-heres-the-truth-about-the-planned-obsolescence-of-tech
9. The marketing guru predicts changes in the life of the consumer. https://sarasotainstitute.global/the-consumer-in-the-age-of-coronavirus/
10. A crisis can jumpstart innovation even in the most siloed cultures. https://www.wsj.com/articles/crisis-has-jumpstarted-americas-innovation-engine-what-took-so-long-11586527243
11. Turning the railway coaches into hospitals was an innovative idea to expand India's hospital capacity for rural areas. https://theprint.in/india/governance/rail-coach-as-icu-how-modi-govt-plans-to-beat-healthcare-gaps-in-remote-areas/388043/
12. Payment apps may make equal sharing between friends more precise, but they lower the trust levels in the relationship. https://ideas.ted.com/the-subtle-surprising-way-that-payment-apps-may-be-affecting-your-relationships/
13. Sales disruptions in the post-COVID world. https://futureofworkjapan.wordpress.com/2020/05/14/top-10-corporate-sales-disruptions-in-2020-covid-japan-how-a-sales-organization-can-survive-and-thrive/
14. The advertisers need Facebook. Despite demands to regulate hate speech and fact-check political campaigns, Facebook has taken no action. https://sanfrancisco.cbslocal.com/2020/07/01/more-than-500-companies-join-facebook-ad-boycott-stop-hate-for-profit/
15. The pandemic is a chance for you to forge deeper relations with the employees and customers. https://www.thinkwithgoogle.com/intl/en-apac/tools-resources/data-measurement/google-search-data-reveals-how-brands-can-help-during-coronavirus-pandemic/
16. Indus Towers case of implementing the Alt-Learning solution provided courtesy PeopleStrong
17. There are seven capabilities that said hi performing salespeople apart. https://hbr.org/2020/05/why-women-are-the-future-of-b2b-sales
18. The sensors can help change your businesses. https://www.networkworld.com/article/3542891/the-internet-of-things-in-2020-more-vital-than-ever.html
19. Every Tesla car has a unique identifier code called a VIN. This number contains vital information about the car, such as its manufacturer, year of production, the plant it was produced in, type of engine, model and more. https://www.industryweek.com/technology-and-iiot/article/21130033/how-digital-twins-are-raising-the-stakes-on-product-development

20. The digital twin. https://www2.deloitte.com/us/en/insights/focus/tech-trends/2020/digital-twin-applications-bridging-the-physical-and-digital.html
21. From pharmaceuticals to airlines read about the possibilities of Digital Twins. https://sloanreview.mit.edu/article/how-digital-twins-are-reinventing-innovation/
22. Digital embalmers are working to create our digital afterlife. https://www.forbes.com/sites/cathyhackl/2020/05/27/meet-the-digital-embalmers-helping-celebrities-brands-individuals-plan-their-digital-afterlives/
23. Campus Placements face uncertainty. https://indianexpress.com/article/education/some-offer-letters-revoked-on-campus-recruitment-postponed-6399443/
24. Campus placement. 66 per cent students are without job offers after they have completed their course. https://indianexpress.com/article/jobs/covid-19-impact-on-campus-placement-66-students-without-job-33-awaiting-response-from-employer-6485029/
25. The internship scenario was bleak everywhere. https://www.cnbc.com/2020/04/22/64percent-of-canceled-job-internships-offer-no-compensation.html
26. Byju's made their learning app free and the pivot paid off. https://www.livemint.com/companies/news/pandemic-is-an-inflection-point-for-education-byju-raveendran-11589828988420.html
27. Hours spent in e-learning get announced. https://www.hrkatha.com/features/learning/air-asia-india-employees-together-clock-2-43-lakh-hours-of-learning-in-april/
28. Edcast built a Learning Health Index that can serve as a quick diagnostic tool https://www.edcast.com/corp/learning-health-index/
29. AI Applications in top four Indian banks. https://emerj.com/ai-sector-overviews/ai-applications-in-the-top-4-indian-banks/
30. Top ten IT Services firms in 2020. https://brandfinance.com/images/upload/brand_finance_it_services_25_2020_preview.pdf
31. MOOCs have poor rates of completion. https://www.edsurge.com/news/2018-11-28-stop-asking-about-completion-rates-better-questions-to-ask-about-moocs-in-2019
32. How much do influencers charge. The answer is, 'it depends' but here is a quick guide. https://tinuiti.com/blog/paid-social/how-much-do-influencers-charge/
33. As selling goes online, the importance of digital influencers will grow. Even traditional retailers have to go online to make up the revenue loss from brick and mortar stores. https://www.marketingweek.com/ms-cuts-marketing-spend-by-a-third-as-it-accelerates-shift-to-digital/
34. How reading has changed in the 2010s by BBC. http://www.bbc.com/culture/story/20191210-how-reading-has-changed-in-the-2010s

35. Population of African continent. https://www.worldometers.info/world-population/africa-population/
36. Disinformation is more corrosive in open societies because it undermines trust in the government. https://www.economist.com/books-and-arts/2020/05/16/the-weapons-of-political-warfare
37. Rani Mani runs the Influencers programme for Adobe called Adobe Insiders. https://www.toprankblog.com/2018/11/interview-rani-mani-adobe/
38. Privacy notices can put off customers. https://hbswk.hbs.edu/item/why-privacy-notices-turn-off-shoppers
39. Andreessen Horowitz did a fabulous podcast about the passion economy that got me to dig into this post. https://a16z.com/2019/10/08/passion-economy/
40. It will not be incumbents who will disrupt. It will be the startups. https://li.substack.com/p/four-implications-of-disruption-theory
41. LinkedIn 2020 report top skills companies are looking for. https://learning.linkedin.com/blog/top-skills/the-skills-companies-need-most-in-2020and-how-to-learn-them

9

Liberating Structures and Roles

A single goose is exhausted after flying 500 miles. But a flock of geese flying in a V-formation can fly 800 to 1,000 miles without resting. Is there something that is special about that structure?

It is the ability of the structure to rotate the role of the leader. Leadership teams spend little or no time taking decisions behind closed doors with no dissenting voices. Then they spend years running change management programmes to get people to adopt the decision. When the intangible social aspects of a decision are respected, the implementation is lightning fast. Isn't that liberating?

The design of workspaces has not been challenged since the industrial revolution. Standardisation of rules governing the workplace means that individuals must conform to the demands of every workplace they participate in. The workplace remains static. The individual needs to adapt.

As consumers demand increasingly individualised solutions, the employees need to be treated as individuals with unique rules of engagement.

The WFH model has created an informal parallel workplace structure, which each individual designs. All the structures of the workplace such as starting time, ending time and vacation days have all merged into one big blur. Instead of employees slacking off at home and watching movies, most experienced total burnout because of the long hours since they were not used to taking their own decisions about when to stop working.

Some organisations started announcing a company-wide holiday in order to coordinate the time to recuperate. Google and Facebook told employees that workers who can do their jobs remotely should plan to do so until 2021. Twitter allowed working from home forever and said, 'Opening offices will be our decision, when and if our employees come back, will be theirs.'

The organisation's structures can either free up or be constraining for the employees and customers.

A print journalist helping the booming web division of a newspaper was told to avoid growing the digital business. Their revenue growth was making life difficult for the dying print business. The print edition has since been shut down and only the digital arm of the newspaper survives. The journalist has joined the ranks of the hundreds of print journalists looking for a job.

The Print is an Indian digital news website launched by journalist Shekhar Gupta in August 2017. They are one of the few business houses who have combined the depth of print media with the breadth of digital. The key lies in thinking about the structures.

Decision-makers and Implementers

Organisations have very clear distinctions of the role that people play. There are decision-makers and others implement what the handful of decision-makers decide. The end result is an enormous amount of time and energy spent in convincing those impacted about the benefit of the decision. If only the decision-making process involved those impacted, the pace of implementation would be dramatically faster and would lead to happier and more engaged employees. Implementing best practices drawn from another organisation and trying to force fit them assumes that there is no ability in the employed group to design solutions to their everyday challenges.

Change cannot be broad enough to make a real difference, unless a large number of people become involved as change agents in SHAPING THEIR OWN FUTURE.

The Mystery of the Geese Solved

The top leadership team decides based on presentations or status reports, leading to discussions only among the few people present in the room. Those impacted are not part of this decision-making process. Is there an alternative to this inefficient but widespread approach?

Henri Lipmanowicz and Kenneth McCandless believe that social structures and relationships embed the levels of respect, empathy and trust that each individual employee experiences in the organisation. Their interest in complexity theory made them focus on interactions and feedback loops to drive better decision-making in the organisations. They created a set of tools which are available under the creative commons license for anyone to use. These tools are simple enough that they do not depend on the skill level of the user. But they have the ability to change the way you meet, plan and decide to relate to colleagues.[1]

Before that, let us solve that the mystery we started with. A flock of geese flying in a V-formation can illustrate what liberating structures make possible to enhance the performance of any group.

'Simply, the geese flying in the back utilise the air currents coming from the wings of the geese in front to lift themselves. The geese rotate leadership at regular intervals. When the leader goose tires, it routinely drops behind in the formation as the geese at the back sequentially move forward. This means that if a goose moves out of formation, the increased drag on its wings provides instant feedback to self-correct its position. When in flight, the geese honk regularly and loudly to identify their respective positions and to encourage others to keep going, especially the leader. If a goose is wounded or unwell, two or three geese accompany it to the ground. Once nourished back to health, they will join another passing flock.'[2]

What if the business needs to be reimagined in the context of changes that have happened because of the lockdown and the new scenario triggered by the pandemic? The 25/10 approach can be used for engaging large groups as a new project is initiated or even for doing reviews, says Henri Lipmanowicz.[3]

When the boss suggests an idea, many people hesitate to oppose the idea. I liked the 25/10 approach that is a non-threatening way to check out an idea. You could try out the 25/10 approach to crowd source ideas.

Want to Scale Up 10x?

Invite participants to think big and bold and discover the most attractive of their ideas together by asking, 'If you were ten times bolder, what big idea would you recommend? What first step would you take to get started?'

How would the 25/10 approach be used?[4] The 25/10 method is especially useful when you have an open ended problem that does not have one single solution. Every solution has a potential payoff and a price to pay. In thirty minutes here is how you can get more people to share their ideas and enthusiasm. The best situation: new, uncertain and complex.

Crowdsourcing Ideas in Thirty Minutes

Most organisational initiatives are designed by the senior leaders in small trusted circles of a handful of people and stay with them. When it comes to implementation the leaders have no choice but to go through elaborate processes of communication in order to convince the employees. Some employees get convinced, some are sceptical, and of course there are always a number of people who remain unimpressed. Is there a way in which we can get ideas from a 'cognitively diverse' (differences in perspective and information processing styles—especially when people have to figure out situations that are complex situations that are rapidly changing in unpredictable ways) group of people? Is there a way in which employees can feel that their suggestions were given due importance and that someone thought through the idea even if it finally does not see the light of day?

Five Structural Elements—Minimum Specifications

1. Structuring invitation

- This is the process when everyone present is invited to think of big bold ideas, and one of the ways to trigger that is to ask them, 'If you are ten times bolder, what ideas would you suggest? What would be the first step you would take?'

2. Arranging the space and the materials

- Open space without chairs or tables
- Participants would be standing and talking in informal groups.
- Each participant would get an index card on which they would write their ideas.

3. What makes this inclusive

- Everyone is included and participates at the same time.
- Everyone has an equal opportunity to contribute.

4. Forming the groups

- Individuals think of their big bold idea and identify the first step they would have to take to implement it. This is written on the index card which was handed to them. No one writes their name on the card.
- The cards can be collected and shuffled and re-distributed. If someone receives their own card after the shuffle, they can exchange it with someone. Everyone should have a card where the idea has been suggested by someone else. The idea could have been suggested by the CEO or the junior-most person present, but since it is anonymous, everyone reads the idea and judges it on its own merit.
- Individuals form pairs and discuss the ideas written in the card they now hold. Then they individually score their card and rate it from 1–5. The score of 1 means the idea was not feasible. A score of 5 is a wholehearted endorsement to implement the idea.
- This sequence is repeated five times. At the end of the five rounds, each card would have five ratings from five different people from 1-5. The maximum score of a card would be 25 (if everyone rated the idea as a 5) and the minimum 5 (if everyone rated it as a 1).

Sequence of Steps and Time Allocation

- Explain the process. First, every participant writes on an index card his or her bold idea and the first step. Then people move around and cards are passed from person to person. The purpose is to ensure that people do not know whose card they are receiving or passing on. After three to four minutes, a bell rings. When the bell rings, people stop passing cards and pair up to exchange thoughts on the cards in their hands. (Another good option is to read the card with no talking.)

- Then participants individually rate the idea/step on their card with a score of 1 to 5 (1 for low and 5 for high) and write it on the back of the card. This is called 'Read and Score'. When the bell rings, cards are passed around a second time, called 'Mill and Pass', until the bell rings and the 'Read and Score' scoring cycle repeats. This is done for a total of five scoring rounds. At the end of cycle five, participants add the five scores on the back of the last card they are holding. Finally, the ideas with the top ten scores are identified and shared with the whole group. *Time needed: three minutes.*
- Demonstrate one exchange-and-scoring interaction using a sample index card to clarify what is expected during the milling, namely no reading of the cards, only passing the cards from person to person so that each person has only one card in hand. The process can be confusing for some people. *Time needed: two minutes.*
- Invite each participant to write a big idea and the first step on his or her card. *Time needed: five minutes.*
- Conduct five three-minute exchange-and-scoring rounds with time for milling (and laughing) in between. *Time needed: fifteen minutes.*
- Ask participants to add the five scores on the back of the card they are holding.

- Find the best-scoring ideas with the whole group by conducting a countdown. Ask, 'Is anyone carrying a card that scored twenty-five?' Invite each participant holding a card scored twenty-five, if any, to read out the idea and action step. Continue with 'Anyone with a card that scored twenty-four?', 'Who has a twenty-three' ... Stop when the top ten ideas have been identified and shared. *Time needed: five minutes.*
- The time needed is approximately twenty-five minutes and you get ten great ideas that everyone endorses. The first couple of times, it may take a little more than twenty-five minutes, but after one or two trials, it works quite well.
- The simple act of involving people to share their ideas can help leverage the expertise of the employees and find solutions to issues. Spending these thirty minutes to get ideas from groups of fifty or hundred people can be an incredibly powerful way to crowd source ideas and involve people in issues that impact them.

Case: The Magic of AFMO (Asking for My Opinion)

A consumer goods company was attempting to change the transportation policy for some of the employees in their Mumbai factory. The usual procedure would have been for the leaders to get together, discuss the policy implementation approach and then 'roll it out'. Someone suggested that they seek the opinions of the employees by posting the policy on its internal social media platform. Most of the leaders were apprehensive that it would lead to a lot of resistance being vocalised, which would lead to an impasse between the leaders and the employees. The managing director (MD) of the company wanted to experiment with the suggestion of seeking feedback from employees. So the policy was posted on the intranet.

As expected, there was an outpouring of responses from the employees—somebody resisting actively and vocally reservations about the new policy. What was interesting was that an equally large number of employees tried to explain the merits of the policy and that led to an open debate. Looking at the barrage of responses, it was impossible to figure out if the employees were clearly against the implementation of the policy or if they had a few apprehensions that could be clarified. After a few days, the MD decided to implement the policy without any changes. He sought the opinion of the employees about the decision, and to his surprise, they agreed and told him how delighted they were.

The MD asked the employees, 'If you support this new policy, why did you all resist it so vehemently when it was announced on the company's intranet?'

One employee's response summarised it best. 'Even if you do not implement my idea, I want to feel assured that you have listened to me with an open mind. I just want my opinion to be heard.'

According to the founders of Liberating Structures, a website that offers an alternative way to approach and design how people work together, 'It is natural for people to resist change that is imposed, change that is someone else's "good idea" or a so-called "best practice". Hence, much effort gets wasted in trying to convince people and to get "buy-in". No such resistance arises when the good idea is their shared idea, one that emerged from a process in which they were a full participant, including choosing the change methods used for the process.'[5]

Case Study: Your Competitor Is GANDALF

I did a workshop for the leadership team of a fairly large and profitable bank in South Africa. We got talking about the startup ecosystem in Kenya with its history of transforming the financial system through its focus on the unbanked millions. Kenya has a growing middle class and is one of the most advanced economies in Africa. Mobile-based money transfer service M-Pesa drove up financial inclusion in Kenya from 23 per cent to 83 per cent within a decade of their launch in 2007.

In addition, Nigeria, South Africa, Rwanda, Ethiopia and Egypt all have startup ecosystems that can comfortably scale up if larger corporate organisations mentor the startups on how to scale the business. Entrepreneurs have to better learn how to work with regulatory issues.

Banks have grown in a breaker in the motor environment because everything from customer acquisition to credit cards or mortgages have been done without any technology. Seventy-five per cent of their IT budget is spent on maintenance, thus making it impossible to lower costs and invest in innovation. The bank passes on increased costs to the customers, making banking a luxury affordable largely by the rich. Sixty-six per cent of the adult population in Africa is unbanked.

One participant pointed out that his previous employer (one of the largest banks in the world and headquartered in New York) employs 210,000 people, of which 30,000 are employed to manually review money laundering and fraudulent transactions. Every new bank they have acquired has increased the bank's footprint but it has been impossible to get the IT systems to talk to one another.

When asked who they viewed as their competition, they listed other banks based on their own divisions and functions. For instance, the retail bank benchmarked another bank in South Africa while their institutional lending business looked up to a different bank in the UK as the gold standard.

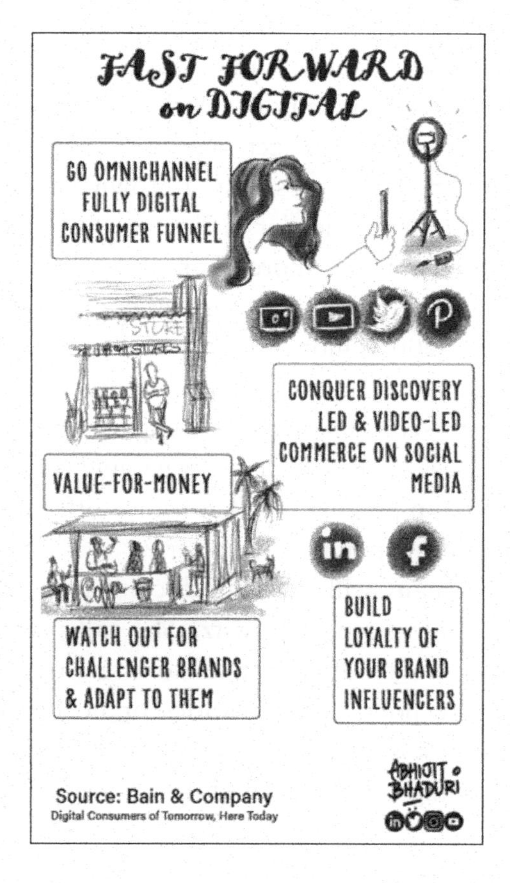

What about Apple as a provider of financial services with its Apple credit card? Uber as the 'bank' for all its drivers with its Uber-Visa debit card? Or Starbucks as the seventh largest bank in the US with its deposits driven by its Starbucks Card?

DBS Bank changed the game by benchmarking not another bank but by aspiring to be the D in GANDALF (a popular character from *The Lord of the Rings*). GANDALF stands for Google, Amazon, Netflix, Apple, LinkedIn and Facebook. The missing D would be DBS bank. It was a simple way to change the competitive canvas.

By the time we ended the conversation, the board had several other 'competitors' marked on it. Flutterwave partnered with Alibaba to get payments from one million Alibaba customers. Kenya's fastest-growing online lender Tala is also the biggest lender in Tanzania. Mobile money's reach is thirteen times more than traditional banks. In Ghana, the initial public offering (IPO) of MTN's mobile money raised $200 million. OPay in Nigeria is driving mass adoption through its motorbike hailing service ORide. The trend is clear—consumer-facing companies can all offer financial services to the consumer. A gaming company takes money for in-app purchases. What if they offered insurance through one of the popular characters?

'Every company will be a fintech company,' says Angela Strange of Andreessen Horowitz. She talks about using many unconventional data sources to assess risks. Millions of people have poor credit histories or no data that can be used to assess their willingness and ability to pay. Machine learning and AI can find the answer in many other datapoints:[6]

- Cell phone bills, rent payment history
- The number of friends you message regularly
- How often you update the operating system of your phone
- If you charge your phone fully at night

The financial services sector is exploding with opportunities. Banking has so far been the privilege of the elite. To get a loan you have to prove that you have enough money and don't really need the loan. A large number of dreamers are trying to address the unbanked with low-cost, innovative products.

The change is everywhere. By the end of 2020, 310 million digital consumers will make up 69 per cent of South East Asia's population that are fifteen years or older.

From 2018 to 2020, the number of digital consumers increased by around 60 million, a compounded annual growth rate of 12 per cent. Almost 70 per cent of the 443 million people in Indonesia, Malaysia, the Philippines, Singapore, Thailand and Vietnam are now digital consumers.[7]

This is the time to press the accelerator on the digital transformation agenda.

Think 'Ecosystems' Like Haier

For more than thirty-five years, Haier has consistently trusted the knowledge of its employees to move the organisation forward. In 2012, Haier divided 12,000 managers among 4,000 small independent companies (microenterprises) within Haier. The new structure has encouraged managers to be far more entrepreneurial.

For its foray into smart homes and appliances, Haier found a way to get the field force to help design the future. They were the people who had first-hand knowledge of the customers. They may not have the right answers but they do have the right questions.

Professor Bill Fischer speaks about the key aspect of organisation design that makes this happen. 'Haier has also made it easy for those same employees to launch new ideas. Only three colleagues are required to endorse a new idea, and invest their own money, in order to propose a possible new startup (microenterprise). If the logic of the proposal makes sense, they are off and running, and these new founders of the microenterprise are given responsibility for hiring, big decisions and distributing rewards. Along with the "zero distance to the customer", there is also "zero approvals" in operating decisions, and so there should be "zero delays" in responsiveness.'[8]

Rethinking Competition, Roles and Job Descriptions

Conway's Law says: 'Any organisation that designs a system (defined broadly) will produce a design whose structure is a copy of the organisation's communication structure.' To be able to thrive in a boundaryless, hyperconnected-ecosystem-led world, an organisation needs to rethink its organisation design. It may be time to question the need for job descriptions to build more fluidity in roles.

Job descriptions have been an essential part of the world of work. Employers use it to tell potential candidates what they are expected to do. Blue-collar jobs or more junior roles have more rigid and defined job descriptions. Each word is carefully chosen and approved by lawyers to ensure that no eventuality is left open for interpretation that may go against the employer. In white-collar jobs, the descriptions are used to hire candidates and is often modified by adding or subtracting responsibilities to make the role attractive. A CHRO job may have responsibilities for facilities, security and administration in some cases and in others, these may be given to a peer. A job description is a boundary that is expected to drive accountability. The CEO's role has outcomes that the board defines. The job description is often fuzzy and open for interpretation and provides leeway to the CEO. When the world is seeing structural changes, maybe it is time to abandon job descriptions—at least until the dust settles. The scenario is too fluid to get people limited to what is described.

Social data points in organisation's design: Consider another scenario that happened during the lockdown. Emergency services across Europe witnessed a sharp rise in domestic abuse calls under sweeping lockdowns imposed across the continent. According to WHO, their offices 'are reporting up to a 60 per cent increase in emergency calls by women subjected to violence by their intimate partners in April this year, compared to last'. The United Nations Population Fund (UNFPA) says there would be thirty-one million more cases of domestic violence worldwide if lockdowns continue for another six months.[9]

Could these data points provide answers in predicting workplace behaviours of how a leader is likely to support the careers of women employees in the team? Does the person's support of a political party that discourages succession planning predict the person's discomfort with building a leadership bench? These are all hypotheses that need to be studied.

Since the sharp dividing line between home and workplace has gotten blurred during the pandemic, if a woman employee becomes a victim of domestic abuse during work hours by her partner, is the employer responsible for making the workplace a safe zone for working? What should be the employer's role if the woman filed a formal complaint? Given that several scenarios are arising that have never happened before, it is time for the role of the employer to be thought through. Maybe it is time to rethink the need for job descriptions given the fluidity in the workplace. When industries are getting redefined, job descriptions also become fluid.

Judgement more than job descriptions may provide better markers in the world of work.

Judgement in a Rapidly Changing World[10]

In a world full of fake news and cybercrime, we need to use our judgement every day. What if you saw a tweet from the verified account of Elon Musk or Obama promising to double the money you send him? Then you see billionaires like Jeff Bezos, Kanye West, Michael Bloomberg and the official accounts of Uber and Apple promising the same. The accounts of all these people got hacked in July 2020. It turned out to be the doing of a seventeen-year-old hacker. What if the hacker had sent out a tweet from the head of a nuclear power declaring war? Or a tweet from Apple's handle announcing the launch of a new device. The trolls, the vitriolic comments and hate speech on social media all demand judgement. How can we get better at it?

Judgement has three components.

1. How we gather information before we decide: To be able to take a decision we have to first gather all the relevant information. During the pandemic we discovered that many of the decisions have unintended consequences. Even the way people gather information depends on their personality. Some people double down on the data, while others look for qualitative information and the insights they can glean from it. Personality determines the approach that we take especially when the stakes are high.

2. The risk appetite, time horizon and data sought while choosing options: The ability to take risks also impacts the choices available while deciding. The choices politicians make depends on the time horizon for which they expect to stay in power. Some people seek data and get paralysed by the complexity of too much data. Others ignore all the data and evidence and go by their own intuition. Both styles have their own benefits and drawbacks. Self-awareness can help a leader understand how their personality plays a powerful role when they make a judgement call in the face of ambiguous and often conflicting data.

3. Responding to feedback when decision has gone wrong: Leaders make hundreds of decisions every day and some of them are likely to be wrong. How do they respond when they get feedback about our decisions going wrong? Some accept the blame and change course, while others dig their heels in and persist in going down a path that is clearly wrong. In the process they drag the rest of the organisation into the abyss. Being able to listen to feedback about a decision can help leaders to make course corrections early.

As a leader, when a decision goes wrong, it is important to be able to listen to feedback and adapt one's world view. It is important to ask if the bridge is powerful enough to survive the hurricane but also note that the course of the river has changed.

How to Hire Great Candidates Who Interview Poorly

Hiring and taking bets on people is one of the skills that takes the longest time to build. When I wrote a book called *Don't Hire The Best* (2012), I found that personality is a far better predictor of a leader's success than previous experience and educational qualifications. Of course, apart from the personality, it is important to decode the elements of the company culture where the leader will operate. Many leaders who have done spectacularly well in one organisation have failed when they were hired to repeat the miracle in another role in the same organisation or in another. Using algorithms to create a wide talent pool is part of the solution. Choosing a candidate who will succeed in a leadership role is a fairly complex decision.

Confidence Is Not the Same As Competence

Although most of us spend more time communicating online than offline, recruitment methods are still heavily skewed towards analogue or physical communication skills, particularly the job interview. Indeed, interviews favour those who can communicate their ideas fluently and come across as likeable. Unfortunately, however, most interviewers have not trained themselves rigorously enough to be able to predict candidates' future job performance.

To make matters worse, once the selected candidates are on the job, they are often evaluated by the same people who interviewed them, which transfers the interview biases to their performance appraisals, conveying the illusion of validity.

For example, behavioural economists have shown quite compellingly that people have a tendency to ignore information that contradicts their initial beliefs while focusing on—and remembering—any events that support them, a reasoning flaw known as confirmation bias. This leads to a large number of hiring mistakes going unnoticed.

Now let us consider the scientific evidence: a rigorous, comprehensive analysis of hundreds of studies with more than 32,000 job applicants over an eighty-five-year period by Frank Schmidt and Jack Hunter examined over 500 different jobs—including salespeople, managers, engineers, teachers, lawyers, accountants, mechanics, reporters, farmers, pharmacists, electricians and musicians—to compare information gathered about applicants with the objective performance that they subsequently achieved on the job. This study simply explains why selecting people through interviews is a flawed process.

In a world where it is still virtually impossible to get hired for any job without going through an interview, this is surely a shocking finding, particularly if we consider the relatively low adoption of psychometric tests in the selection process.

Clearly, interviewers have to depend on the candidate to provide evidence that they can do the job and would be a good fit with the company's culture. This encourages candidates to give socially desirable responses rather than speaking their mind. If someone is not articulate, then it is even harder to convince the interview panel. On the other hand, people who feel very comfortable and come across as charismatic may actually have some antisocial tendencies.

For example, people with antisocial and psychopathic tendencies are generally fearless and they often come across as charming and socially skilled in short-term interactions, which can contribute to favourable evaluations by interviewers. Yet, just like you don't marry someone after a first date—at least, most people don't—you should not hire someone based largely on their interview performance. Unless that performance is closely linked to what they need to do on the job—e.g., face-to-face sales, acting, public speaking, being a politician, etc.

So what should you actually do? Here are some data-driven recommendations for minimising biases against strong candidates who may not do so well during interviews.

1. Analyse the job and the candidate's development needs

- How much of the job's success actually depends on communication and interpersonal skills? Is impression management a key driver of job performance, or should it be treated as noise?
- What aspect of the written communication, interpersonal communication or client presentations does the candidate need help with?

- How often would that gap pose challenges? How can that risk be mitigated? Can someone coach this person? Can that part of the job be given to someone who does it well?

2. Use multiple assessment tools

- Ask your star employees—and be sure to work out who they actually are—to go through the hiring process and see if the process would have eliminated some of them. If not, use this data to benchmark future candidates.
- Ensure that your performance evaluation systems focus on actual job performance rather than individual career success. In a perfect world, there would be a strong overlap between the two. But in the real world, they are only marginally related—many top performers don't attain high levels of career success, and some of the most successful individuals are not that good at their job.
- The most effective interview questions are called situational judgement questions. Instead of asking candidates to describe how they handled a unique situation in a previous job or organisation, it's more fruitful to describe consistent situations that candidates could face in this job or organisation, and ask them what they would do or how they would reason. These can be done online, though the key is to use a data-driven approach to link each answer with a meaningful and robust candidate profile: 'people who pick X are more likely to do Y', and so on.

3. Let the algorithms do the work

- The rise of AI-based platforms are helping companies sift through millions of resumes to find the right candidates.
- Skillate, an AI-based recruitment solution platform, helps companies do just that for SAP. Their next feature aims to update candidates' resumes based on their posts from Facebook, GitHub, etc. This will help candidates who may have expertise but do not know how to express it in a way that catches the attention of the employer.
- Bangalore-based startup Belong helps employers seek passive candidates based on their social media posts. PayPal is using Belong's algorithm to eliminate recruiter bias. Humantic already offers tools based on natural language processing to create instant candidate profiles for recruiters and employers. The companies say that the technology is based on traditional personality tests, including DiSC, a behavioural assessment tool, and the Big Five, which measures five personality traits. Instead of applicants filling out long questionnaires, an algorithm creates a personality analysis based on publicly available content written by the candidate, say, on LinkedIn.[11]

While the general public is usually concerned about these automated methodologies, it is important to understand that the current paradigm of humans rating other humans is not only flawed but also much more likely to result in biased selection decisions and unfair and non-competitive outcomes for both the candidate and the organisation.

People have a similar reaction when it comes to self-driving cars. Although it is estimated that they would save almost two million lives a year, most people think of themselves as better drivers than AI, even if they are willing to accept that self-driving cars would probably drive better than other people.[12]

Can Someone Do a Job They Have Never Done?

There are many good reasons for predicting human performance at work.

The vital few are truly different

First, at any level and in any job and industry, there is substantial variability in people's performance, which explains the near universality of the Pareto effect, whereby fewer than 20 per cent of people tend to account for around 80 per cent of group or organisational performance. Identifying these 'vital few' in advance is crucial if you want to compete in the war for talent. Compare the number of Olympic golds Michael Phelps has got with whoever you think qualifies to be the next best. That is the difference.

Most people cannot assess their own potential

Second, people will be happier and more productive if they end up in jobs that are a good fit for them, but you cannot rely on them to work this out by themselves. Indeed, most people have a fairly inaccurate sense of their own talents, especially when the question is how good they are in comparison to other people. As a consequence, too many employees end up in jobs they detest. Self-awareness helps people choose career options where they have the maximum probability of success.

Traditional talent criteria are obsolete

Third, many of the traditional indicators or 'signals' used to predict future job performance have been devaluated by the changing landscape of work, and this will only intensify in the future. In broad terms, we have transitioned from a world where academic expertise, hard skills and formal qualifications were essential to predict whether someone would fit a given role, to a world where experience, soft skills and broad talent traits have come to represent the cornerstone of human potential.

In addition, innovations in HR technologies are also changing how we evaluate these new vital attributes of potential. If AI and science can join forces, we will soon live in a world where a substantial proportion of the workforce will not need to be assessed because of the amount of data we will have on people.[13]

Personality Assessment Alone May Not Be Enough

What personality assessment can provide is a great insight into the strengths, derailers and motivators and values of a person. What is missing in this equation is the context in which an individual functions. One individual may shine in an entry-level role and flame out as a middle manager or in the C-suite. The CEO may have been a good performer (not exceptional) in another organisation. The organisation's culture and the chemistry with the other colleagues is the missing factor that often determine success or failure of the new hires.

Being able to frame success factors not just in terms of the prior experience that a person has, but also to add information about what matters most in the organisation's culture is important. Uber under Travis Kalanick celebrated colleagues who stole credit. Travis encouraged colleagues to be the first one to steal the limelight from the rest of the team. The charges of sexual harassment, bending the law and backstabbing was part of the toxic culture at Uber under Kalanick. The person who is successful in such an environment will be very different from someone who will shine in Uber when it is led by a different CEO.

Jack Welch didn't think of GE as merely a manufacturing company. By the time he stepped down in 2001, GE had grown from a $25 billion business to a $130 billion behemoth that was known for Welch's flamboyant leadership style and the slash-and-burn model he became synonymous with. Jeff Immelt took over from Welch and wanted to make GE one of the top software firms. He left under a cloud, and GE, which was known for being a leadership factory with its legendary investment in leadership development, had to hire a CEO from outside.[14]

When the business canvas changes, a strategy that may have been applauded a few years ago may come in for criticism. It is not uncommon for the judgement of the best of CEOs to be questioned when things go wrong.

Fortune magazine's 'CEO Daily' dated 3 March 2020 added some more colour to Jack Welch's legacy:

- Welch focused on shareholder returns. Today's CEOs are advocating a much broader view of 'stakeholder' capitalism.
- The best leaders are focusing on how to completely rethink their processes and disrupt their businesses. It's a very different skill set from using Six Sigma, which Welch loved, to reduce costs.
- Even the leadership development model of Welch seems to have become obsolete. 'Top 21st century leaders believe their managers need to look outward to find direction for the future, not focus inward,' says the article.

The leader sets the cultural norms in which talent of a certain kind will thrive. That in turn attracts more people who have similar values. Most organisations will write that they hire for values, yet when it comes to a choice between competency and values, businesses routinely vote for someone who can do the job—the tangible, measurable results. The intangible elements that explain how the results were achieved are seen after a leader leaves.

The Economist says, 'For decades GE managers had an over-exalted sense of their own abilities, which led to narcissism, hubris and the bending, if not breaking, of accounting rules to hit their profit targets. This eclipsed any strategic vision they may have had.'

Assessing for Jobs That Don't Exist Today

Digital embalmers help people plan their digital afterlife long after they are dead. That could mean continuing to monetise their social media accounts by engaging fans. If you are looking to hire a digital embalmer, what would you write in the job description to be handed to a search firm?

What if the job involves 'working with ocean farmers to develop an underwater camera system and a set of machine perception tools'. You want to know more about the employer, and this is what their website tells you:[15]

'X is a diverse group of inventors and entrepreneurs who build and launch technologies that aim to improve the lives of millions, even billions, of people. Our goal: 10x impact on the world's most intractable problems, not just 10 per cent improvement. We approach projects that have the aspiration and riskiness of research with the speed and ambition of a startup.'

Businesses will have to chart new territories if they have to stay relevant in the post-pandemic world. It is much like what people are talking about when it comes to taming the virus. People have to find new ways of assessing talent. New methods of tracking performance will have to be found especially when many of the tasks remain ambiguous. In parallel, learning teams will have to help people build the skills they need to do tasks that increasingly make their skills irrelevant.

To be sure, not much has changed when it comes to predicting someone's ability to do something they have done in the past. People have always been creatures of habit—and they always will be—so past behaviour is a very good predictor of future behaviour. However, if we are interested in working out whether someone is able to do something they haven't done before, let alone predict their performance on jobs that do not exist yet, things get a lot more complicated.

According to a Manpower Group and World Economic Forum report, 65 per cent of the jobs that await Generation Z (anyone born after 1996) will be jobs that do not exist today, and a recent report by Dell estimated by 2030 only 15 per cent of today's jobs will still exist.[16]

Fortunately, science provides a well-established solution to address this challenge. In fact, there is a fairly formulaic process for quantifying someone's potential for performing a job they have not done before, even if we don't know what that role might actually be.

Ability, Likeability and Drive

The first and most important recommendation is to focus on generic and universal ingredients of talent, such as ability, likeability and drive. As we have shown in our own research, these are the most important qualities for predicting not only people's job performance but also their career success. We may not know what the future jobs will look like, but it is safe to assume that people who are generally smarter, better able to deal with people and more hard-working, will be able to perform them better than their less able, likeable and driven counterparts, and it is relatively easy to measure the degree to which people possess these qualities. Furthermore, this simple formula can be applied at all levels of job complexity and seniority, including the C-suite.

For instance, when a large steel conglomerate decided to hire a CFO, it identified a candidate who had previously worked in a petroleum company and then for a major energy firm. While the functional competencies for the role would have been common to most CFOs, the hiring team chose to use those merely as gating criteria. What got the candidate hired was the ability to lead a business transformation. The steel manufacturer was about to undertake a large transformation to respond to the change in the global market conditions.

The CHRO told us that they were looking for a terrific business leader who could collaborate with others in the C-suite and lead the transformation. They specifically assessed their ability to analyse the barriers they would face with the frontline, middle management and senior leaders.

They viewed the candidate's analytical skills as a great asset. The CFO was skilled at analysing data and finding patterns and trends. The person came across as likeable and respectful without compromising on the agenda, and viewed by colleagues as persuasive and charming. During town hall meetings, this candidate listened to people without imposing his/her own ideas, and none of this stopped this candidate from driving an ambitious agenda of 10x revenue growth.

Willingness to Learn What They Don't Know

A second key recommendation is to bet on trainability. First, because what people know is less relevant than what they are likely to learn. Second, because the only sure way to avoid being automated is to keep learning new things, broadening one's skill range to remain employable and competitive.

Unsurprisingly, there has recently been a great deal of emphasis on the importance of human curiosity—often referred to as learnability—vis-à-vis jobs and careers. Curious people are more likely to question things, which helps them solve problems and arrive at smarter answers. They are also more comfortable with ambiguity, which makes them receptive to change and adaptable. Finally, curious people are more likely to be self-critical and to seek out and pay attention to feedback from others, which is essential for developing and getting better.

Naturally, it is not possible for organisations to expect to hire only curious people, so investing in developmental and coaching interventions that boost trainability is also necessary. Such interventions can be expected to be more successful if they manage to prepare people for management and leadership roles, which will depend largely on their ability to coach or develop people skills.

Ability to Develop People Skills

Ironically, in the age of AI and digital automation, humans will mostly compete on their emotional or social skills, as these are the hardest abilities for technology to emulate.

A $43 billion corporation, the Aditya Birla Group is in the league of the Fortune 500. They employ almost 120,000 employees, belonging to forty-two nationalities. A couple of years ago, they took a bold stand. They decided to stop hiring external talent at the top of the pyramid and to instead invest heavily in transition coaching to prepare their leaders for success in top roles.

As Ganesh Chella, a leading coach, noted, 'The most common area where leaders need coaching is in the area of emotional intelligence. Self-regulation and impulse control matters a lot at the top.' At the middle level, attention to detail can be a strength. At the senior level, the same quality would be a derailer. Getting them to operate as a leader who empowers, not micromanages, is another important area of development.

Recruiters have always found roles for people where they can leverage their competencies. Could they start using their understanding of personality to identify opportunities for candidates? Talent is, after all, personality in the right place. It is hard to think of the brilliant soccer player Lionel Messi as a banker. After the end of the 1993–94 basketball season, Michael Jordan announced his retirement from basketball to pursue baseball. Jordan's magic on the basketball court was never replicated on the baseball field. That is why personality is such a great predictor of careers where the individual can find purpose and personal fulfilment. This is where good recruiters should still be able to add value and help decide which roles can leverage the strengths and weaknesses of the individual. A strength in one job (taking initiative) can be a huge weakness in a job where following procedures can be the difference between life and death, e.g., air traffic controller.

Three Factors that Should Define All Roles

Almost every white-collar role can be plotted along three parameters:

1. Cognitive ability

This includes everything to do with analytical thinking, understanding complexity and complex data, and ease and ability with new skills. At the lower end of the spectrum

Cognitive Skills
DATA, ANALYSIS, ABILITY TO LEARN

Strong

CUTTING EDGE TECH
MULTIDISCIPLINARY

BASIC QUERY HANDLING
TECHNICALLY LOW COMPLEXITY TASKS
SIMPLE AUTOMATION/ CODING

Weak

the tasks are rule based and repetitive. Most of the jobs that are getting automated and replacing human beings tend to be at the lower end of this spectrum. A mechanical calculator is a good example of this ability. Quite often we see such jobs being automated and done by software or machines. It gives the ability of the machine to create generic responses to common questions. Chatbots on many websites can respond to routine queries. It needs someone to build the rules into the software or the machine, and the machine can replace the human being doing the task.

At the opposite end of the spectrum we have tasks that require complex cognitive capability. People working at the cutting edge of the discipline operate in this zone. The extreme end of this capability can describe jobs where the problem being solved is loosely defined and the solution may require interdisciplinary thinking. Think of the people who won the Nobel Prize in physics, chemistry, biology, economics (but not the Peace Prize, which is in a different category). Or someone who won the Fields Medal in math would represent the highest end of the cognitive ability spectrum.

2. Emotional and relationship-building ability

This refers to the ability to navigate the world of emotions and diversity in relationships. As social animals we need to continuously interact with other people in the course of our day-to-day existence. This requires a certain dexterity in trying to understand our own emotions and that of the others we are interacting with. In order to do that we use verbal and non-verbal cues and modify our own responses accordingly. It involves the ability to use our language skills in a manner that does not antagonise the other person.

Emotional Agility

HUMAN RELATIONSHIPS & EMOTIONS WITH PEOPLE

Strong

CROSS-CULTURAL ADAPTABILITY
EMPATHY, RESILIENCE, OPTIMISM
SELF-CONTROL IN HIGH STAKES ENVIRONMENT

LOW INTERPERSONAL SKILLS
UNABLE TO CONVEY DIFFICULT MESSAGES WITH EMPATHY
LEAVES OTHERS WITH NEGATIVE FEELINGS AFTER AN INTERACTION

Weak

Voice assistants like Alexa or Siri are examples of machines learning to build relationships with human beings through natural language processing and machine learning. When Siri or Alexa respond to our voice commands with some emotions like humour, they are simply activating the appropriate response that has been programmed into them.

But this is just what endears them to humans. If that little bit of programmed humour does so much for a machine, imagine what it would do for human beings who have a much wider range of emotions to understand and work with as they deal with others.

As we think of emotions, visualise the range of colours that any brand of lipsticks can offer. As one site puts it, 'There is scarlet and crimson, cerise and magenta, maroon, carmine, claret and burgundy, as well as carnelian and cherry and cardinal red. To say nothing of ruby or garnet or vermilion, and wine-red, rust-red, rufous-red, terracotta-red.'[17]

We can have the same set of shades for emotions. Happy can have many shades too. Gleeful, joyous, delighted, delirious, happy, cheerful, ecstatic ... you can see that there can be hundreds of shades of the primary emotion just like there can be many shades of the same colour. People who are able to see more nuances of the emotions and understand different demographic chunks spread across multiple cross-cultural contexts are experts in understanding emotions and relationships.

It is harder to quantify emotional and relational skills. The ability to convey bad news to someone without leaving them bruised or emotionally scarred is an important element of relationship and emotional skills. Jobs that involve giving and receiving feedback, dealing with challenging relationships, not having enough resources to meet multiple and impossible deadlines, dealing with change and emotional trauma, job losses, setbacks and failure all need high degrees of resilience and emotional intelligence.

Think of how many people managers whimper while sharing bad news with their team members and say, 'I had recommended it, but, you know, senior management knocked it off.' Or the CEOs who are at the forefront while giving the 'We are here to change the world' speech and then put the HR team to announce layoffs or no increase in salary. Having a powerful network inside the organisation and outside the business and across industries and geographies is a sign of great relational and emotional skills. So is being able to manage (successfully) a matrix reporting structure where the two bosses sitting across two different time zones may push their own priorities on you. Managing these successfully requires immense emotional maturity and skills.

In some cases, when dealing with complex scenarios like a hostage negotiation or when working with emotionally distressed clients, people have to be highly skilled in understanding emotions and relationships. To be a skilled special needs teacher, a psychotherapist, a mental health professional needs an exceptionally high degree of empathy, resilience and optimism. I will put it at the same level as the emotional and relational skills of a hostage negotiator. It is a high-stakes moment, and one false move can be devastating. Emotional and relational skills can be either used in group settings or in individual interactions. The post-pandemic setting adds another dimension of complexity—the ability to be equally effective on video.

In Asian countries, the ability to balance a network of relationships across hierarchies and interest groups forms the basis of many successful business empires. Many tycoons have realised that it is far easier to pass on their wealth than their network to their children. Friends cannot be inherited. Succession planning becomes very complex

Creative Agility
DIVERSITY OF CONTENT,
AUDIENCE APPEAL & MEDIA

Strong

ABILITY TO SHAPE & SHIFT EMOTIONS
INFLUENCER, CREATOR & SENSEMAKER

LOW ABILITY TO UNDERSTAND BIG
PICTURE, METAPHORS, IMAGERY ETC
UNABLE TO READ THE AUDIENCE

Weak

because many Asian patriarchs cultivate a personal relationship with the politicians and financiers that is hard to pass on to the children.[18]

3. Creative storytellers and social media

This is a new dimension that is getting added to many roles. CEOs need to communicate with the employees as well as the stakeholders outside the organisation. Freelancers have to make videos to showcase their work. Experts in the organisation need to make videos to showcase their skills and teach other employees.

This method is especially powerful for building skills which Degreed describes as 'emergent skills'.[19] These are skills that are not well understood and the descriptions are ambiguous. There is no curriculum that can be followed. These are usually hybrid skills and are cross-functional. They emerge faster than institutions are able to teach them.

In the post-pandemic world, this has to be done over video. At the lower end of the scale, it could refer to the millions of creators who are using WhatsApp, Facebook, YouTube, TikTok and Instagram to create content in the form of stories, visuals and videos. This is the area that is the hardest to automate—even the lowest end of the skill spectrum.

The biggest skill lies in being able to understand the emotional state of the audience and make every member feel that the story being told is specific to their individual context. The creative process has to act in conjunction with the emotional state of the consumer. Facebook shows audience engagement level; with each live video the rise and fall of the graph shows the level of engagement as it changes from moment to moment. The creator can also figure out at which point of time the audience dropped off or were hyper engaged during the conversation.

This is the moment reserved for the creators. Every platform is wooing them and partnering with them to push their imagination and creative boundaries. Typically, creators on YouTube with at least 10,000 subscribers will have received an invite from their YouTube partner manager to join an event in a city's 'Pop-up Space'.[20]

Think of these as temporary studio spaces providing creators with opportunities to create content and attend platform and production workshops. It becomes a community lounge space for co-working or socialising with other visiting creators and artists. Adobe partnering with YouTube Space is a wonderful opportunity for creators to take their skills to the next level with Creative Cloud, said Kevin Towes, global head of business development for

Adobe Video. 'We're thrilled to empower creativity for next-generation creators by teaching them video editing, motion graphics, design, sound, colour grading, mobile production, and more.'

At the top end of this spectrum are people who are emotion shapers. They are able to create content that change the opinions and beliefs of people. These are powerful roles and are attractive to brands who use them as influencers or to politicians who leverage their social media following to shape the popular discourse. The stand-up comedian uses this factor to make people aware of their biases and encourage them to adopt new behaviours without making them feeling threatened. The comedian is able to point out the hypocrisy and double-speak in leaders in a manner that is hard to replicate.

Being able to change the content and the emotion that it generates based on the media format or platform being used is an emergent skill. If you look at the follower count and engagement levels you have across Facebook, LinkedIn, Twitter and Instagram, you will see that your effectiveness is different across each platform. Every post generates a different level of engagement and sharing even across the platform where your follower count is the highest.

While AI has made many blue-collar jobs redundant, could it do the same for creative fields like music and art? Technology may create new art forms that are pushing the boundaries and definitions of creative forms of expression. David Bowie played with a digital lyrics randomiser in the 1990s. Songwriter Holly Herndon created an album in which she harmonised with an AI version of herself. The demand for music is increasing exponentially with the need for background music for films, TV show, mobile phones and video games.

Endel is a company that specialises in creating technology with personalised sound environments to reduce stress, increase focus and improve sleep. The sounds are generated in real time based on various inputs such as one's location, time, weather, cadence, heart-rate, etc.[21]

The area that is struggling to keep up with these changes are copyright laws. Who owns the rights to an AI song? The programmer who created the AI system, the original musician whose works provided the training data or maybe even the AI itself?

IMPLEMENTATION CHALLENGE

What if you plot your own role on just these three factors? Jobs that involve a lot of data crunching, analytical thinking, specific professional degrees, specialised skills and ability to keep learning push them towards the higher end of the scale.

The emotional/relational complexity the role demands increases if you manage people and teams (but sadly, most people managers have a massive skill gap in this area). A geographically distributed team that needs very high cross-cultural sensitivity will move the role to the higher end.

Similarly, plot the demands of the role in terms of creativity and proficiency in creating content on different topics across different platforms for different moods and different audiences.

Now plot the actual skill levels in these three areas and you get a good view of where you can leverage a coach to strengthen your skills. This can be a useful way to prepare yourself for the next big role you are looking to take up.

0 cognitive complexity 100

0 emotional complexity 100

0 creative complexity 100

References

1. The 33 options suggested can change the manner of decision making (and hence the acceptance rate of decisions) in the organisations. Try out some in your next meeting. http://www.liberatingstructures.com/ls-menu/
2. This reading was suggested by Arvind Singhal, one of the co-authors of this paper. He shared it on LinkedIn. https://www.linkedin.com/posts/abhijitbhaduri_conversation-listen-theconversation-activity-6666196502693629952-DtJ3
3. Personal interview with Henri on 27 May 2020
4. There are several variations and tips listed on the website which you may find useful as you try it out. http://www.liberatingstructures.com/12-2510-crowd-sourcing/
5. If you want to read a primer on the methodology this is a good place to start. https://medium.com/@keithmccandless/liberating-structures-change-methods-for-everybody-every-day-648e9c0d04a7
6. Every company will be a FinTech Company—a must listen podcast. https://a16z.simplecast.com/episodes/every-company-fintech-company
7. Bain says 70 per cent of SE Asian consumers will go digital in 2020, a growth that was scheduled to be done in 2025. https://www.bain.com/globalassets/noindex/2020/facebook_and_bain_and_company_report_digital_consumers_of_tomorrow_here_today.pdf
8. Prof. Bill Fischer speaks about Haier's ecosystem in this Thinkers 50 publication. https://thinkers50.com/thinkers50-books/ecosystems-inc/
9. Domestic violence and abuse increase sharply during the lockdowns. https://www.thehindu.com/news/international/coronavirus-lockdown-surge-in-domestic-violence-says-who/article31529111.ece
10. Personality plays a big role in each of the three aspects of decision-making and judgement. http://www.hoganjudgment.com/
11. How job interviews are getting transformed. https://www.wsj.com/articles/how-job-interviews-will-transform-in-the-next-decade-11578409136

12. How to hire great candidates that interview poorly. https://www.hrexaminer.com/how-to-hire-great-candidates-that-interview-poorly/
13. From smartphone apps to solving games, number of new methods are evolving but academia still treats them as one day wonders. https://info.hoganassessments.com/hubfs/TalentIdentification.pdf
14. The leadership style of Jack Welch. https://www.businessinsider.in/slideshows/miscellaneous/triumphant-rise-spectacular-fall-general-electrics-127-year-journey-from-cutting-edge-american-icon-to-possible-fraud-case/slidelist/70706379.cms#slideid=70706384
15. There are many jobs which are really fluent in their description because they are dealing with problems that are still ambiguous. https://x.company/projects/
16. As the world of work evolves, many new roles will get created. There is a way to predict if someone can do a job they have never done before. https://recruitingdaily.com/how-to-tell-if-someone-can-do-a-job-theyve-never-done/
17. I never knew there were so many shades of red with names. https://turbofuture.com/graphic-design-video/Shades-Red-Greensleeves
18. It is easier to pass on your wealth to the children than to pass on the relationships built over the years that imapct success especially in Asian businesses. https://www.economist.com/business/2020/05/28/why-asian-business-dynasties-struggle-with-succession
19. Emergent skills are hard to teach and need to be learnt by creating content. https://blog.degreed.com/the-innovators-guide-to-emerging-skills-download/
20. YouTube and Adobe partnered to create these opportunities for creators. https://www.youtube.com/space/pop-ups/
21. AI is redefining what 'composing music' really means. https://time.com/5774723/ai-music/

10

'Sensemaking' and Algorithms

Sensemaking is a method of practical wisdom grounded in the humanities. We can think of sensemaking as the exact opposite of algorithmic thinking. It is entirely situated in the concrete, while algorithmic thinking exists in a no-man's-land of information stripped of its specificity. Algorithmic thinking can go wide—processing trillions of terabytes of data per second—but only sensemaking can go deep.[1]

'Sensemaking'—The Essence of Success in India

The founder of a very large Indian firm was telling me about the challenge of expanding the firm's geographical footprint. The Australian team of the firm would serve beer in the office on Friday afternoons. In the summer months, the second half of the Friday was unofficially spent drinking beer. When the founder showed up in the Sydney office on a Friday, the Australian employees invited the founder to join them for beer. The founder jokingly asked if the team would make up for the Friday beer session by working on Saturday instead. The head of the business in Australia quickly stepped in and said that it was meant to be a joke, but the damage was done. Making 'sense' is an intuitive process. It comes from sensibilities sharpened over many meandering conversations. Sensemaking is not efficient but is effective.

Sensemaking for 'Multiple Truths'

India is especially complex for anyone to make sense of—even Indians. The people in the northern states cannot make sense of the south Indians. The 'south Indians' are not one single homogenous group but many different states and union territories—Andhra Pradesh, Karnataka, Kerala, Tamil Nadu and Telangana as well as the union territories of Lakshadweep and Puducherry, each having their own cuisine, dance forms, language (not to mention dialects) and script. Many Indians would stumble if asked to name the seven (some say eight Northeastern states if you include Sikkim) states in Northeast India—Arunachal Pradesh, Assam, Meghalaya, Manipur, Mizoram, Nagaland and Tripura.

Starbucks offers many more versions of tea in India. McDonalds offers a 'vegetarian burger'. There is no commonly understood definition of the term 'vegetarian' in

India. It changes by the day of the week—some meat eaters do not eat meat on a specific day of the week; some do not eat fish during the monsoon season; some eat meat and eggs if cooked outside the home or in a restaurant ... the combinations are endless. Sensemaking is about the nuances of emotions without getting caught in the literal meaning of the word. The meaning is conveyed using language. That is just what separates humans from algorithms.

You suggest an option in a team meeting. A colleague says, 'Of course!' That phrase could convey many emotions from agreement to sarcasm or can even be trivialising. The meaning can be grasped only by someone who understands the layers of context—the nature of the relationship between the people, the relative importance of the matter, the career trajectory of the people involved, who is currently being seen in positive light and even how that response will be interpreted. That is how we are tuned to sensemaking all the time.

I was part of the team that worked on the implementation of SAP (HR) module in the Asia Pacific region for Colgate-Palmolive in the late 1990s. 'Data will give us one version of the truth,' was the rallying cry. One of the first challenges in building the database was to standardise the names and surnames. In some states, people use the father's name as the last name, in some states it is a middle name, in some states the caste names are used, while others have dropped them. In some cases the name of the village is part of the name. While the West is all about 'one version of truth', India is all about the co-existence of many truths. That's where sensemaking works.

Using Sensemaking to Understand the Customer

Christian Madsbjerg, the author of *Sensemaking*, says, 'Knowing how to build things is great, but if you have no idea for whom you're building them—how these inventions will connect with people's aspirations and challenges—you will fail, no matter how many coding geniuses and data scientists you employ.' He goes on to say, 'Literatures—like in-depth journalism, plays, music, art, and even activities like cooking—can put you in the shoes of people unlike you in profound, empathetic ways.'

Sensemaking sometimes shows up in strange ways. When the level of uncertainty goes up, as it has during the pandemic, humans need to figure out how to make sense of the deluge of information (often contradictory). Even the authorities seem to be contradicting themselves. One doctor has advice on how to stay safe, but another dismisses that as rubbish. The WHO itself has backtracked on its numbers and recommendations. So have the most credible sources. Then there is news that Bill Gates spoke about 'microbes, not missiles'. Conspiracy theorists then try to look for patterns by connecting the dots and playing on people's scepticism and fears. It is much like seeing your loved one's face in the clouds. A new conspiracy theory is then created to help us make sense of this chaos. And Gates is blamed for having caused the pandemic to profit from it.[2]

In several TV reality shows, we see talented singers who are able to sing every note to perfection. Yet, when you think of the greats, the difference is that they know the words and music just as well as the novice. What differentiates the maestro is that they can sense intangible elements, like the mood of the audience, the impact of world events, the impact of previous singers they have heard, and then improvise.

Culture and Context Matters

Algorithms can turn seven and a half billion people into 1 and 0. While Silicon Valley has created many products, they are all created for people who are like them. That may be completely far removed from the reality of someone in Ivory Coast or Jodhpur.

Samsung discovered that even though men in most families believed themselves to be the decision-makers when buying a television, it was actually the women who made that decision. When women bought televisions, they did so by matching it with the furniture at home, while men looked at it purely as an electronic gadget. Understanding this may have profound implications on how the television is to be sold and displayed in the shop.[3]

The Consumer Is Always a Step Ahead

The search firm ABC Consultants invited five leaders in early June 2020 for a fireside chat to decode their observations about the Indian consumer.

Here were some ideas this group shared:[4]

- When the lockdown was announced, many people had to rush out and beat long queues to buy products just in time before the stores were shut. Even after the lockdown was eased, consumers decided to continue keeping some stock of essential items at home. This is a newly developed 'just-in-case' purchase behaviour that will continue.

- Viewing time on television increased substantially and is now more than the viewing time on digital platforms. Before the lockdown, general entertainment used to be the number one category, but post pandemic, what was watched most often were news channels, followed by movies, kids programming and then general entertainment shows like reality shows, etc.
- While online shopping has understandably gone up during the lockdown, the neighbourhood kirana stores have also thrived. The lack of availability of anything not categorised as 'essential' changed browsing habits on platforms like Amazon. Pre-pandemic browsing was for a specific product (called 'spear-fishing').
- Health, hygiene and protection have gone up in importance. Beauty salons are asking for single-serve tubes of shampoos and creams.
- Staying at home meant keeping the children busy, and that explains the 300x growth in ludo and carrom boards sold. Buying products related to hobbies went up as did orders for gourmet home-cooking kits.
- As schools and tuition classes moved online, 90 per cent of the students rated the experience 'good'. When the lockdown gets over, only 10 per cent want classes to be entirely online. Forty per cent students want a hybrid experience (online plus in-person interaction). This has interesting implications for schools and

coaching classes. Making the best teachers available online can dramatically improve learning options for students in rural areas. The school need not cater only to students in the neighbourhood.

Many of the changes that have taken place might well become permanent shifts in consumer behaviour. The pandemic has pushed everyone out of their comfort zones. While videoconference options have been available on every phone, businesses have resisted adoption. The lockdown prioritised speed and agility in adoption and usage rather than waiting for a perfect solution. Had it not been for the pandemic, Zoom would have never become part of the business lexicon.

All these examples have interesting implications for organisations in terms of the choices they have to make as employees come back to what used to be the workplace. A distributed workforce working from different locations will have profound implications for leaders in the way they communicate and manage. Everybody working from their homes, combined with the uncertainty of jobs, will have huge implications for talent strategies. If everybody works from home, is there any such thing as workplace culture anymore?

1. Can storytellers be more prophetic than business analysts?
Many people describe the pandemic as a black swan event. Storytellers and computer geeks had both predicted the pandemic. Take the movie *Contagion* that was made in 2011. It predicts a pandemic caused by a virus that originates when meat is contaminated by exposure to bats. The disease spreads when people come in contact with an infected

person or touch infected surfaces and then touching their faces. We have seen a hundred examples of science fiction where something that seemed implausible turns out to be prophetic.[5]

'If anything kills over 10 million people in the next few decades, it's likely to be a highly infectious virus rather than a war. Not missiles, but microbes,' Gates said during his Ted Talk in 2015.[6] He repeated his warning in 2017. Almost 30 million people have watched the talk but that does not seem to have impacted the scenario-planning teams of any corporation—big or small.

Leadership development itself will need to change in the post-pandemic world.

2. From broadcasting to individual conversations: Most businesses take a 'broadcast'-style communication approach as they guide customers in their journey. When it comes to employees, organisations are a lot less inclined to invest in anything that does not have a 'business case'. This creates a transactional view of the employer-employee relationships that no offsite team-building can make up for.

As individuals move away from being co-located in the office to working from home, leaders have to address each employee as an individual. This is different from using mail merge and feeling delighted at each employee getting a letter that addresses him or her by their first name. It is a feeling that gets generated as the employee goes about working every day that matters.

A group of new hires (including me) were invited for lunch with the chairman of the company and told to answer a series of questions about our hobbies and interests, where we grew up, etc. I had joined two weeks ago and was looking forward to the lunch meeting. It was hugely orchestrated. We had to sit in designated places and were not allowed to change seats (they were numbered). During the lunch meeting, the chairman referred to each of us by name and asked a question each, potentially from the information card that had been prepared for him. That the chairman had actually taken the trouble to learn so many things about me seemed impressive to me. It was a deeply personal experience.

The next morning, I happened to walk into the elevator and was taken aback to see the chairman standing there. Fresh from the lunch meeting of the previous afternoon, I greeted him like an old friend. He gave me the look reserved for an animal you never knew existed. His cover was blown. I was a faceless employee who had no business behaving like a long-lost friend.

With a teleprompter, even a nervous speaker can create the illusion of being a spontaneous one. When the bank sends me a birthday greeting at the stroke of midnight, it does not make me weep with joy. Human relationships hinge on authenticity.

The competitive advantage is shifting in the post-COVID world of work from the tangible to the INTANGIBLE factors

A Customised Workspace Called Home

The world of work is going to undergo a massive shift. When everyone went to the same workplace, one set of rules applied to all. Well, almost ... women got a ladies' watch and men got a matching pair when they hit retirement age. That was the world of customisation (by gender).

Some organisations attempted to get to the next level by allowing the retiree to choose a watch from the showroom and pay the difference if it exceeded the budget allocated for a retiree watch. If someone did not want a watch, he or she was given one anyway. If the person gifted that watch to someone else, no one was wiser. That was an example of personalisation. What if someone did not want a watch as a retirement gift? For example, the Chinese believe it is bad luck to gift someone a clock or watch on their retirement. 'We cannot make separate rules for each employee,' the employer would then say.

Since workers went to the same workplace, it made sense to have one set of rules for everyone. Making an exception to the rule was a sign of privilege and hierarchy. A separate dining room with a different menu served to the senior managers was accepted. But now, work has become location- and time-independent. Work has been brought home, and the office thinks nothing of telling the employee, 'Think of the time you have saved by not commuting.' Does that time saved belong to the employee or the employer?

Elsewhere, Switzerland's top court has ruled that employers are required to contribute to employees' rent payments if they are expected to work from home. The decision applies to employees who work from home upon the employer's request. However, employees who ask the employer to work from home on their own would not be eligible to get reimbursed.[7]

The Similarity between Retail and Education

Retail and education have both been designed for the in-person experience. In the post-pandemic world, both are learning to adapt to the parallel universe of digital experiences.

Retail

On 25 February 2020, India's biggest mall owner, the Phoenix Mills Ltd., was galloping. The stock had touched a lifetime high and their market valuation topped $2 billion. In the first nine months of 2019–20, revenue was growing at 23 per cent and net profit was up 50 per cent. With almost 6 million sq. ft. of mall space to lease, they were able to attract the high-end brands that also generate footfalls.[8]

Post-pandemic, the scenario is vastly different. Even after the malls reopened, the density of footfall was lower. That coupled with the unsold stock of retailers makes it difficult for them to pay rentals and yet remain committed to long-term contracts. The supply chains of many firms have been impacted because of labour unavailability and skill gaps impacting every manufacturer.

Education

Education is going through a churn at every level from kindergarten to universities. India's new education policy wants students to learn coding from Class 6. Whitehat Jr, an eighteen-month-old startup, was bought for $300 million by the decacorn Byju's (currently valued at more than $10 billion). Whitehat Jr created a new category in ed-tech—teaching coding skills via a live-learning model. All its 5,000-plus teachers are women. They teach students to code and help them build commercial-ready games, animations and apps. Online is thriving.

College education in the US, Australia, Canada and Britain has been an attractive option for wealthy Asian parents. It is great for the colleges too. International students pay more than 20x in fees than locals. That money has been spent on lavish buildings, giant auditoria (yes, many auditoriums), Olympic-size, heated swimming pools, a bloated set of admin staff, etc. The salaries of many deans and presidents of colleges will shock you. Post-secondary education in the US is an almost $700-billion-a-year business, and tuition and fees associated with residential colleges are a primary and critical pillar of this educational economy.

Where do colleges save money? In teaching! Yes, the classes are taught by inexperienced hourly gig workers called teaching assistants. Professors and teachers are getting laid off. The swimming pools and auditoriums are empty because of geopolitical tensions, COVID and no travel.

Higher Education could be a synonym for the next big streaming service.

Besides the pandemic, many US universities are also impacted by geopolitical issues like the US-China face-off. Ivy League colleges have their endowment funds from the alumni, but revenue from overseas students (especially Indian and Chinese) keeps many second-rung colleges financially viable. The returning Chinese students may discover racially motivated 'social distancing' on campus given the geopolitical stress between the US and China.

Until it is safe for people to move about unfettered, education will go online. It is likely that we will settle for a hybrid model of education, sports, and much of white collar work. Think of what a 20 per cent drop in the market cap of Amazon and Apple on the same day would do to the stock market.

The pandemic is also impacting the training of defence officers. While the pre-commissioned training of cadets across the three defence services entails a focus on physical training, as the officers grow in service, the emphasis largely shifts to the knowledge domain. The cadets undergo training at the National Defence Academy (NDA) in Pune. The NDA is now conducting its academic courses mostly online, through intranet connections. Weapons handling is being carried out in a staggered manner. Games and drill competitions have been put on hold. Non-contact sports activities, such as horse riding, volleyball and hockey, have been postponed to a later date.[9]

- Businesses need to identify allocation of resources to create digital infrastructure.
- The ecosystem of suppliers needs to be adapted or recreated for the new reality.

- The skill building of employees and the adjacent ecosystem needs to be built in.

WICKED PROBLEM

Could the challenges of the real-estate-based sectors like retail and education get solved by disaggregating the space problem from the value-creation problem? Or by designing the experience of shopping or eating out or learning, independent of the economics of it?

Case: Serum Institute of India

In a world impacted deeply by the downturn, low cost and high volume is a winning combination, especially when it comes to who will win the race for a vaccine for this dreaded disease.

The most likely candidate is the Serum Institute of India, a relatively unknown fifty-year-old company tucked away in Pune. You probably don't know that they manufacture about 60 to 70 per cent of all the vaccines sold worldwide. If all goes well, millions of Indians will get the vaccine by early 2021.

Their network runs deep within the pharma and biosciences companies. They have tie-ups with Astra Zeneca to take the vaccine to poorer countries. They had a partnership with Novavax (for anti-malarial vaccine) and the Austrian firm Themis. The Gates Foundation trusts them as does the Indian government.

The secret sauce of Serum Institute may be a combination of factors. Their employees have expertise and are relatively

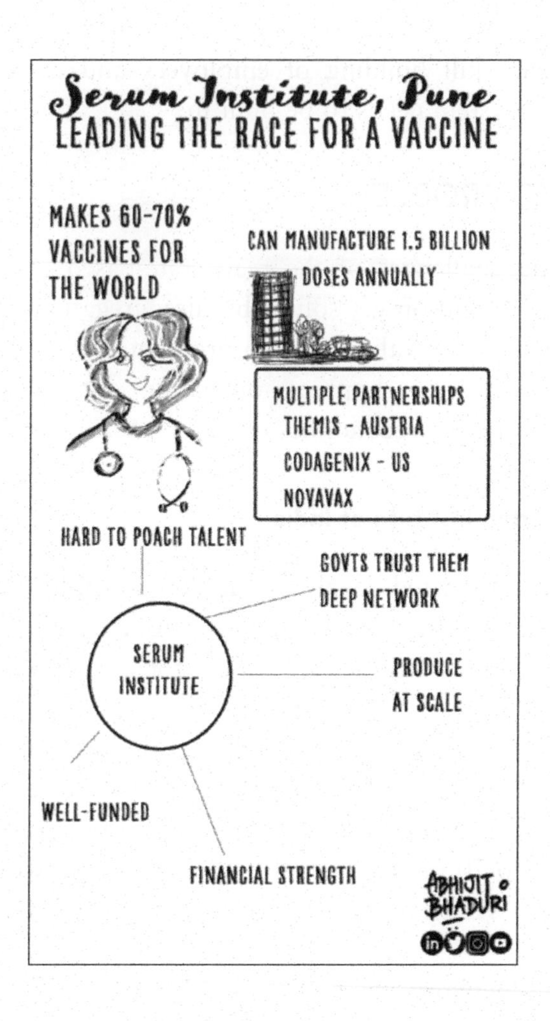

well paid. Their work environments are described as 'stress-free and stable'. The company invested Rs 4,000 crore to build the world's largest multifunctional product facility in Pune. It can produce up to 500 million doses of vaccines a year.[10]

If a business is doing something of consequence, it will have to deal with the politics of business. Will the government hunker down and insist that the Serum Institute makes sure that every Indian is vaccinated as a way to build our competitive advantage in the world? Could this be the bargaining chip India will use to, say, get visa waivers for Indians in the US?

Sanofi S.A. is a French multinational pharmaceutical company headquartered in Paris, France. As of 2013, it is the world's fifth largest by prescription sales. They are one of the pharmaceutical companies in the race to make the COVID vaccine.

Sanofi's COVID-19 vaccine research is partly funded by the US Biomedical Advanced Research and Development Authority (BARDA), but in recent years, Sanofi received tens of millions of euros in tax credits from the French government to help its research. Both French (and the European Union) and US citizens feel that they have the moral right to get the vaccine, having funded the research.

When Sanofi CEO Paul Hudson said that the US government had 'the right to the largest pre-order because it's invested in taking the risk', the French politicians pointed out the €150 million (£133 million; $162 million) in research tax credit and millions more in other tax credit that Sanofi got from the French government. The French prime minister said that access for all was 'non-negotiable'. Sanofi's chief in France responded like an exhausted parent mediating a fight between children. He said that Sanofi's goal was to have a vaccine 'available to the US as well as France and Europe at the same time'.

Whoever makes the vaccine has to be prepared for a tsunami of challenges. Expect to see questions about the efficacy of the vaccine, questions about the safety of the vaccine, the claims of success and a flood of conflicting emotions, leading us to wonder if we should celebrate or be suspicious.

A group of developing countries like Senegal, Pakistan and Ghana are pushing to limit patent protections for COVID-19 vaccines from the pharma giants. It will let poorer nations produce cheaper generics. Pharma companies claim allowing for cheaper clones of the vaccine will curb innovation.

Sensemaking for the World of Work

As businesses face rapid downturns and no revenue, they have to let go of employees. Some struggle to spell 'furlough' even as they explain the policy to their employees. Many human stories are getting buried in the largest unemployment the world has seen since the Great Depression. This is a moment for leaders to stop using legalese and instead discuss the merits of 'V-shaped' or 'saw-shaped' recovery. The world's Nobel laureates and data scientists using quantum computing could not predict anything about the pandemic's spread and impact.

Trimming costs by lowering them is a natural response to a significant dip in the company's revenues. A number of firms have had to lay off a number of employees. Uber went through 6,700 job cuts—almost a quarter of its workforce. Even Silicon Valley was not spared. Tech startups have seen more than 56,000 layoffs while the economy in the US has shed more than 36 million jobs.[11]

In India, the tourism value chain—hotels and restaurants, airlines, tour operators, transport providers and other allied businesses—alone has felt the impact on 38 million to 50 million jobs.[12]

The Organisation's Empathy Muscle Is Being Tested

A job loss is hard no matter how logically you explain it to yourself. It is particularly important for employers to think about having empathy for those impacted. It is easy to be insensitive like the electric scooter-maker Bird that axed about 400 employees over a Zoom call that was over in few minutes even before everyone could log in.[13]

On a Zoom call, when the employees are reduced to thumbnails, it is easy to say anything. It requires much more empathy to look someone in the eye and say the same thing. The discomfort of telling someone that they do not have a job anymore is managed by depersonalising the entire process, which a Zoom call allows for. That is why students and teachers find it equally dissatisfying to turn education to a 100 per cent online experience. That is also why most massive open online courses (MOOC) have abysmally low completion rates. Technology is all about efficiency, while human beings are all about human connection.

Unpleasant Memories of the Office

Lack of empathy shows up in multiple places in the corporate world. To say that people must read every clause in the appointment letter before they sign it is not fair. When you need a job, you don't wish to start off on the wrong foot by squabbling with a new employer. Think about the number of times you have clicked 'I Agree' on the end-user license agreement just so you can get started.

If you have used Apple's iTunes, you may have agreed not to use it to develop, design, manufacture or produce biological weapons, remember? If you use iTunes, you agreed to the following clause:

> You also agree that you will not use these products for any purposes prohibited by United States law, including, without limitation, the development, design, manufacture, or production of nuclear, missile, or chemical or biological weapons.[14]

The same principle is being applied by employers as they lay off employees in the most insensitive manner. The layoffs at most media outlets including legacy organisations like the *Hindu*, *Hindustan Times*, the *Times of India* and *Mint* come across as insensitive. A news report on the layoffs in Indian media stated: 'Employees are asked to either resign with offered terms, or be terminated. Often, this message is conveyed via a phone or video call. Those who have not been axed continue to work in uncertainty, anxious about their job security.'[15]

While layoff is a business decision. and, yes, people do sign employment contracts (much like you sign the end-user license agreement to instal software on your device), employees expect dignity during the layoff, although employers want a clinical sawing-off. What is even more painful is that while these media outlets write about layoffs in other sectors, they follow the unwritten code of not reporting on the unfair and inhuman treatment of fellow scribes. The shoemaker's children do not have shoes.

IMPLEMENTATION CHALLENGE

If you want to build empathy and passion in the workplace, ask your decision-makers to read more literary fiction. Findings from neuroscience show that reading and social cognition improves our capacity to simulate hypothetical scenes and mental states.[16]

Ten Dimensions about the Workplace You Must Rethink

The Society for Human Resource Management (SHRM) is the largest HR professional organisation in the world with 300,000 members in over 165 countries. The SHRM India office includes the following:

1. Organisational Purpose
2. Business Strategy
3. Values and Culture
4. Organisation Structure (span of control, reporting structure, etc.)
5. Performance Management
6. Learning and Development
7. Coordination and teamwork
8. Innovation
9. Decision-Making
10. Office Space

IMPLEMENTATION CHALLENGE

To track the effectiveness of your onboarding programme for new hires, track the number of days it takes for them to learn all the TLAs (three letter acronyms) that are used among the colleagues in the workplace. Then figure out creative ways to reduce the number of days. New hires begin to feel a sense of belonging when they understand all the insider jokes and the TLAs.

The invisible majority: There is an invisible majority in the workplace too. The organisation of the future will need to create work contracts with each person based on the 'workplace' settings they operate from. The workplace will be like the set of a play that changes according to the characters and the roles they are playing. If the nature of the work needs more people, a virtual collaboration zone will be set up. Solo work, teamwork, town hall, offsites—the possibilities are infinite. As organisations create hybrid talent models with a small number of generalists on their rolls and a range of specialists whom they can engage as freelancers, remote working will slowly become a part of the mix.

Assuming that the entire talent pool is location-independent, creating the technology needed to secure the data, the IP and working will be an option organisations must increasingly view as a business continuity plan.

Unrestrained by the limitations of co-location, organisations have a chance to make their talent pool truly boundaryless. That requires two more factors to be aligned—a new model of leadership and a workplace culture that may have to be nuanced for the different kinds of talent to thrive.

Organisational culture is a summation of all 'workplace relationships': The head of one of the largest search firms had once told me, 'The culture of the organisation acts like super-glue. If it is very easy for me to hire somebody to go work for a competitor, it tells me volumes about the firm's culture. There are some firms where it is virtually impossible to place them in any other organisation because they have such a strong set of workplace bonds. In organisations which have a strong culture of shared values, the candidates want to know many more things about the prospective employer's culture before they even read the job description.'

Organisational Culture is a summation of all 'workplace relationships'

Organisational Culture in a WFA World

Physical assets such as plants, property or machines no longer account for a company's value. Today, IP such as patents, trademarks, goodwill and even data and software have become more precious. Intangible assets make up much more than tangible assets. The office space is no longer the homogenous concept of where workers assembled to get work done. In that case, what happens to the organisational culture and hiring for culture fit?

Today, however, 32 per cent of the big American firms in the S&P 500 invest more in intangible assets than physical ones, and 61 per cent of the market value of the S&P 500 sits in intangibles such as R&D, customers linked by network effects, brands and data.[17]

Organisational culture can be seen in many different ways—tangible aspects like furniture, use of space (who gets how much space), ratio between space allocated for individual work versus teamwork are all interesting ways to observe company culture.

Any discussion about workplace design has to keep in mind that while in the pre-pandemic era the entire workforce was located together, in most businesses in the post-pandemic era, an increasing number of people will work from home. The role of the workplace has changed sharply. It is no longer the place where almost all the work is done or stored. It is not the place where colleagues bond and relationships are formed. Proximity to the boss used to result in greater mindshare compared to peers. That was the basis of office politics.

Workplace Design Shapes Relationships

1. Offices are a signalling device for the culture: The concept of office culture changes from when it is a small team huddled together in the office of a dreamer to a time when the organisation establishes its offices across cities when it hits the unicorn phase of growth. Market shapers like Apple, Google, Microsoft and Amazon flaunt their own culture through their office buildings, campuses and even the paintings on the wall. The Google campus is known for its lavish space and recreational opportunities. The Apple spaceship office campus got as much press for its cost as its unique design. Amazon's offices are frugal and functional to the point of being impersonal. The desks are made out of discarded doors. Netflix office culture celebrates 'no rules' around vacation and businesses expenses. Employees do what they believe is the right thing to do. Dealing with ambiguity is part of the culture.

Hierarchy and space are an integral part of human nature. Taking up more space signals the importance of the person occupying that space. The extra space in business class or the enclosed cabin in the first-class section signals status. Even a notional increase in space as compared to peers signals privilege.

The king's palace and mausoleum signalled the exalted position of royalty in a world where millions were homeless. Even in a democracy like ours, the official residence of the president of India has 340 rooms spread over four floors and five acres. The government allocates large bungalows to top officials in prime locations. In office buildings, the corner office and sometimes the entire floor or the top floor of a building is occupied by a few or sometimes, just one single person. The size of the leader's office is a give-away. It is often reflective of the wage inequality prevailing in the organisation.

2. Office designs reflect four dimensions of privacy: Jim Keane is the CEO of Steelcase, the largest office furniture manufacturer in the world. At the company's headquarters in Grand Rapids, Michigan, his office is located in the building where customers are received. Changing the office location to that area was a way for the company to make a statement about the importance of being where the customer is.

Proxemics is the study of human use of space and how population density affects behaviour, communication and social interaction. The research done by Steelcase finds that the workspace must create four privacy dimensions.

- Acoustical—what you hear
- Visual—what you see
- Territorial—the boundaries of space
- Informational—what is revealed and concealed from each other

In the Western world, privacy at work is defined in terms of the degree of sensory stimulation, whereas the extent of access to information defines privacy in Asian settings. Some companies like Apple actively limit information sharing across work silos on a 'need-to-know' basis. Your colleagues may be working on a secret product launch that others may read about only in the newspaper.

3. Employee experience drives engagement: Workplace designs still remain horribly non-egalitarian and non-inclusive. Most HR leaders never ask employees if the workplace helps them do better work. When employees are told to move to a new office, they are almost never asked if they like the new office layout. Yet, workplaces play a prominent role in employee engagement.

In the digital business, where speed matters, it is important that the leader works alongside the rest of the employees and perhaps even customers. Startups often cram workstations cheek by jowl, and the founder is seated inconspicuously pecking away like any other employee. That may signal an egalitarian work culture, but is it effective?

The LinkedIn Global Talent Trends Report for 2020 talks about employee experience as one of the four biggest trends driving talent. Employee experience, they found, was driven by the four Ps—people, place, product and process. The relationships with colleagues and customers are described as 'people'. The physical environment, whether in an office or remote place, which impacts employee experience, is referred to as 'place'.[18]

'When the employees are engaged, the signs are visible in the workplace. They display their toys, trinkets and trophies,' says Praveen Rawal, the MD of Steelcase for India, APAC (Asia Pacific) and the SAARC (South Asian Association for Regional Cooperation) regions. Toys and trinkets refer to stuffed toys and photos. Photos can be of the employee with their colleagues or with family. Trophies refer to the awards they may have won or the certificates of recognition.[19]

The increasing importance of workplace design as a strategic lever for shaping culture needs to become part of the CXO vocabulary. Work settings that enhance the feeling of engagement with colleagues and those that encourage individual contribution time need to be consciously designed. How we do our work has changed. The workplace design has to catch up.

4. Interdisciplinary collaboration: Workplaces need to foster more interdisciplinary collaboration and creativity. Teams need to engage with each other constantly to iterate and build on everybody's ideas. One of the IT majors in Bengaluru has more than twenty-five buildings that came up as the business and employee strength grew. The challenge of crawling through the city's traffic snarls means that most teams can't be co-located. The employees of that office suddenly had to experience the alternative reality of video-conferencing as an alternative to commuting between offices to attend meetings.

Companies that have been successful in working remotely attribute their success to the majority of employees already knowing each other. Prior familiarity can help decipher colleagues' facial expressions on video calls. New hires who are remote, who have not developed such bonds, may have trouble acclimatising or an organisation's core culture could deteriorate.

Open offices make it impossible to do deep, undisturbed work. It takes almost twenty-three minutes to go back to the same degree of depth after an interruption from a colleague or the beep of a message. People need different kinds of space to do different kinds of tasks. Some need a group. Some need isolated space to do deep work.

Multitasking is inefficient. So is the overdose of collaboration. Too many team meetings lead to fatigue, stress and burnout. In the case of creative work, the initial phase of brainstorming needs people to bounce ideas off each other. In the execution phase, the ability to do long stretches of deep solitary work needs isolation. The office has to support both phases.

IMPLEMENTATION CHALLENGE

Want an easy method to evaluate organisational culture? Just look at who gets promoted. They are the heroes of the organisation. Are the promotions announced or are they held in confidence until the person invites just a few friends to celebrate his or her success? You could also note if there is a discrepancy between the official reason given for the promotion (which is usually all the hard work done, numbers achieved, etc.) and the informal gossip which tells you, sometimes really accurately, what went on in the room when the promotion was decided!

Same Organisation, Different Country

Many multinational corporations are an interesting mix of the culture of the country where the headquarters are located and the culture of the country where the subsidiary is. When I worked for Colgate-Palmolive, a company headquartered in New York, I lived and worked in Malaysia in a role that gave me a chance to observe American culture blend with South East Asian culture. After a few years, when I was transferred from Malaysia to work at the headquarters in the US, some interesting differences that came up were:

- Presentation slides: In the US, the slide designs are minimalistic. It signifies: 'Tell me the time, don't build the clock'. In India and China, slides densely packed with words and graphs are meant to convey the seriousness of the subject or that 'the presenter is very knowledgeable'.
- After-office socialisation matters equally in the US as well as in India and South East Asian countries. In the US, it is all about networking. But skipping an office event to attend the parent-teacher meeting is socially acceptable. 'The family comes first' is an accepted norm. Asian countries look at it as a show of solidarity with the team. Missing an office dinner is frowned upon and avoided, especially by men.
- In the US, the manager focuses on the strengths of the team member. It is okay to describe a colleague's strengths, but using the term 'weakness' is taboo. The opposite of strength is 'development opportunity'. In Asian culture, the manager is far more measured in praising the team member. 'You have to keep them

grounded' is the guiding principle. Any 'weakness' will be pointed out frequently as an opportunity to improve.

For each one of these observations, there are exceptions and nuances. An entire country or continent cannot be generalised. But what we do need is a formal structure to decode what matters to people when it comes to organisational culture.

When business leaders think of digital transformation, they need to focus on four levers—business model, talent strategy, leadership style and organisation culture. Changing the culture of the organisation is arguably the toughest lever of the four. Talent strategy complements the business model, and the leader's role lies in leveraging the team at the top to change how every employee drives the transformation in everyday behaviour.

When Ed Catmull of Pixar made *Incredibles*, he took a bold bet. Disney was already successful. Yet, he decided to move from 2D animation to creating 3D animation through code. He took a bet on a director whose last movie had been a giant failure. That action created the cultural DNA of the organisation. It changed the behavioural norms.

Every employee must understand the behaviours that drive the outcomes that are expected.

Do the Value Statements Reflect the Culture of the Organisation?

When you look at the values that organisations articulate on their posters, most sound the same. Customer obsession, integrity, teamwork, innovation, diversity, courage, saving the planet ... these have all been used. The posters have now become almost interchangeable.

1. The nature of work determines workplace culture: The nature of work must be facilitated by the culture of the organisation. When you read what employees say anonymously, you get a clear sense that the same value may get implemented differently in different organisations. Amazon and Pixar may both have innovation as a value, but in the context of their cultures, the behaviours may be completely different.

2. Employee feedback: Employees are often the best people to tell you what it feels like to work in an organisation. What makes them stay and what makes them leave can be a rich source of insight about the culture, leadership style, etc.

Microsoft: Culture Change Is a Trillion-Dollar Opportunity

When Satya Nadella took over, this was a company that was stagnating. Nadella's predecessor Steve Ballmer had shouted to all 13,000 employees on the day of his retirement, 'Soak it in, all of you. You work for the greatest company in the world.' Microsoft had a know-it-all culture. Employees were hesitant to float new ideas for fear of breaking from the charted course.

A new leader often has to translate values into norms of behaviour, an abstract concept into tangible behavioural norms.

Nadella translated the cultural shifts into three norms:

1. *Customer-centricity:* He hired almost 5,000 specialists to make people understand how customers were using cloud-based services. This told the employees that the customer mattered.
2. *Speed of response:* Meetings are often the by-product of hierarchical structures. Nadella freed up the sales people from several obligatory meetings. That greased up the organisation and built speed.
3. *Incentivise the new norms:* Nadella used performance bonuses to encourage sales people to go beyond selling fixed contracts. This is a great example of partnering with HR to change culture.

Measuring Culture: The Nine Values that Matter

If Microsoft's growth is a by-product of the company's culture, so is it with Wells Fargo, the third-largest bank in the US. In February 2018, Wells Fargo lost nearly $30 billion in market capitalisation in a single day. The company had reportedly opened more than 2 million accounts without authorisation from customers. The bank's financial fraud was an extension of the porous norms of corporate ethics at Wells Fargo that existed much before the fraud was discovered. The feedback from Wells Fargo employees, on job site Glassdoor, had been consistently pointing out the toxic culture that encouraged such behaviours.

Glassdoor has collected more than 49 million reviews and employee insights, covering approximately 900,000 organisations over more than a decade. Employees submit anonymous reviews, which employers cannot remove (especially the critical ones). Employee feedback can often be the weak signal that describes the organisation's culture.

The Massachusetts Institute of Technology (MIT) partnered with Glassdoor to understand if they could create a measure of organisational culture. Using machine learning and human judgement, the employee feedback was used to make this. They identified nine cultural values in the study they term as Culture 500.[20] These are:

1. Agility/nimbleness: Employees can respond quickly and effectively to changes in the marketplace and seize new opportunities. Does the organisation's internal bureaucracy come in the way of course corrections?
2. Collaboration/teamwork: Employees work well together within their team and across different parts of the organisation.
3. Customer focus: Employees put customers at the centre of everything they do, listening to them and prioritising their needs.
4. Diversity: The company promotes a diverse and inclusive workplace where no one is disadvantaged because of gender, race, ethnicity, sexual orientation, religion, or nationality.
5. Execution excellence: Employees are empowered to act, given the resources they need, adhere to process discipline and held accountable for results.
6. Innovation: The company pioneers novel products, services, technologies or ways of working.
7. Integrity: Playing by the rules and honesty are valued.
8. Performance-driven: The company rewards results through compensation, informal recognition and

promotions, and deals effectively with under-performing employees.

9. Respect: Employees demonstrate consideration and courtesy for others and treat each other with dignity.

When someone asks you if culture change can help the company make money, you can point to the Microsoft market cap and share the evidence.

Leadership Now Goes beyond the Aquarium

> *'A decade or two ago, CEOs could be in their offices with spreadsheets, executing on strategy. Now, if you're not out listening to the market and catching market transitions ... if you're not understanding that you need to constantly reinvent yourself every three to five years, you as a CEO will not survive.'*
>
> —John Chambers in 2017

While Travis Kalanick was the CEO, Uber taught its new hires the fourteen values at Ubervarsity. The world celebrated the valuation of Uber and ascribed it to its values like 'Always be hustling' and 'Step on toes'. It was built on a view that for you to succeed, you must kill your peers. The value of 'principled confrontation' was designed to encourage employees to challenge authority without fear. On the ground, it translated to bullying the weak colleague. When Travis was sacked, there were over 200 cases of harassment, bullying, gender discrimination, reports of interns working a hundred hours a week and being paid for forty.

In a remarkably short span of time, WeWork went from an unknown startup to a celebrated unicorn to a place people were ashamed to have on their resumes.

WeWork had offices in thirty-two countries and a private-market valuation bigger than the GDP of Serbia. It all crumbled in September 2019, after WeWork's IPO failed. Its founder Adam Neumann was pushed out—in a deal that made him a billionaire—and the company was taken over by the Japanese conglomerate SoftBank, its largest investor, at a valuation well below the $13 billion that the investor has now put into it. Describing a boring office-space-leasing company as a tech unicorn was Neumann's idea. The stock options and twenty-five-year-old bosses, 'hackathons' and free beer all disappeared as quickly as the marijuana smoke that used to follow Neumann.[21]

These are two great examples of how the leaders can destroy value. But there is a company in India that was formed in its current avatar in 1958. Since 1958, India's economy has multiplied 1400x, but this company's earnings has grown 6000x giving it a 15 per cent compound annual growth rate (CAGR). Nine out of ten Indians use at least one of its products every month. The company in question has given 400 CEOs and CXOs to the Indian industry. What makes them consistently successful? The company I am talking about is Hindustan Unilever.

Could Hindustan Unilever's Values Be Their Secret Sauce?

Sudhir Sitapati, the author of *The CEO Factory* talks about the values of Hindustan Unilever that were crafted almost seventy years ago by Unilever. Sitapati spoke about them in a podcast with leadership coach Deepak Jayaraman:[22]

In early 2000s, we were having a really bad time in business and our CEO, Chairman at that time, Vindi Banga came to one of our annual conferences and said, 'It's time to go back to our values of action, caring, courage and truth. Every time in the canteen, we would keep making fun and to us it just sounded like jargon. One of the techniques I use in market research is to ask people what their favourite memories and stories about HUL are. There were four kinds of stories.

A lot of them were in the buckets of action, which is the same 'entrepreneur-professional' thing. Caring demonstrated itself mainly in terms of how the business dealt with employees who are either ill or passed away in the course of service. Courage means that the culture lets mavericks stand up to power and speaking truth to power. Truth is basically honesty.

What is the best way to perpetuate the values?

I can think of only two things.

1. Recruitment: Recruitment, both into the company and the team that you are in. You must recruit people with the values and character that you're really looking for.

2. Living the values: The second way is you have to live it. If you live it and your senior teams live it, then everybody sees it. If you don't find enough evidence of it in the organisation, you're not living it, not doing enough. You might be talking about it; you're not doing enough about it.

The Aquarium Is Now a Part of the Ocean

The leader's role has changed sharply in recent times. In the analogue era, the leader had all the answers. In the digital world, every employee, including the CEO, is equally clueless. Ironically, in many businesses, the most digitally savvy people are at the bottom of the pyramid. Yet, in many analogue organisations, the decisions are still taken by the leader who may know the least about how the digital world works.

The organisation is no longer like an aquarium that has a solid boundary wall. They share three characteristics especially if they have to survive.

1. **Boundaryless:** Anything that gets digitised behaves differently. What used to be called a car is best thought of as an internet-connected computer on wheels. Netflix has made internet-connected entertainment accessible to 139 million paid subscribers in 190 countries. The digital organisation is boundaryless. It is not limited by geography or even its initial business model. We are in a world where e-commerce companies are winning Oscars.

2. **In perpetual beta:** Everything that can be digitised is being done. Facebook has digitised our friendship and news. Tinder is digitising romance. Amazon started by digitising the book and then went on to digitise the reading experience along with the experience of buying and selling anything. When they had online retail figured out, they reimagined the grocery store and removed cashiers and check-out lines. Microsoft has gone beyond office software. Apple has moved from hardware to services. Disney is thinking beyond theme parks.

3. **Hyperconnected:** People are no longer content with having a phone to just make calls. They now expect a phone

to be connected to the internet and capable of running apps, which are the symbol of the digital world. We are now able to 'talk' to machines and make them carry out tasks that are repetitive and rule-based. One forecast is that by 2035 the world will have a trillion connected computers, built into everything from food packaging to bridges and clothes.

Combine these three forces and you have a cocktail of possibilities that will change business models. Some existing ones will disappear or become unviable and some new possibilities will win over customers. The organisation is no longer like an aquarium that has a solid defined boundary wall. The organisation is part of an ecosystem. Leading the fish in an aquarium is different from navigating the ocean.

Why Do Leaders Need New Skills?

Hyperconnected employees and consumers: The organisation's brand is not owned by the organisation. It is created every single day in real time by the employees and consumers or customers who are hyperconnected. What they say about you online is what everyone knows and believes about you.

In a hyperconnected world, problems get solved and innovations happen differently. To find the best algorithm to predict user ratings for films, Netflix offered a million-dollar prize to anyone. The result was that the best brains competed for it and solved the problem. General Electric (GE) challenged the public to redesign a metal jet-engine bracket to make it 30 per cent lighter while preserving its integrity and mechanical properties like stiffness. The contest was announced on GrabCad. The winner was a participant from Indonesia who managed to make it lighter by 84 per cent. This was way beyond what GE had been able to achieve with their own employees and consultants.

The new media is changing communication: Social media has changed how people consume media and how they form opinions and take decisions. Leaders have to understand how to communicate on social media platforms like Twitter, Instagram, Facebook, etc., where each platform has its unique unspoken rules. The always-on, hyperconnected media demands authentic responses in real time. Angry customers will vent on social media. They expect instant redressal. Employees will share their views about their experience at work or even with their managers through photos and posts on social media.

The boss no longer has the power to silence employees. They can hit back punch for punch.

The double-edged sword: CEOs are often expected to take a stance on social issues as well as political issues. Whether it is climate change or sustainability or racism, leaders are expected to speak up. As the protests on the killing of George Floyd rocked the US, CEOs had to decide if they should comment on an issue such as race. If so, should it be a statement on social media or should they address the employees and give them time off to protest? Wouldn't they be doing this anyway, since so many were working from home? Would they be setting a precedent they would regret?

Netflix said on Twitter that 'to be silent is to be complicit. Black lives matter. We have a platform, and we have a duty to our Black members, employees, creators and talent to speak up.' Because consumers are quick to punish brands that are seen not being socially conscious, there is a rush of 'performative brand allyships' as Katie Martell describes it. A range of businesses spoke up.[23]

But when they do, it encourages scrutiny over much more. People questioned the CEO and asked why there were not enough Black leaders in their leadership team. Goldman Sachs's boss wants to 'accelerate economic progress for all', but it faces a huge fine for its role in the 1MDB corruption scandal in Malaysia.

The CEOs of Apple, Google and Starbucks have had to take a stance on issues ranging from immigration to data privacy to LGBTQ issues. Candidates seem to think positively about the CEOs who take a stance on sociopolitical issues even when their personal views do not concur with the leaders. 'CEOs campaigning for humanistic values will increase job pursuit intentions when compared to CEOs remaining neutral, while CEOs campaigning for non-humanistic values will decrease job pursuit intentions when compared to neutral or humanistic CEOs.'

Most Problems Are 'Wicked Problems'

A 'wicked problem' is a social or cultural problem that is difficult or impossible to solve for as many as four reasons: incomplete or contradictory knowledge, the number of people and opinions involved, the large economic burden, and the interconnected nature of these problems with other problems. The leaders are seeing an increasing proportion of 'wicked problems' as part of what they have to do every day.

In the analogue world, experience mattered. The leader had all the answers whenever the team members had questions. In the digital world, the problems that are coming up are often wicked. If you are a pharmaceutical company, how do you respond to the threat of Amazon buying Pillpack—an online pharmacy that lets users buy medications in pre-made doses? How does an automobile giant like Tata Motors deal with the new emission standards that the regulators introduce? How does the *New York Times* deal with consumers' preference to get their news on Facebook?

Toys"R"Us (founded in 1948) filed for bankruptcy in September 2017. Another company LEGO reinvented itself by making sense of the wicked problem. They found: 'Shoppers are not the same as consumers. Consumers are usually kids without the ability to buy things. At the same time, we want them to tell their parents, and we want their parents to have a good experience as they shop.' The company learned that there were often two journeys: one for those who love LEGOs and another for those who purchase them on behalf of someone else. As a result, LEGO mapped two customer journeys, one for children and one for parents. Insights from each helped the company focus on developing touchpoints within each journey while also ensuring synergy and intersection between them.

Microsoft missed the mobile revolution altogether under Steve Ballmer's leadership. He also dismissed the iPhone when it was launched because he looked at the future through the lens of the past. The leader's role is to ask better questions—not to be the one-stop-shop for answers. Having the humility to say, 'I don't know,' may be the greatest value-add by a leader so that the rest of the organisation stops trying to second-guess the leader. Satya Nadella has described this shift as a 'learn-it-all' culture—not a know-it-all culture. In the digital world, the knowledge and skills may lie with people who are much younger in age and often without prior experience and credentials because there are new jobs being created that have never existed before. The leader's role has changed.

The New Role of Leaders

1. Mindset—not tech: Most organisations get excited by a technology (e.g. robotics or AI) and try to bolt it on to analogue processes. When we think of the word 'transformation', we have to remember the best example of the process—the caterpillar turning into a butterfly. Transformation is irreversible. Change is not easy, and the butterfly is a completely different creature than the caterpillar. The digital transformation of an organisation cannot be thought of as a tech project. It is about reimagining the business model and the value proposition by putting the customer at the centre. It is about designing an experience.

2. Leaders have to navigate ecosystems: Think of talent in a boundaryless manner. Like the hyperconnected world, it is www, i.e., whoever, wherever, whenever. Whoever is the best person to do the job (employee, supplier or gig worker), wherever the person may be located in the world, make it easy to collaborate whenever needed. Leaders have to learn how to communicate and engage talent. This is a new skill that every leader needs to learn. Collaborations with tech startups can help legacy organisations get access to cutting-edge technology. Startups get access to a large customer base that legacy organisations have. It can be a great win-win.

3. Balancing polarities: Digital businesses are often built on gathering vast amounts of data that are then used to personalise the service. Leaders have to be ethical about what data is being collected, how it is stored and how it is being used. They have to set the limits themselves. Tim Cook of Apple says, 'Data assembled to create a digital profile lets companies know you better than you know yourself. This is surveillance.'

Digital organisations are as different from legacy organisations as the butterfly is to the caterpillar. Leading these organisations needs not just a new set of skills and competencies but also a different mindset. The hyperconnected customer is more aware and makes decisions and choices differently. The power balance has tilted in favour of employees and consumers. They own the brand. The leader's role is now about helping the organisation go from the aquarium to becoming a part of the ocean.

Honesty-humility is a new personality element that is made up of five attributes: sincerity, modesty, fairness, truthfulness and unpretentious behaviour. Leaders who are high on the H factor put the spotlight on the team rather than on themselves. While such leaders are high on ambition, they liberally seek help from others and listen to feedback from others. Such leaders handle success without glowing in the I-did-it-all feeling.[24]

We have all seen scores of examples of leaders who will attribute all success to themselves and ascribe failure to reasons outside of themselves. When others ignore their accomplishments, most leaders feel annoyed. They feel that they are more talented than the others around and are entitled to being treated as special. Humble leaders are aware of their own weaknesses and are eager to improve themselves. These leaders acknowledge others' strengths and appreciate them; the upper management team listens to divergent views and collaborates better.

Be the Inventor-in-Chief

Most CEOs trying to lead the digital transformation faced the challenge of their own obsolescence. A study of Jeff Bezos (Amazon), Larry Page and Sergey Brin (Google), Steve Jobs (Apple) and Bill Gates (Microsoft) shows that when it comes to expertise and innovation, these leaders are role models that other employees can look up to. Customers are impressed with their technical knowledge.

Bezos filed for eighteen patents in 2017, a minor drop from the twenty patents he was granted in 2009. He holds a total of 155 patents and was the designer-in-chief for Kindle. Elon Musk got five patents after becoming the CEO of Tesla. Jobs filed for eighty-seven patents in 2010. He held 620 patents in all, including more than 200 patents that were approved after his death. Since the process of filing for patents and getting accepted takes almost two years, it is not surprising that Jobs obtained 219 patents even *after* his death. Brin (thirty-three patents), and Page (twenty-one patents) wrote the page-rank algorithm of Google. Between 1997 and 2011, they filed 400 patents. Jun Young-hyun, CEO of Samsung SDI, in the renewable energy sphere, registered 145 patents.[25]

These CEOs provide the prototype for the leaders that will impress customers and employees alike.

The way such leaders would have to be developed would have to change. That means a fundamental rethink in management development.

We have to think beyond skills and build the culture that allows an organisation to be resilient and understand emotions of consumers and employees alike. Sensemaking needs a different method of development.

Shiv Shivakumar, group executive president (strategy) for Aditya Birla group suggests changing the focus of management development in the context of a future society. Management development in the future will be a joint responsibility between the manager and the company in which each has to do their part. Leaders and companies have to think through the three As in their own development:

1. **Awareness:** The key to future leadership is to be self-aware. Leaders of the past in most organisations are short on this because they grew up in a relatively stable environment. Building self-awareness will make for a better set of future leaders, who can deal with adversity and ambiguity in a more thoughtful way.

2. **Agility:** The pace of a future world is lightning quick. So, future leaders need to be agile learners and be equally adept at unlearning. New skills will be needed every eighteen months if leaders have to stay relevant to a future world. The onus of this squarely rests with the leader. Mental agility will lead to physical agility and will help when the leader has to go through a series of pivots for his organisation.

3. **Alignment:** Society is demanding a lot more from every company and leader. The role of a company in society is challenged on inequality, diversity, inclusion, sustainability and ecology. Leaders need to be able to align and serve society interests while stewarding their companies. This will need more sensitivity than leaders exhibit today.

'Darshan'—Seeing the Unseen

We go to the temple to do the 'darshan' of the deity, i.e., to see the deity. According to mythologist Devdutt Pattanaik, to be able to see beyond the obvious, the devotee needs to have 'drishti' which is 'the ability to see the visible and tangible, the saguna. But there is also divya-drishti, the ability to see the invisible and the intangible, the nirguna. It is the ability to see what no one else could see and join the dots, create patterns and observe rhythms. This led to insight, hearing the inner voice that makes no sound but still can be heard.'[26]

Mythology may help us make sense of the future. History is as much about the future as the past.

Adaptability—Not 'Culture Fit'

When organisations look for a new hire who is a 'good culture fit', the assumption built in is that the employee has to fit the culture. So any cognitive diversity is discarded as the people hired are those that do not need to change themselves. They fit in. Is it any surprise that the same organisation struggles to change?

It may be better to look for the new hire's ability to adapt and to drive change that enables the rest of the organisation to adapt. The ability to adapt needs the ability to make sense of context.

That means actively tuning the hiring system to evaluate the sensemaking ability of people.

References

1. Madsbjerg, Christian. Sensemaking: What Makes Human Intelligence Essential in the Age of the Algorithm . Little, Brown Book Group. Kindle Edition.
2. Bill Gates is the voodoo doll of the COVID-19 pandemic. https://www.bbc.com/news/technology-52833706
3. Brian. X: *Solis The Experience When Business Meets Design*, Wiley
4. The fireside chat had Sudhanshu Vats of Essel Propack, Manish Tiwary of Amazon, Amit Dalmia of Blackstone, Vivek Gambhir of Godrej Consumer Products and Abheek Singhi of BCG. It was held on 4 June 2020 over a Zoom call which was by invitation.
5. It is interesting to see how many elements of the current pandemic seem strangely accurate and prophetic by a film released nine years ago. https://www.thequint.com/entertainment/contagion-and-everything-it-predicted-right-about-2020-coronavirus-covid
6. Bill Gates's talk seemed improbable then and prophetic now. https://youtu.be/6Af6b_wyiwI
7. This ruling drew a gasp of disbelief from many employers. https://www.swissinfo.ch/eng/court-decision_companies-must-pay-share-of-rent-for-employees-working-from-home/45781126
8. Pandemic hit Phoenix Mills. https://themorningcontext.com/pandemic-hit-phoenix-mills-faces-its-biggest-battle-yet/
9. Training of the cadets has a large physical training component that has to be redesigned. https://theprint.in/defence/online-courses-non-contact-sports-how-military-training-is-taking-on-covid-challenge/437365/
10. The Serum Institute of India and its partnerships are the best bet for humanity to get the vaccine for COVID-19 at scale. https://www.moneycontrol.com/news/coronavirus/serum-institute-raises-hopes-of-india-getting-its-covid-19-vaccine-before-end-of-2020-5364781.html
11. Except for the digital giants like Amazon that hired during the slowdown, every other organisation froze or reduced its payroll even in Silicon Valley. https://www.wsj.com/articles/coronavirus-layoffs-remake-silicon-valley-job-market-11589968800
12. One of the hardest hit industries by the paranoia around hygiene in public spaces is the travel and hospitality industry. https://economictimes.indiatimes.com/jobs/tourism-hospitality-industry-begins-layoffs/articleshow/75854257.cms
13. Fired over a Zoom call. https://www.bbc.com/news/technology-52091615
14. I did not believe that this was a clause that was put in iTunes. Check out for yourself. https://www.apple.com/legal/internet-services/itunes/us/terms.html

15. Opacity of layoffs in the media. https://www.newslaundry.com/2020/07/04/stop-press-the-opacity-of-indian-media-layoffs
16. The ability of the business leaders to make sense of social phenomenon like shifts in consumer behavior can be significantly enhanced by reading fiction according to research. https://www.ncbi.nlm.nih.gov/pmc/articles/PMC4733342/
17. The role of the CEO is to understand the value of intangibles in the workplace that account for the largest proportion of the firm's value. https://www.economist.com/leaders/2020/02/06/what-it-takes-to-be-a-ceo-in-the-2020s
18. The LinkedIn Report highlighted the importance of employee experience design. https://business.linkedin.com/talent-solutions/recruiting-tips/global-talent-trends-2020
19. Toys, Trinkets and Trophies in the workplace. What do they reveal? https://www.thehindubusinessline.com/specials/people-at-work/are-there-toys-trinkets-and-trophies-at-your-workplace/article30802773.ece
20. These nine dimensions can be used to compare peers in the same industry. https://sloanreview.mit.edu/culture500
21. The rise and fall of WeWork. https://www.newyorker.com/culture/culture-desk/the-rise-and-fall-of-wework
22. I recommend you read the book *The CEO Factory—Management Lessons from Hindustan Unilever*. Meanwhile, this is a good place to get started. https://youtu.be/Z7Cni9jdZ3g
23. Brands invite scrutiny when they take a stand on a social issue. But staying silent is not an option. https://www.katie-martell.com/blog/2020/6/6/promises-promises-7-risks-of-performative-brand-allyship-blm
24. The H Factor of Leadership. https://abhijitbhaduri.com/2018/11/08/the-h-factor-of-leadership/
25. How tech CEOs are defining the top job. https://sloanreview.mit.edu/article/how-tech-ceos-are-redefining-the-top-job/
26. Seeing the invisible. https://devdutt.com/articles/seeing-the-invisible/

11

Top Talent—Not on Your Payroll

There are new models of engaging talent that defy categorisation. Uber's four million drivers are not employees. Millions of mission-critical workers in Apple's supply chain are not employed by Apple. The influencers who shape brand perceptions and drive more sales than some people in the sales team are freelancers. The top talent in any field is not on your payroll. How do you broaden your view on talent, beyond the obvious?

Market Shapers Follow the Talent Trail

The factory that manufactures Apple products, specifically iPhones, has approximately 230,000 workers. Only eighty-three cities in the US have a population that big. The market shapers will follow the talent pools.

'There's a confusion about China. The popular conception is that companies come to China because of low labour cost. I am not sure what part of China they go to, but the truth is China stopped being the low-labour-cost country many years ago. And that is not the reason to come to China from a supply point of view. The reason is because of the skill, and the quantity of skill in one location and the type of skill it is.' That is Tim Cook talking about why Apple makes its products in China. 'It is a combination of quality and quantity,' he explains.

'The products we do require really advanced tooling, and the precision that you have to have, the tooling and working with the materials that we do are state-of-the-art. And the tooling skill is very deep here. In the US, you could have a meeting of tooling engineers and I'm not sure we could fill the room. In China, you could fill multiple football fields.'[1]

Tony Hseih described Zappos as a customer service company that happened to sell shoes. The definition is interesting because it puts the human being at the centre. That is what the digital age is about. You cannot turn a business from analogue to digital if you don't put employees first.

What business is a chef in? If you said, 'Food', you are wrong. Chefs are in the business of hospitality. What they need to sell is the food. To build a human-centred view of the business you are in, focus on making yours the place where top talent will queue up.

Your job as a leader is to simply ensure that they have other bright people to work with—that's your talent strategy. The hallways where these people come together to have energising conversations are called workspaces (virtual or otherwise). The leader's job is to remind everyone that they are in the business of talent—who happen to sell a product or service. It is all about talent.

Talent—How to Recognise It and Measure It

In ancient times, the word talent was referred to as a measure of silver that was paid in exchange for someone's work. Better output by the person resulted in more payment—hence more 'talent'.

We believe that since we spend a lot of time with human beings we must be good at evaluating their talent and potential. We have all heard many jokes over the years. But that does not automatically make us terrific stand-up comedians.

Putting much more effort to assess and evaluate the talent pool before hiring is cheaper than fixing the damage a wrong hire can do. Organisations have moved from being at the top to becoming irrelevant in the span of four to five years because of the choice of a poor CEO. A CEO may have the perfect strategy crafted, but getting an organisation to execute that vision needs a leader whose vision the employees trust.

A simple heuristic is the ease of hiring top talent in the organisation. The leader's bad reputation makes it harder for the business to attract and retain talent. A qualitative analysis of the exits is a good measure of the leader's reputation. The leader has to hire people who can translate the vision into reality. The talent pool and the leader together create the culture that sustains that vision.

'COVID changed how we view talent.'

—Rashmi Daga

FreshMenu describes itself as the 'go-to neighbourhood food delivery option you can turn to when you're famished. Our chefs create a variety of plated meals on demand, to make sure that you are spoilt for choice.' I ask Rashmi Daga, the founder, what has changed in the post-pandemic world.[2]

1. Dealing with ambiguity: The pandemic has highlighted the people in the talent pool who are self-driven and motivated. Whether they are working at home or their hometown or anywhere else. That means it is all about being able to work without having a supervisor micromanage you or pamper you. The self-driven take charge. The rest feel lost. The difference is stark.

2. Greater usage of gig workers: Bangalore was seen as the startup capital of India. So, we would expect people to move to Bangalore if they wanted to work with the startup ecosystem. Given Bangalore's traffic jams, we would prefer people who would be able to stay close to the office. COVID changed everything that we believed about talent. Location does not matter anymore. In the early stage, having a full time designer burns cash. Startups are using more gig workers for projects before the project turns into something long term. That is when they would hire a full-time person. Gig workers have become more mainstream.

3. Bringing the team culture online—work-in-progress: The future will look more like a hybrid model. When people work from remote locations, spontaneous interactions are limited. Fun and camaraderie is missing, and that is what defines office culture. Many people spend their time functioning like 'individual contributors'. How to work like a team and bring the team culture online is something that we have not figured out.

Some Design Principles in Talent Management

1. Talent is not uniformly distributed: Marie Curie got the Nobel Prize twice. The first was for physics (1903), which she shared with her husband Pierre and physicist Henri Becquerel. She then got it again for chemistry (1911) and was the sole recipient. Her daughter Irene shared the Nobel Prize in 1935 for chemistry with her husband, thus making the Nobel Prize seem like a family monopoly with five medals between the three of them.

Walt Disney won twenty-six Oscars over the course of his career and was nominated a grand total of fifty-nine times.

Michael Fred Phelps (born 1985) is the most successful and most decorated Olympian of all time, with a total of twenty-eight medals. Phelps also holds the all-time records for Olympic gold medals (twenty-three), Olympic gold medals in individual events (thirteen) and Olympic medals in individual events (sixteen).

Wolfgang Mozart was competent on the piano and a violin player by the time he was five. He also began composing at that age and performed before European royalty.

Not everyone is equally talented, and the rough measure is that the top 20 per cent performers contribute to 80 per cent of an organisation's results. The next 30 per cent contribute 10 per cent to the total result; leaving the last 50 per cent to contribute only 10 per cent.

Your BEST performance is a measure of your ABILITY.
Your average performance is a measure of your MOTIVATION

2. Hiring is a test of the hiring panel's competence—not the new hire's:[3] When a new head feels that a new hire has failed, instead of firing the new hire, it may be worth asking the interviewing panel some uncomfortable questions. The selection process must identify the candidate's fit for the role. It must be a comfortable fit—not too tight and not too loose. The second test is the person's personality—strengths and weaknesses (instead of weaknesses, you can use the word 'derailers'). In high stress jobs, especially at senior levels, the person's personality has a disproportionate impact. Peak performance is a measure of ability while average performance is the result of motivation.[4]

3. Talent is personality in the right place: Think of any two successive presidents of countries or companies, and you will see that even though the job description was the same, the two did the role in very different ways. Your best salesperson may make the worst possible people manager. It often happens that an organisation's topmost technical talent does not enjoy managing a team.

Job crafting* may enhance some elements of the role or give away some parts to another colleague, and that can

*Job crafting—redesigning different elements of a job, e.g. the client set, the skill set, the team, etc., to make it meaningful.

dramatically change the outcome. Having a coach can often help leaders get that clarity. Everything that the person can do well may not be what the person enjoys doing. By crafting roles that leverage the person's strengths and weaknesses, we can create better outcomes.

Autism spectrum disorder refers to a set of neurological disabilities that interfere with a person's social interactions, their ability to communicate, and their repetitive repertoire of interests and activities. They can excel at jobs that need little or no social interaction and need a keen eye for details. SAP has employed autistic people in roles that involve quality control in software. It leverages their strength and weakness. Autistic candidates lack social skills to interact and communicate their ideas during an interview. But they possess intelligence, skills and technical expertise necessary to thrive in the IT industry. SAP simply changed the interview process to be able to tap into this talent pool. The successful candidates are put in jobs that involve quality checks for software but don't need interaction with others.[5]

What to Measure while Hiring

I am not going to use HR speak by employing terms like competencies, competency maps, skills versus traits, etc. I will attempt to put it in business language even if it is not 100 per cent accurate as per the pundits.

What makes someone an effective hire boils down to three characteristics. Do they have the knowledge to do the job? Are they motivated to work hard (on their own)? Do they have social skills that will make it easy for them to work with others?[6]

1. Are they learners and problem-solvers? Assess for actual problems that they will need to solve in the role. Ask them how they would go about solving the biggest problem they will have to solve when they start. Assess their approach to problem-solving by giving them a problem that was solved and compare their approach to what was done. How do they react when faced with a question they do not know? Do they bluff their way through or will they teach themselves? Curious people are great learners. Leonardo da Vinci wrote and drew on subjects including geology, anatomy (which he studied in order to paint the human form more accurately), flight, gravity and optics, often flitting from subject to subject on a single page and writing in left-handed mirror script. He 'invented' the bicycle, airplane, helicopter and parachute some 500 years before they were actually invented. Elon Musk literally taught himself rocket science by reading every textbook on the subject. Then he cold-called experts and learned from them.[7]

2. Are they willing to work hard? Energetic people who are self-driven are an asset. In the scenario when everyone is working from home, this is a particularly valuable trait to look for in people. When they are on their own, will they continue to set equally high standards and drive themselves just as hard? There will be deadlines to meet that need extending beyond the usual. There will be a crisis with a team member that needs everyone to pitch in. People who set high standards for themselves also set the bar high for others. They are comfortable perfecting their routine over years. Or spend a day polishing up a short speech until it is perfect. Willingness to work hard matters. It matters a lot. Consider two cricketers who started their careers at the same time—Vinod Kambli and Sachin Tendulkar. Kambli did better than Tendulkar in school and college cricket. He scored two double centuries and two centuries in his first few international Test matches. Kambli also had a better ODI average than Tendulkar when both were playing. But, it was Tendulkar who became a legend. He just worked way harder than anyone else.

3. Are they likeable and pleasant in their interactions with others? Satyajit Mohanty of Crompton, a consumer goods company (and a client) told me that when he became a CHRO of a company for the first time, he sought advice from various CHROs. One common advice he received was: 'The CEO has to like you and should be able to talk to you.' Likeability comes from the ability of the person to understand others' emotions and needs. Being able to adapt to the emotions of the others makes us likeable.

We feel good after interacting with them. They are pleasant and easy to understand. Emotionally agile people are often viewed by others as being very tactful and even 'politically savvy'. If the term 'political' makes you uncomfortable, replace that word with 'influential'. People with high emotional quotient (EQ) can work with many different kinds of team members because they can build trust and are predictable. Likeable people can take large groups of diverse opinions and interests along on their own journey. Likeable people can give someone disappointing or difficult news without demolishing their self-worth.

Very few people are equally strong in all the three areas, but to have a really successful career, one must be extremely strong in at least two of the three areas.

Unconventional Talent Pools

Finding the right number of people to harvest sugarcane at the right time is a problem that sugar manufacturers have to solve every year. The job has traditionally been done by migrant population coming from different states of the country. 'The pattern is unpredictable,' the head of the business in a sugar company told me. The pandemic made this worse because the migrant population decided to go back to their roots.

'Sometimes the entire village from one corner of the country will come to work with us for one season. But in another year, they do not. We have to find a way to build predictability of people. We provide them housing and medical facilities. Sometimes we get the entire village because having their social support system is good for the mental well-being of the workers. Yet, it is so hard to find people to do this work in a country like India where so many people are unemployed,' he stated.

Someone in the company suggested they employ transgender people for this job and make them a part of the permanent workforce. Transgender people find it hard to get employment, leave alone any alternate employment. Finding housing and hospitals is a challenge for them. This would be a win-win for everyone.

There was a step missing before this brilliant idea could be implemented. Having a transgender workforce also meant training the supervisors and other employees on integrating and managing this cohort in the workforce. Think about it keeping in mind what makes Gen Z employees and millennials different from more experienced employees.

When SAP hired autistic techies, their supervisors and colleagues had to learn how to adapt to the talent pool. When Wipro hired people with disabilities (PWD), it checked the performance rating distribution of the PWD employees with other employees to ensure their performance distribution is no different from any other group doing the same job.

The same principle would apply for integrating transgender people in the workplace. Their needs and views about rewards, recognitions, compensation, employee engagement and even what they consider 'fair' is different. Without building a truly inclusive and accepting culture, it is hard to get the best out of anyone. It is even more important to do it when the talent pool is diverse.

Rethinking Assumptions about Talent

- *How work will be done, especially keeping social distancing norms in mind:* The paranoia about hygiene and safety will need every business to rethink their workplace. Restaurants, travel, hospitality, hair salons, fashion, performing arts, retail and traditional manufacturing are all industries. The MD of ABC Consultants, Shiv Agrawal, mentions how hiring for even CXOs has gone virtual and part-time. 'We did eighteen CXO appointments without any in-person meetings. In January 2020, I never thought it could happen. We have got mandates to look for a part-time CEO for a company that could potentially translate to a full-time role in a few months if the project materialises.'
- *Think skills—not degree or pedigree:* The WFH possibilities mean that talent beyond the metros and

big cities can be part of the talent pool. If someone's skills are valuable, where the person is working from will be irrelevant for most jobs (not all jobs though). It may mean more opportunities for people with disabilities, women and even people who do not have credentials from top universities. Apple, Google, Netflix and many top technical employers do not need college degrees for many of the jobs that they advertise. Alphabet, Google's parent company, is also among a long list of companies emphasising skills over schools. Google's certificate programmes can be completed in months and cost a few hundred dollars. They are more likely to get you a job that pays an annual salary of $50000. Do you need to go to college for four years? Google offers 100,000 need-based scholarships, to complete any of these career certificates. That is such a market shaper—like move! In many of its job listings, Alphabet's subsidiaries require applicants to have bachelor degrees 'or equivalent practical experience'.

- *The post-COVID talent brand and the employer brand:* The leaders and people who represent the employer in public forums and social media shape the employer brand of the organisation. Employees and candidates are two stakeholders who actively shape the talent brand. The brand is the reason:
  - The talent practices of the organisation differentiate the organisation as an employer. If the employer has had to let go of people during the pandemic, the way it was done would have a big impact on the talent brand.

    - The impact of the advertised role on the organisation's goals and vision tells potential employees that the work they will be hired to do will be considered as valuable and that it matters.
    - Employers who take special measures to coach and mentor their employees have a big impact on the talent brand.
    - The overall experience of being an employee and the extent to which the employee is an evangelist for the brand also helps.
- How the talent brand is communicated: Leaders shape the employer brand. It is what employees say crafts the talent brand. Many leaders feel threatened to see employees represent the brand. Smart employers leverage them. They help employees learn about social media and handhold them as they grow their clout. Employees are the most credible source of brand advocacy, perhaps even more than the CEO of the brand. Yet others add influencers to boost the talent brand. If done well, the results are inspiring.

The TALENT BRAND is the reason why talent chooses to work with an employer. BRAND perception shapes the decision

Influencers + Employees: A Combined Force

In most organisations, the decision-makers and leaders have no presence on social media. When one employee becomes very powerful on social media, the decision-makers worry that the person's brand will enable the employee move to a competitor. It is quite likely that a junior employee may have more followers on social media than the CEO. Instead of helping the employee's voice to grow even more powerful, the insecure CEO would stifle the employee. Salesforce employee Vala Afshar works as a brand influencer for his employer.

His Twitter bio describes him as 'Chief Digital Evangelist @Salesforce | Columnist: @ZDNet | Show: @DisrupTVShow'.

With more than 460,000 followers on Twitter, Afshar is a powerful voice shaping perceptions of customers and other stakeholders alike. The CEO of Salesforce, Marc Benioff, has a million followers on Twitter. What a powerful combination that is! Together, they communicate directly with their employees, customers, media, government and fans. They communicate directly—human to human. This is the most powerful method of communication in the digital age.

Add to that mix a set of influencers, and you have the kind of brand strength that is unbeatable. Rani Mani of Adobe runs their influencer programme. She says, 'Influencers provide a trusted, authentic, believable level of evangelism to the brand that employees on your payroll simply don't, and they also bring a fresh outside in POV that forces you to evolve and improve.'[8]

Nevertheless, leveraging influencers for building trust in the employer brand is not something that too many organisations have done. This is a white space waiting to be exploited. Several companies use testimonials from influencers on their webpage when purchasers want to get advice from influencers. Most buyers turn to online advice for their purchase decisions.

By working with the right influencers, the CHRO can train a handful of the C-suite and a few employees who are active on social platforms to be brand evangelists. This can be a powerful tool for social listening

The Activists Are in the Office

Employee activism is going mainstream. Blue-collar workers have had their unions for a long while, and white-collar employees now have social media. The latter are vocal about what they think is right or wrong and are not shy about posting their views online. But things were not always the same. Reasons for protest have also changed.

Employees expect the leaders to play 'fair'. That translates to several areas where white-collar employee-activists have put their foot down in recent times.

1. Executive compensation and job cuts: Compensation, from that of the executive to the junior-most worker, has been increasingly under question. Decisions taken by senior leaders lead to low profits, but it is lower-paid workers who get the axe. That does not seem right. Many protests are triggered by that.

When the bosses at Air France decided in October 2015 to cut costs by $2 billion over two years, they did not anticipate the backlash. Hundreds of workers protested against the plans to cut almost 3,000 jobs and increase pilots' working hours while reducing the size of the fleet. At some stage during the protest, the workers almost lynched two executives, including the HR manager. Historically, in such scenarios, the employer strikes back. Five of the offending protestors were identified from video footage and arrested. The backlash from the employees and media made the employer soft pedal the issue and the matter was resolved. In a similar incident in October 2008, Jet Airways employees protested and managed to get all the impacted employees reinstated.*

2. Sexual harassment: On 1 November 2018, almost 20,000 employees of Google walked out and left this note on their desk: 'Hi. I'm not at my desk because I'm walking out in solidarity with other Googlers and contractors to protest sexual harassment, misconduct, lack of transparency, and a workplace culture that's not working for everyone. I'll be back at my desk later. I walked out for real change.'

The protest came one week after Andy Rubin (the 'father of Android') who had been accused of sexual misconduct, was paid a $90 million severance package.[9] The employees demanded five changes from the company: an end to forced arbitration, a commitment to ending pay inequality, a transparent sexual harassment report, an inclusive process for reporting sexual misconduct, elevation of the chief of diversity to answer directly to the CEO and creating a position for an employee representative.

In the middle of 2017, Arunabh Kumar, the founder of The Viral Fever (TVF for short), which licenses its content to

*In this book the term layoff/retrenchment/job cuts/fired etc., are used interchangeably though they have different meanings in law.

giants such as Netflix and Amazon Prime Video, as well as Times Internet–owned MX Player,[10] was accused of sexual misconduct by several former TVF employees; the company dug in its heels at first, but Kumar eventually resigned as CEO, and receded to the background.

3. Tech that could harm a group: In 2018, research showed that commercial facial recognition systems (including IBM's) were biased. IBM officially dropped all projects pertaining to facial recognition. Clearview AI built its facial recognition tool with more than three billion images compiled in part from scraping social media sites. This tool was being used by private sector companies and law enforcement agencies. Clearview is at the centre of a number of privacy lawsuits. While tech startups have celebrated their perpetual beta culture, when imperfect technology gets false positives, it can put marginalised groups at further risk.[11]

4. Militarisation of AI: In April 2018, some employees petitioned Sundar Pichai, urging him to drop out of the Pentagon project. This was not just another geeky problem where Google's top-notch team of engineers would churn big data from hours and hours of video footage to glean actionable insights. What started as a murmur at the fringes soon seemed to take on a life of its own.

That month, the *New York Times* published the letter that Google's employees had written to the CEO. They rejected the argument that the likes of Microsoft and Amazon were also partners in the project. Google's unique history and influence set it apart from everyone else. More than 4,000 employees signed the letter.

It was the resignations of key talent that finally made Google's leadership decide to drop the project whose value was expected to go up to $250 million. High-end, specialised tech talent is scarce. Losing these valuable resources was not an option. It forced a rethink at Google.

5. Transgender rights: Transgender activist Liz Fong-Jones forced Google to allow users to use pseudonyms for Google+. Using their legal names makes the space inaccessible to some teachers, therapists, LGBT+ people and others who need to use a different identity for privacy and safety.[12]

6. Unsafe working conditions: While the Indian government has been working on 'labour reforms' for the past few years, the trade unions have been resisting their implementation. Then came the pandemic. Citing a public emergency, the labour departments of Gujarat, Madhya Pradesh and Himachal Pradesh simultaneously issued notifications extending the work hours of factory workers to a maximum of twelve hours a day and seventy-two hours a week.

This may set a dangerous precedent of creating periods when the guardrails of governance are removed and anarchy sets in in various pockets. Imagine if following traffic rules were to be made optional for six months to allow people to reach hospitals faster during the pandemic. The chaos that would follow would be unimaginable and would be hard to reverse.

The trade unions feel that the COVID-19 crisis is being used as a pretext to push through the unfinished 'reforms agenda' of increasing the hours of work, restricting wages to the bare minimum, reducing social security benefits, permitting the engagement of contract labour for any kind of work, easing norms for firing workers, clamping down on trade union rights and minimising labour inspection.[13]

What Skills Will You Need Soon that You Have not Hired for Before

Ramesh Menon, the president (HR) of the Rs 40,000 crore Murugappa Group, reached out to me in December 2018. The group, headquartered in Chennai, has nine listed companies and nineteen unlisted businesses that range from agri-business to metal tubes (that go into making cycles) to finance. The leaders of the group had just concluded their business plans for 2025. They now wanted to create a talent strategy for 2025. The group's ambitious plans included expanding to new categories, new customer segments and so on. The talent strategy had to drive the growth agenda of the conglomerate.

This would have to identify the acquisition strategy and the strategy to upskill the current workforce. The HR landscape would need to be reimagined for the millennial and Gen Z population. What should be the talent-mix of generalists and specialists? For which functions should they look for specialists?

I spent time with the CEO and CHRO of each business to understand the talent challenges unique to their business and what would be different about the business model in future and the kind of skills they would need to run the business. That meant drawing up a palette of hard skills and soft skills.

Business leaders find it easy to articulate the hard skills they would need to have but struggle to identify the soft skills needed for future business scenarios.

The group of business leaders and CHROs were divided into mixed groups and asked to identify: 'Who do you not employ today but would need to in future?' The simple exercise can be a trigger for businesses to think of all the possible skills that they will need in future and the kind of groups they could draw the skills from.

It can throw up challenges in brand perceptions or company policies, which need to be modified. Hiring people you have never hired before requires policies in place to retain the people who bring in the new skills. Their performance assessment systems need to be agreed upon. They may need a different set of policies and benefits. The supervisor may need to be trained on how to manage such a team.

That exercise with Murugappa Group's leaders generated a huge range of ideas that the leaders then went back to their teams to put into practice.

The Talent Canvas in the Post-Pandemic World

The co-founder of TeamLease, Manish Sabharwal, says, 'Shareholders do not pay salaries, customers do.' For countries like India where the per capita income is barely $2500, the ability to handle the lockdown depends on the resources you have. India has 63 million enterprises of which only 19,500 have a paid-up capital of more than Rs 10 crore. The vast majority of MSMEs have no margins or working capital to provide a safety net to the vast majority of the half a billion workers in India. While India may be the 4th largest economy in the world, in terms of per capita GDP, India features at the 138th place.[14]

Talent Marketplaces—From Horizontal to Vertical[15]

The mobile phone enabled the creation of many marketplaces. A parallel universe is being created with marketplaces of all kinds going virtual. From entertainment to education there is a virtual marketplace for everything, where geographical boundaries become irrelevant.

Marketplaces Follow a Pattern

The $70 billion global market in healthcare logistics is being increasingly populated by drones. In Rwanda, over 150 medical products have been delivered to remote areas by Zipline drones since 2016. They are expanding their service to Ghana and are establishing their presence in the US. The use of drones is expanding. Bhutan, Malawi, Papua New Guinea and Switzerland have all been using drones.

The mobile phone also created the base for new industries. Several technologies like drones have used mobile phones to create new markets and new opportunities. Talent markets are growing along the same patterns.

Phase 1 and Phase 2

Technology follows the same path. Markets are first created horizontally. A new product or service has to have several different use cases to build a big enough customer base. Once the customer base hits the critical mass, it then starts to create niche clusters.

When spreadsheets were created, adoption was rapid because a wide variety of scenarios could be handled using a spreadsheet. The spreadsheet could be used by accountants and chefs alike. One could use it to do financial analysis or run the balance sheet of the firm. Another could use it to create a database of their books. Think of this as phase one of development.

In phase two, the same spreadsheet concept was used to create specialised software for accounting. That is an example of the use of cases going from a wide customer base to serving a niche user. The spreadsheet can serve as a base for building specialised software. The pattern is always the same—vertical niche follows horizontal growth.

Vertical Talent Pools

Connectivity has created a marketplace for skills. LinkedIn alone has a user base of half a billion people of which 44 per cent are women. It is the marketplace for many working professionals. The accountant, the HR person, the digital marketer have their resumes on the site, making it easy to get discovered by an employer. As more sellers of skills join the network, it attracts more buyers who start signing up to get access to the talent pools.

There is a parallel universe coming up for skills. These are marketplaces for skills that are niche. Imagine a LinkedIn just for your field. Already, there are marketplaces for niche skills popping up all over the world. There are marketplaces for those who are not looking for full-time employment. StyleSheet can help you find hairstylists for the local salon. TrustedHealth is a portal that provides nurses to the healthcare industry.

There have been search firms that operate within a specific industry. In a hyperconnected world, the buyer and seller can find each other without having to look only in the neighbourhood. The talent marketplace becomes boundaryless.

Phase 2 of Talent Markets

LinkedIn solved the first problem by organising unorganised professional workers across the world. While that database will continue to grow, the marketplace will evolve to create clusters for specific skill sets and demographic segments. This is the phase two of talent marketplaces. Having experienced horizontal expansion, it is time to get vertical.

These markets can be set up by geography, specific skill sets or even demographic commonalities (e.g. women re-entering the workforce). The vertical markets for talent are growing consistently for blue-collar skills. UrbanCompany offers hyperlocal services in several metros and major cities. Wedding photographers, yoga trainers, interior designers, dieticians, beauticians, plumbers are all hired, screened, trained and deployed. When it comes to white-collar jobs, the marketplace gets more nuanced.

Some platforms fix the price the customer has to pay and do not allow the service provider to negotiate the price. This is where the marketplace for high-end talent gets messy.

Five Problems a Talent Marketplace Must Solve

1. Make it easy to discover: Gig-work platforms like Upwork have made it easy for the buyer and seller to find each other in case of low- to medium-skilled jobs. The gig worker gets listed and the jobs are allocated by the algorithm. The buyer sets the budget for the job. The seller can apply for the job he/she wishes to apply for. There is little room for individual negotiation. The platform ensures that the buyer and seller cannot post any personal information to enable direct contact. Work is also transacted through the site.

2. Background verification: This is a vital trust-building process if a service provider has to thrive in the marketplace. Marketplaces need to find ways to verify credentials for work that requires specific licenses and experience. Imagine being able to see the doctor's credentials and licences before they undertake surgery for someone (even if they are employed by a hospital).

Knowing the expertise levels of the gig worker can help to build trust in the buyer. SpareHire is an online work marketplace that connects organisations with top-tier finance and consulting professionals for project-based work. They offer investment bankers, management consultants or investment professionals on demand. CTO on Demand provides chief technology officers (CTOs) for non-tech founders. OrthoCare on Demand connects patients in need of urgent orthopaedic care directly to orthopaedic surgeons in their local area for an affordable, one-time fee set by that physician.

3. Customer ratings to evaluate proficiency: This is the equivalent of performance appraisal in organisations. Employers want to know what it was like to work with a gig worker they had deployed. A bad rating by a customer must be fixed immediately. Talent markets run on reputation.

Is the person easy to work with? Does the gig worker have a track record of happy customers? This is where customer reviews help. Uber and Ola driver ratings are available for all to see. The drivers in turn can see the reputation of the customers they have been assigned. Star ratings, comments, being tagged as a 'ninja' are all key ways to find people who have the skills and have a string of happy customers who can vouch for them. LinkedIn encourages people to write recommendations for people they have worked with. Gig work is extremely dependent on someone verifying the quality of work done.

4. Seamless payment for all: The payment system for gig workers must be made friction-free. Upwork and Uber have solved the payment problem by making payments instantaneous. Uber and Ola set the base wages for the gig worker. The payment for most workers is fairly uniform with limited opportunity for the individual to negotiate.

Experts like to set their own price. They can work across the world. Knowledge search firms like GLG or AlphaSights provide such opportunities to experts. While GLG and AlphaSights set the tiered, hourly rate for experts, freelance marketplace Fiverr is aimed at sellers who are often highly skilled, and determine the terms of the job and payment themselves.

5. Reskilling and upskilling: Professionals must be able to stay employable by upgrading their skills and knowledge in real time. Sometimes that may mean upgrading skills by being an apprentice to an expert. This is still an unsolved problem in most specialised marketplaces. LinkedIn has LinkedIn Learning as a way to keep upskilling. This is still an unsolved problem for most niche talent marketplaces. Here lies a massive opportunity for each niche skills marketplace.

LinkedIn is a horizontal talent market for all professions. Several niche talent markets are coming up for every profession, e.g., HR, lawyer, doctor, MBAs interns...

The talent marketplace is evolving. No single talent platform has so far solved all the five problems. Therein lies a big opportunity. The transition from looking at general talent pools to expertise-based talent pools for each profession (e.g., lawyers, architects); by demographics (e.g. women, retirees, disability, LGBTQ); by previous experience (e.g. military service) or even by duration of employment expected (e.g. gig workers); etc. The list goes on.

Talent in a Location-Agnostic Workplace

Traditionally, white-collar job opportunities have been clustered in urban areas and in big cities or hubs. These grew to become traditionally hot job markets that offered the best opportunities.

The Invisible Talent Pool—Women

About sixty million people are looking for life partners at any given time in India, of which some ten to twelve million people get married a year, which means five to six million couples. Some six to seven million people register on online matchmaking sites, of which 20 per cent find a match. Lockdown has accelerated online matchmaking sign-ups and engagements by at least 30 per cent. A lot of it is led by Tier III cities when compared to the metros.[16]

This may not be good news for working women in India as the pandemic wipes out decades of gains. Seventy per cent of women in India are employed by the informal sector, and it is not surprising that the downturn impacted women much more than men. When it came to deciding who had to be made redundant, many employees chose to axe women and people who were relatively older.

Between 2005 and 2018, the number of women in the labour force of India dropped from 32 per cent to 21 per cent. Some sociologists attribute it to improved economic gains. It is a symbol of status in some segments to tell the others that women in their family do not need to work because the family is well off.[17]

With the world's second-largest population, India also has the second-largest digital market. India's online population of 400 million is expected to hit 650 million by 2020. Smartphone ownership has tripled between 2016 and 2020.

Yet, in many fast-growing sectors, women remain underrepresented. It is still an industry where almost three out of four game developers are male. The talent pool for women game developers is growing thanks to movements like Girls Who Code. Gaming generated $145 billion in revenue in 2019. There are almost 1.33 billion gamers worldwide, of which 38 per cent are women. The mobile phone has become the most popular platform among female gamers. Female gamers account for 35 per cent of mobile games revenue, which is expected to be close to 40 per cent in 2020. Women players like games that have a strong strategy element, visually appealing design and diverse characters.[18]

It makes sense in every business to have a workforce that mirrors the customer base, and nowhere is it more applicable than in gaming, where women are fast gaining wallet share.

Women are under-represented in leadership roles. So, the main question we should be asking is not why there aren't any more women leaders, but why do so many incompetent men become leaders? That is because our mental model of a leader has three characteristics:

1. We tend to view confidence as a sign of competence.
2. Charismatic people are seen to be 'leader-like'.
3. Narcissistic people who claim that their vision is to 'change the world' is who we define as a leader.

'Instead of falling for people who are confident, narcissistic and charismatic, we should promote people because of competence, humility and integrity. Incidentally, this would also lead to a higher proportion of female than male leaders—large-scale scientific studies show that women score higher than men on measures of competence, humility and integrity. But the point is that we would significantly improve the quality of our leaders,' says Tomas Chamorro-Premuzic.'[19]

The solution may be to use a selection method that helps us evaluate competence, humility and integrity—in men or women. And not expect women, too, to behave like incompetent men instead.

Gen Z

It is one thing to graduate virtually in your living room and have your degree couriered to your home address. It is quite another thing to have job offers withdrawn leaving you uncertain about your visa status, ability to pay back student loans and even choose a role. Gen Z is particularly hard hit by the pandemic as they are entering the labour force.

Some of them have not yet reached the legal age to work. Many of them will work with millennial managers. Gen Z is as different from the millennials as chalk and cheese. This is the group that is just about entering their twenties.

Gen Z does not remember a time when the internet did not exist—and as such, it's not surprising to learn that 50 per cent of Gen Z spends ten hours a day online, and 70 per cent watches YouTube for two hours a day or more. Their method of learning and sharing is shaped by digital media that they have always used. But put aside this ultra-connectivity, and Gen Zers have other unique and possibly unexpected traits.

Gen Z prefers face-to-face interactions in the workplace and also expects to work harder than past groups. For Gen Z, equality is a top issue. Finally, Gen Z is possibly one of the most practical generations, valuing things like saving money and getting stable jobs.[20]

Case Study: How Adobe Is Engaging Gen Z

Adobe runs a large-scale conference on digital marketing called Adobe Summit. Their programme Adobe Max brings together storytellers, designers, digital marketers and delirious fans who swear by their entire range of products like Photoshop, Acrobat, Premier Pro and Audition, to name a few. Adobe's collaboration with Microsoft help turn Word documents, Excel sheets and PowerPoints into PDFs that cannot be tampered with. Photoshop has been used by photographers for decades to edit and enhance their photographs. The power of the product is such that it is now a verb in the English language. 'Has this picture been photoshopped?' is now considered legitimate usage.

Adobe has now added a layer of AI called Sensei to their offering to be at the bleeding edge of technology. Their video editing software uses natural language processing, and hence, the user can search through a library of stock images that automatically matches the style of what is being created.

Several of these products, like Adobe Sketch, enables the user to create breathtaking content on their mobiles. Did I mention that so many of these cool products are free? Adobe donates their products to a million students in India for free as part of their education initiative.

What they have done better than most companies is the way they run their influencer programme that includes Gen Z influencers. The 'influencers' are brought in to these conferences to watch, participate, narrate and amplify the brand voice through their social media channels. Through the stories, visuals and interviews that the influencers share, their followers participate and learn from these global conferences.

During the conferences, Gen Z influencers can attend workshops on how to use Adobe products to tell better stories online or run digital marketing campaigns that are personalised.

Many of the Gen Z influencers are gifted and accomplished. Esabella Karena (@EsabellaKarena) from Canada is an ambassador who advocates for the cause of learning disabilities, has published a novel and has made films that have won awards. She has been attending the Adobe events with her parents since she was about fourteen years old, when I first met her.

As an Adobe 'insider' (that's what they call the influencers), Karena has ringside seats to the Adobe conference, and opportunities to interview celebrities, CEOs and keynote speakers. Over the past four years, she has remained an integral part of the influencers who connect Adobe to other Gen Z consumers. That provides a great opportunity for Adobe to understand the mindshare of this group before anyone else has had a chance to engage them.

IMPLEMENTING THE IDEA

Invite a diverse group of eighteen- to twenty-five-year-olds to learn about what they expect from work, their choice of careers, their views of money and the role models they have. Let the interviews be carried out by millennials who are managing teams. Video record the interviews and share it with everyone. Watch the film together and discuss what it could mean for your organisation to have them as employees and consumers/customers. Have Gen Z lead some timebound exercises, and watch how they lead and give instructions. Watch how they deal with success, failure and teamwork. Ask them to solve some of your workplace challenges. Nurture these relationships over time. They may drive the biggest changes in your culture that are needed to attract the future talent pool.

Gig Worker, Freelancer and Gig Artistes

India has fifteen to twenty million freelancers, and its sharing economy could be worth $20 billion to $30 billion by 2025. The report indicates that one in four freelancers in the world is from India. A gig is a one-off assignment that has a defined start and end. The output and the fee for the gig is agreed upon. The duration could vary depending on the nature of the work being delivered.

The term 'gig worker' has become an umbrella term, thanks to ride-sharing companies like Uber and Ola that defined them to be independent entrepreneurs who can choose when they work, for how long and for whom. I believe it is a convenient business model that avoids paying health benefits and insurance to the most vulnerable sections of the workforce. The food delivery personnel and everyone else who gets labelled as an 'essential worker' during the pandemic need to be covered by health insurance for themselves and the family.

A gig worker can often work for competitors. While gig work has been very common in India for blue-collar work, even white-collar jobs today are available as gigs.

Gig workers show up in the most unexpected places—like education. The extra tuitions that students take are all offered by gig workers. In the US, where a four-year undergraduate degree costs $200,000, tenured professors make up less than 29 per cent of the teaching staff, leaving 71 per cent of them to be non-tenured or adjuncts. Stand-up comedian Hasan Minhaj's show *The Patriot Act* refers to adjuncts as the 'gig workers of higher education'. They get no time off, no sick leave, no health insurance and most have to work gruelling hours every day to get by.[21]

There are two factors that determine whether the service or product is being offered by a gig worker, freelancer or gig artiste.

1. The gig worker: A platform allocates the work to a gig worker. The platform decides the fee and takes a percentage of the earning. The customer does not care about the individual who is delivering the service or product. The individual worker is interchangeable and faceless.

This process is the same for blue-collar and white-collar work that get allocated automatically through the platform. Customer rating is possible only after the transaction is over. The person delivering the service is left at the mercy of the platform. The pandemic exposed just how vulnerable this group is with no paid time-off or medical insurance. They are called 'essential services' and are often the least paid.

A platform like TapChief is tapped by several large employers to find niche coders or even content writers, editors, UI/UX specialists, etc. Noble House claims to have created a network of over 400 independent HR professionals with 30+ skill sets across India and Asia.[22]

2. The freelancer: Getting discovered is the biggest problem a freelancer faces. There is no platform to allocate work. So, the freelancer must hunt if they want to eat. Building a brand becomes an essential activity for a freelancer to ensure they periodically show up in the newsfeed of people to stay on top of their minds. In case of a freelancer, the service provider cannot be replaced. When someone buys tickets to see a specific singer perform, they wait impatiently for the opening acts to get over until the star of the show is on stage.

Being a freelancer means that everything from filing taxes to marketing to answering queries is to be done by the freelancer. Sometimes, the freelancer creates a hybrid model where they employ other freelancers to help them out in specialised tasks like research, accounting or digital marketing. Freelancers who do sustain their business over time are the ones who have deep expertise in some area, for instance, designing sales incentives. Some freelancers create a niche for themselves by addressing the unique needs of a client category, say, MSMEs.

A PayPal report (2018) talked about the growing numbers of freelancers in Vietnam, India, the Philippines, Mexico, Argentina, Hong Kong, Russia and South Africa. Their biggest challenge is irregular income. Some freelancers list themselves with platforms if they are unable to secure steady flow of work.

3. The gig artiste: The CHRO of Sony Pictures Networks India, Manu Wadhwa, says, 'Eighty per cent of Bollywood (or creative content producers) works with gig artistes. Being employed (by a studio or network) is an exception rather than the norm.' Authors, columnists and journalists fall in this group along with everyone who produces creative content. So are the daily-wage workers in Bollywood, estimated to be around 650,000, whose livelihoods have been thrown into a downward spiral amid the coronavirus pandemic that has brought India's prolific Hindi film industry to a standstill.[23]

Street magicians and gymnasts, bahurupiyas (quick-change artistes across India who physically metamorphose into many characters), storytellers and singers in the villages are all gig artistes. Writers, sound engineers, musicians, art directors and all the roles that scroll up at the end of a movie or series you have watched are all part of the gig artistes' community who fuel our senses.

Wedding photographers, sketch artists, TikTok sensations, YouTube stars whose payments depend on the number of 'likes' they can notch up, stand-up comedians who entertain you at the restaurant, and actors on radio, television, OTT (over-the-top), broadcast and satellite television platforms are the gig artistes who lose money when we listen to or watch pirated content.

Accenture used the term 'liquid workforce' as a way for organisations to look beyond their own employees. Companies must look beyond just updating skills. To drive change, they will need to become agile at each level of their business: their skills, projects and organisations. By embedding the assumption of constant change enterprise-wide, companies will be able to access critical skills sooner, innovate faster and operate more effectively. This digitally powered workforce isn't just changing what businesses do; crucially, it's changing how they do it.

Remote Workers and Digital Nomads[24]

Startups like Automattic, Buffer, GitLab, Invision, Toptal and Zapier all have from 100 to nearly 1,000 remote employees. These organisations are fully, or almost fully, remote, with employees distributed around the world. There are also nomadic founders with no fixed location and who do not wish to move to Silicon Valley because they have a startup to nurture. The emergence of accelerators and investors worldwide has made it possible for a business to be location agnostic.

As @Suvarchala, a digital nomad, wrote about her experience of working in Bangalore, 'I've been offered incredibly exciting projects based on a conversation, word of mouth, and even a late mobile bill payment. I've slept in hostels, airbnbs, rented places, and my car. My offices in the city have been almost every cafe on the Indiranagar 100 Feet Road stretch, friends' terraces, a treehouse, and my car.'[25]

Technology and connectivity have supported these new categories of workers. But it is the social acceptance of work being done in locations other than under physical supervision that is going to shape the future of talent.

Activism Is a Feature—Not a Bug

Madan Nagaldinne, chief procurement officer (CPO) for Blink Health, says, 'If you want talented employees, you will need to manage the level of activism that exists in the company. You cannot be managing through power, title or position. Any company is a mini-country or a mini-ecosystem. You will have some employees strongly agreeing or disagreeing with certain policies of the company. As a smart business person, you will have to factor that in.

'Neither can one be an activist company nor a my-way-or-the-highway one. One needs to balance it out. My advice to founder-CEOs is not to think of activism as a drag. Instead, look at it as a tailwind you can appropriately manage to increase employee satisfaction.'[26]

Build Distraction-Free Time to Think about Talent

Telling others how busy we are has become like a badge of honour. People enjoy telling others how hard they are working. Having free chunks of time is a matter of shame for most people. That may be another relic of the past we may need to leave behind in the post-pandemic world. Maybe you can do what one of the founders of one of the biggest market shapers has done for years.

Bill Gates has devoted one week, twice a year, to lock himself up in a secret cabin somewhere in a forest in the

Pacific Northwest. The 'think week' is his time to spend a distraction-free seven days reading about ideas that different employees have shared with him. It is an easy way to hear ideas from people who are close to the ground. Those papers, handwritten notes and ideas are all compiled and read.

If Gates can find time to take fourteen days off to read and reflect, can't you? That works out to spending roughly one day a month. Maybe you can start by taking a week off to read and reflect. Too hard? How about three days? Maybe you can spend time for half an hour every day to read and reflect ...

Just get started. Plan how you can devote a think week devoted to talent.

References

1. Tim Cook on why Apple manufactures in China. https://www.inc.com/glenn-leibowitz/apple-ceo-tim-cook-this-is-number-1-reason-we-make-iphones-in-china-its-not-what-you-think.html
2. Phone interview on 10 Aug 2020
3. *Don't Hire the Best* explains why personality is a much better predictor of performance especially in high stress or senior level jobs. https://www.amazon.in/Dont-Hire-Best-Abhijit-Bhaduri-ebook/dp/B00BAMKCT6
4. *The Talent Delusion* by Tomas Chamorro-Premuzic is my recommendation for the best book you will find on the subject. https://hbr.org/podcast/2017/04/our-delusions-about-talent
5. Tapping the autistic talent pool for tech jobs. https://www.cio.com/article/3013221/how-sap-is-hiring-autistic-adults-for-tech-jobs.html
6. These three characteristics form the basis of every role. https://abhijitbhaduri.com/2017/09/23/3-hiring-secrets/
7. Elon Musk taught himself rocket science. https://www.businessinsider.in/Former-SpaceX-Exec-Explains-How-Elon-Musk-Taught-Himself-Rocket-Science/articleshow/44918922.cms
8. Adobe has one of the best run influencer programmes. https://abhijitbhaduri.com/2018/11/17/how-to-work-with-influencers/

9. Google paid $90 million to Andy Rubin when he was fired for sexual misconduct. https://www.nytimes.com/2018/10/25/technology/google-sexual-harassment-andy-rubin.html
10. The founder of TVF had to quit from his own company over charges of sexual misconduct. https://themorningcontext.com/a-coup-at-the-viral-fever
11. Employees have been the driving force behind employers dropping projects involving technologies like facial recognition. https://www.theverge.com/2020/6/8/21284683/ibm-no-longer-general-purpose-facial-recognition-analysis-software
12. Transgender rights. https://medium.com/s/story/google-workers-lost-a-leader-but-the-fight-will-continue-c487aa5fd2ba
13. Labour laws are being put away for a while by various states. This is undesirable. https://thewire.in/labour/labour-laws-changes-turning-clock-back
14. The pain of the pub will be far worse than the 2008 crisis says the founder of TeamLease. https://youtu.be/N1MlzX2Ei5g
15. Talent market places will first be a patchwork of general skills and then niche market places will appear. https://www.thehindubusinessline.com/specials/people-at-work/here-come-vertical-talent-markets/article28077589.ece
16. The rise in traffic for matrimonial sites may mean bad news for women. https://www.thehindu.com/business/online-matchmaker-sign-ups-increase-30/article31434245.ece
17. The pandemic has clearly impacted more women than men. https://www.nytimes.com/2020/06/09/world/asia/india-coronavirus-women-economy.html
18. Think with Google provides a look at the growing numbers of women gamers. https://www.thinkwithgoogle.com/intl/en-apac/trends-and-insights/play-like-a-girl-key-ways-to-engage-one-of-asias-fastest-growing-gaming-audiences/
19. Tomas Chamorro-Premuzic's book *Why do so many incompetent men become leaders* explores the research underlying this phenomenon. https://ideas.ted.com/why-do-so-many-incompetent-men-become-leaders-and-what-can-we-do-about-it/
20. Gen Z in the workplace. https://www.visualcapitalist.com/meet-generation-z-the-newest-member-to-the-workforce/
21. *The Patriot Act*. https://youtu.be/YytF2v7Vvw0
22. Noble House is an example of a vertical talent market in the gig economy. https://yourstory.com/2018/08/hr-talent-marketplace-noble-house-driving-gig-economy
23. The creative content producers have been hard hit by the pandemic. https://

www.straitstimes.com/asia/south-asia/casual-workers-hit-as-bollywood-comes-to-a-standstill

24. https://techcrunch.com/2019/03/30/remote-workers-and-nomads-represent-the-next-tech-hub/
25. I met Suvarchala while she working for Factor Daily, a media startup. https://factordaily.com/not-all-those-who-wander-are-lost-digital-nomads/
26. Madan Nagaldinne describes employee activism here. https://www.hrkatha.com/people/dialogue/the-right-people-policy-for-startups/

12

Dreamers, Unicorns, Market Shapers and Incumbents

If you view the growth of an enterprise through tangible measures like revenue, growth, profitability, etc., then the terms like Dreamers, Unicorns, Market Shapers and Incumbents would be limited to organisations. If you use the new drivers of growth—leadership, talent and culture, the human side of work, then, workers and workplaces starts emerging. Your focus turns from the tangible to the intangible. It is more about the mindset than anything else. The categorisation is more future-focused and up for debate. Inside every 'Market Shaper' is a brewing team of 'Incumbents'. In every 'Incumbent' business

lies a set of 'Dreamers' who could become 'Market Shapers'. The biggest Market Shaper in the history of business has to be COVID-19.

The Human Version of Growth

In my experience, I find organisations to be a lot like human beings. They start off as infants where they learn languages that help them communicate with the world. It is a combination of nature and nurture that explains how they behave as adults. During the phase of adolescence, human beings experience rapid growth in their body structure—they gain height and build muscle. The invisible hormonal changes drive what is externally visible. As humans grow into adulthood, they make choices, and these choices impact their future growth options.

The American-German psychologist Erik Erikson found that our personality develops through eight stages of development from infancy to adulthood. At each stage, the person experiences a challenge that impacts the psychosocial development of the individual.[1]

1. Trust: In the first eighteen months, a child develops a basic belief on whether others can be trusted or not. Later on in life, this assures the child that if there is a problem, others can be relied upon to help.

2. Independence: From eighteen months to three years, the child focuses on being independent. They exercise their free will and choice. This develops confidence in their ability to handle the world.

3. Purpose: During the three-to-five-years age range, children learn about interpersonal skills by playing with other children. They learn to experiment and take initiative. These are early experiences of leading others and of handling scenarios when others refuse to play by their rules.

4. Competency: During the five-to-twelve period, the peer group becomes very important in children's life. This is the time they discover early signs of their skills as they show signs of being a 'natural' in some areas. These could be sports or language or arts or some other field. At this stage, when they compete with their peers, they realise that they are better than others in some areas and average or below average in some others.

5. Identity: The period of adolescence, between twelve and eighteen, is when gender identity gets formed as a way of preparation for life as an adult. This is the time when occupational choices and gender choices get shaped. In some cultures, a certain occupation is associated with being a male. In another culture, the same occupation would be linked to being a female. This is the time for children to rebel and challenge the norms.

6. Love: Between the ages of eighteen and forty, people start to build deep relations with those outside of the family. They learn to experience love, warmth, safety and care in relationships. Avoiding intimacy, fearing commitment and relationships, can lead to isolation and loneliness.

7. Altruism: There is a time to leave a legacy, and it gets triggered between the ages of forty and sixty-five. The mid-life crisis often gets us to think of going beyond the self.

At this stage, people experience a need to create something that will outlast them. This is also a time when those who feel successful actively mentor and find successors. They get involved in community-building activities. At this stage, people create positive changes that will benefit other people.

8. Wisdom: This is the stage when people look back at their lives and take stock. This stage sets in around sixty-five years of age and lasts till death. When people feel theirs was a life well lived, it gives a feeling of completion. Else, it may lead to a feeling of having wasted one's life and that not enough time is left to make amends. Wisdom comes from a life lived fully.

Human to Human not B2B or B2C: Build Trust

When an organisation is formed, the leaders have to focus on gaining the trust of the employees, investors and customers. As we enter the post-pandemic world of work, trust between the employer and employee will need to be regenerated because many promises have been broken. When employers install keystroke tracking software or scan employee emails, rather than do it stealthily, employees must be given the freedom to opt out, if they so choose. Employees may feel the need to assure the employer that productivity will not suffer when they work out of remote locations. Many employers initially promised to treat the employees 'like family members' and then axed them when they were least expecting it. Every new beginning triggers the need for building trust in a relationship. That would be the first task of the leader.

Erikson's model can be a useful guide that connects the dots on why Silicon Valley is being questioned on its version of exploitative capitalism.

1. Consistent action—not slogans: Slogans generate scepticism unless backed up by action. Consistent action builds trust. Unlike when the Fortune 500 companies were questioned for leveraging the Black Lives Matter movement to show their social conscience only on social media. 'The number of female CEOs in the Fortune 500 hits an all-time record,' says *Fortune* magazine. We are impressed with the list initially, until we see that only thirty-seven out of 500 companies are led by women.[2]

2. Stay in sync with social issues: Responding to social issues is now an important element of organisations having to take a stance. It builds trust. Especially in a scenario when people are working from home, there is no distinction between social and business issues. Leaders have to be authentic and respond to social issues. Authentic responses build human connections. The Black Lives Matter movement resonated with the bias across consumers in Asia where fair skin is seen to be the universal definition of beauty. Unilever will rename Fair & Lovely, a skin-lightening cream that has been criticised for promoting negative stereotypes around dark skin tones. It will also remove references to 'whitening' or 'lightening' on the products, which are sold across Asia.

3. From B2B or B2C, it is now H2H: While organisations often try to cash in on social occasions to sell their products, they also rose to the challenge the pandemic posed. Indian brands like Fevicol and Santoor, and global brands like Audi, Volkswagen and McDonald's distanced parts of their logos to emphasise the message of social distancing.[3]

Leaders have to stop thinking of customers and employees in a hierarchical setting where they are almost servile in the way they respond to customers and insensitive to employees' needs. This is the time to make the organisation human. That is the common baseline that connects customers and employees.

It is no longer about B2B (business to business) or B2C (business to consumer). Everything is H2H (human to human).

The Four-Speed Model Is Driven by Intangible Factors

The convergence of social shifts, wealth distribution, political movements and technological innovations has created the perfect storm. The COVID-19 crisis simply accelerated the changes that were already underway. When we look at 2020, we will see this as the year when an irreversible shift happened.

Managing polarities and intangibles: It is the time of many polarities. Many businesses have gone bankrupt, while some have made profits. Yet others raised billions of dollars in cash. Alliances built over decades were broken. It is a time when the work-worker-workplace equilibrium has seen radical shifts simultaneously. The Four-Speed growth model is a simple categorisation that can help decision makers think of the intangible and invisible aspects that have often been given inadequate attention.

We have been told that what gets measured gets done. This has created a hierarchy in the organisation where quantifiable measures decide the relative importance of functions. It has given rise to a form of capitalism that is corrosive. The leaders of listed companies are overtly driven by quarterly profits incentivised by compensations that reward profits at all costs. Often, the result is products that are good for the shareholders but are bad for the environment, societies and employees.

We built products that incentivise hatred, divisive behaviour, self-harm and nudge consumerism among those who can ill afford it. Businesses have used loopholes in the law to keep workers on third party rolls so that they can remove one single 'vendor' and get rid of hundreds of workers without catching the attention of the media or whistle-blowers.

The pandemic has given us a chance to rethink what matters. Organisations, nations and individuals can use the four categories to find patterns. This is much like Erikson's model where the baby decides whether the world can largely be trusted or if it should be sceptical. That shapes behaviour.

Intangible factors create value: While financial metrics, supply chain and product-market fit remain crucial, these are areas where decades of leaders have documented their experiences, thousands of case studies have been written and the path has been well trodden. The tangible factors are well known. The intangibles are the new growth drivers. In *Prosperity*, Colin Mayer says, 'Forty years ago, 80 per cent of the market value of US corporations was attributable to tangible assets—plant, machinery, and buildings—as against intangibles—licenses, patents, and research and development. Today, intangibles account for 85 per cent of the market value of US corporations.' The power and influence of firms used to come from tangible things that could be measured and counted—number of employees, number of offices across the world, goods sold, return on investment, etc. The tangible factors remain important, but much of the firm's value comes from intangible factors like brand power (like Nike), design (think Apple), sustainability (think Tesla), data (think Google), influence- and opinion-shaping (think Facebook), boundarylessness (think Amazon), payments (think crypto currency), entertainment (think Netflix), creativity (think Adobe) ... the list goes on. These Market Shapers are changing how we live. In each one of the categories, there are Unicorns (like Space X) who are creating new categories of work that have never existed before.

Leveraging ecosystems: The healthcare ecosystem is a good example of the future we are heading towards. Life sciences is being influenced by major innovations in diverse fields like Big Data, Analytics, Artificial Intelligence, Virtual Reality, the Internet of Things. It is giving rise to new fields like Digital Therapeutics. Regulatory bodies are often stumped by these changes. The field of Digital Therapeutics is an example of a Dreamer. The field itself is evolving—even though the research in many of these fields has been going on for decades. Spurred by the travel restrictions during the pandemic, telemedicine is thriving. There are apps being developed that leverage the mobile phone to replace lab tests.

When something moves online, a new ecosystem has to be created. Education is in that twilight zone. There will be many iterations as the world figures out how to engage learners across all ages. This may need an ecosystem that brings together different fields of psychology, neuroscience, behavioural economists, incentive designers, storytellers, mobile platform creators, augmented reality and virtual reality ecosystems, and video game designers. The current model on speaking to a camera and transferring content is severely limiting and flawed.

The learner is distracted, time starved and has a parallel universe of choices that are more engaging. The content creators must leverage the best technology and their creativity to shape the learning experience. The role of the teacher will be to motivate, inspire and coach the learner. The ecosystem of learning has to be reconfigured to make learning a deeply rewarding experience.

The top talent always knows which employer's name is a liability on the resume and which one is something to be proud of.

The work ecosystem is a work-in-progress: The ecosystem of work must be designed to rethink what it means to work. Work must be more than a source of livelihood. The ecosystem must be designed to make it a source of dignity, inclusion and meaning. Maybe there is a need to bring in ethicists and philosophers as we get back to the drawing board. Geography and demography are the parents of innovation. Japanese marine scientists built a simulator to train shipping captains. But now, they are using the simulator to build algorithms that could potentially go into 'autonomous ships'. Mitsui and many other Japanese firms have been working on similar efforts since 2016. Japan has 400 islands that are hard to reach other than by ship. More than half of the 21,000 mariners in Japan's coastal shipping industry are over fifty years old. More than 25 per cent are more than sixty years old. Shipping firms are not attracting talent. In the future, we may see a different kind of shipping industry.[4]

Stay Relevant. Stay Interesting

The 'Dreamers and Unicorns' framework gives us a chance to rethink the underexplored growth levers.

Dreamers, Unicorns, Market Shapers and, of course, Incumbents are rough categories. They are not prison walls. In each stage of growth, one of the three drivers—leadership, talent strategy and culture—become the starting point of driving change. Every Dreamer wants to experience scaling up like a Unicorn and have the global presence of a Market Shaper. Every Market Shaper and Incumbent wants to have the agility of a Dreamer and the scale-up pace of a Unicorn.

Is it harder for a startup to scale or is it tougher for a large organisation to be nimble? Both have their unique strengths. The giant enterprises have great brand awareness, and a stable set of customers and presence across geographies and markets. That is just what a startup does not have. Imagine the power of such collaborations. But when a large firm acquires a smaller firm, the firm becomes an insignificant part of the new ecosystem. The band of Dreamers feel dwarfed by the bureaucracy and scale of the big firm. Their founders get disillusioned and the innovation machine of the Dreamers stop.

A vibrant talent brand that attracts the best must be a great combination of strong tangible factors like finance, supply chain, product development, etc., along with strong intangible factors like leadership, talent and culture, and leaders who lead by vision rather than supervision. A talent brand that is a talent magnet for not only the current skills but also the ones that will be needed in the future. Investments in learning and development make that happen. A culture of inclusion and openness makes it valuable.

The Relevant-Interesting Framework to Build the Talent Brand

1. Being relevant: Organisations have to stay relevant so that the product-market fit is retained across their businesses. That means being relevant to customers across different demographics and geographies. This can be done through product innovations and making wise choices about the product and service portfolio or the technologies being invested in. It is based on logic, analysis, science, data and technology, quantitative research excellence and big data analysis. These are tangible areas that firms have had to address as they grew. Brands who aspire to position themselves as Thought Leaders release white papers, research reports and presentations that have millions of slides packed with dense content. In an attention-deficit world, boredom is a trigger to start surfing for options.

2. Being interesting: We live in times when people have had an opportunity to listen to the best storytellers of the world through TED talks, YouTube or Instagram videos and millions of movies from the world's best directors. When we watch a movie in the theatres, we have to sit through the entire movie even if we do not like it. Now, we simply choose a different movie or show to watch. Even if the content is relevant, if it does not grab your attention, people switch to something more engaging. A talent brand must avoid becoming frivolous by not taking steps that the talent base views as relevant. 'Employee engagement' not backed by meaningful work, skill development and opportunities for growth are also ineffective. Being interesting builds an emotional connect that is hard to substitute with the competitor's cold facts.

The below two-by-two matrix serves as a quick summary of the idea. Which quadrant would describe the talent brand of your organisation?

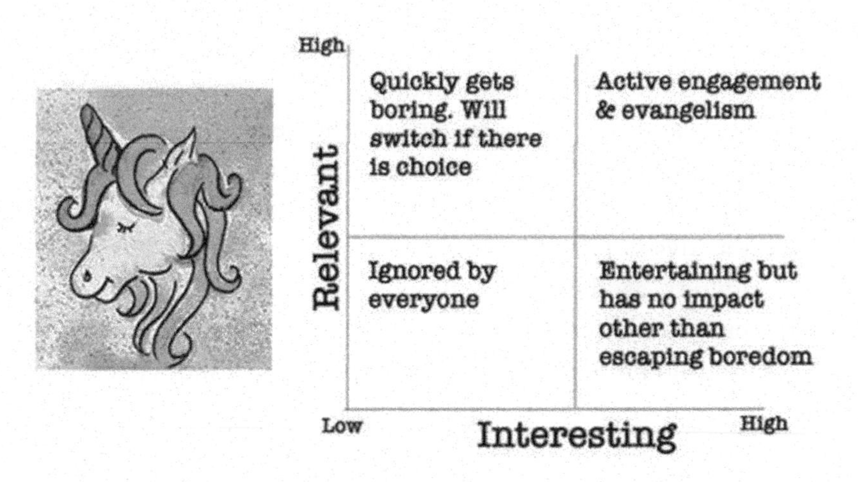

Low on Relevance-Low on Interest: You are on your way to becoming irrelevant to the current consumer—if you already are not. The Ambassador car in India used to be synonymous with India. Not anymore. The old fleet of cars will slowly fade away and have only nostalgia value. The graveyard of the business world is littered with the corpses of businesses that have stopped having relevance. They never invested in innovation, their corporate governance structures were weak and the leadership teams were incompetent because they failed to adapt and arrest the slide. The company neither appeals to the consumer's reasoning nor emotions. When an organisation starts getting ignored by top talent, that should be a moment for the leader to formally assess their leadership team's capabilities and succession planning systems. Without addressing the product-market fit, flawless operations and a robust financial system, it is hard to be relevant. Or attract great talent. Chances are that the board is made up of friends and family who are either incompetent or conniving with those pushing the business over the edge.

High on Relevance-Low on Interest: This is typical of a company that has competed only on outdoing the rest by simply putting their head down and working. The leadership may not have noticed the competitive arena getting crowded by many emerging players. Paytm is in that category. It grew to be a Unicorn and built enormous goodwill as a first mover. But now, the product differentiation is getting more and more blurred. Investing in growing leaders at all levels, a talent strategy that grows more leaders beyond the corporate office and a culture that makes rapid growth sustainable would create the reputation of Paytm being a talent magnet. Growth on steroids as a Dreamer may come from everyone putting in crazy hours at work. As a Unicorn, when everyone is working from home, the people managers have to be trained to work with a distributed team. Focusing on the talent brand and other intangibles would be the way to go. Most successful B2B brands are guilty of living in a world where they limit themselves to communicating their information in the most depressingly boring and uncreative way possible. Here is a simple test to know if you are uninteresting. Interchange your company logo with the five biggest competitors and ask your employees to figure out which website content belongs to your company. If most of your employees fail the 'website test', your clients find your products undifferentiated. The intangible elements take the product to new pockets of consumers.

Low on Relevance-High on Interest: These are the businesses where the CEO is better known than the product itself. The leaders invest in brand-building by making noise on social media and the business press. Unfortunately, that makes it harder and harder for the business to succeed. Chances are that the business model needs to be looked at closely to see if the assumptions that got the business started have changed. Rethink the competitive landscape and strategy. Startups often use a moment like this to pivot. Odeo began as a place to find podcasts. When Apple's iTunes began to take over the podcast space, Odeo did a pivot and focused on building a microblogging platform called Twitter. The founding team of Burbn had built a check-in app that had gaming elements from Mafia Wars and a photo element as well. They removed everything except the photo element that allowed people to use 'filters' to improve the look of their photos. That is the origin story of Instagram. Relevance gets built by focusing on the tangible, time-tested aspects of running a business—making it cash positive much like the way the founders of Nutrikraft did. The collapse of WeWork in recent times left Masayoshi Son red-faced. After Softbank signed a billion-dollar cheque, 8,000 'WeWorkers' were transported to a field outside of London, where they camped in tents for three days. Lorde performed, and the new-age guru Deepak Chopra led a meditation. The cost was estimated by some at $2,500 per head just for flights.

DREAMERS & UNICORNS ...

A bunch of friends in college or a group of colleagues or a few like-minded people come together to solve a problem. They have a fresh new way of addressing a gap in the market. The desire to solve an unsolved problem creates a Dreamer. A group of people who are equally enthused come together to form a startup. They work like a group of possessed people. A Dreamer can be a project team trying to create a new process or a project, or turn around a business everyone has given up on. Dreamers try to solve problems that have no known solutions. They symbolise new beginnings. They operate in places that are empty maps. They see what is unseen, try to decipher languages which no one is aware of. Every Dreamer is a 'Tech-Humanist' as Kate O'Neil would put it.

Most founders know how to build a PRODUCT They rarely learn how to BUILD AN ORGANISATION

A Dreamer Creates New Definitions

A Dreamer is just a way of reframing an idea, a product or a novice in a field. It is someone who can become a novice ever so often—even in a field where they have spent a lifetime. It is about the obsessive desire to build something new and walk down the path less travelled. For Dreamers, the size of their dreams is bigger than the resources they have.

After seven years of clinical trials, the FDA approved EndeavorRX (made by Akili Interactive) as a medicine for children between eight and twelve years of age suffering from attention deficit hyperactivity disorder (ADHD). It is the first video game that can legally be marketed and prescribed as a medicine in the US. This changes the definition of what a drug is. It blurs the lines of several fields. It has been designed by video-gamers working with scientists and experts to create a game that aims to stimulate those parts of the brain that help a person focus. Digital therapeutics is a thing now.[5]

Every startup is a Dreamer. But every Dreamer is not a startup. A business organisation may be born from the dreams of a single individual, but a Dreamer organisation or team is born when a group of people work together to address an opportunity. Dreamers are everywhere. They are working inside Unicorns thinking of the next big idea or fine-tuning the current product. The Dreamer symbolises the perpetual beta mindset. When the startup starts reaching consumers across multiple cities or maybe even a couple of countries, they are treading the path to become a Unicorn. When consumers in every country line up to welcome the Unicorn, a Market Shaper is born. A Market Shaper combines the innovation of a Dreamer and the speed and scale of a Unicorn to become a benchmark in leadership, talent pool and unique culture.

Never Stop Dreaming

But being a Market Shaper is no insurance against becoming irrelevant. Hindustan Motors Limited (HM), part of the Birla group, was India's pioneering car manufacturing company set up in 1942. Their car design never changed for the sixty years that it spent on the roads of India. Once the consumer had a choice of cars, it was a slow, lingering death for the organisation. Arguably, even their research and development section did not have a single innovation to boast of. Not having the Dreamer's DNA is a recipe for irrelevance. Unicorns have to ensure that they do not lose the hunger of the Dreamer. If Incumbents have to become relevant all over again, they need to be able to partner with a Dreamer to rethink their business model and culture.

A rock band like The Beatles began performing live in England in 1961 and continued to perform in various clubs during their visit to Hamburg, West Germany, until 1962. During this phase, the line-up was John Lennon, Paul McCartney, George Harrison, Stuart Sutcliffe and Pete Best. Sutcliffe left, Best was fired and Ringo Starr became the drummer. The popularity of songs like 'Love Me Do' and 'She Loves You' established their appeal beyond England. These chart-topping numbers established them as a Unicorn to watch out for. It was during their appearance on the Ed Sullivan Show in 1964 that their screaming hysterical fans turned them into Market Shapers.[6]

The product-market fit turns the Dreamer into a Unicorn and then a Market Shaper. But the ability to focus on the human element sustains the organisation over time. The intense friendship between the four members of The Beatles helped them create the greatest body of work in the next seven years. Their strength was also the reason why they did not survive as an organisation. In 2012, Harvard Business School professor Noam Wasserman studied 10,000 founders for his book *The Founder's Dilemma*. His research found that 65 per cent of startups fail as a result of co-founder conflict.[7]

The Rolling Stones are an English rock band formed in 1962. They have not been very creative but have survived as a band for decades. They have consciously or otherwise run themselves as a business and not as a group of friends who make music. They are colleagues in a corporation whose product is music. One of the most striking differences between The Rolling Stones and The Beatles is this: 'The Beatles split up after a mere seven years at the top, whereas the Stones are still going. One startup flashed brightly and burned out; the other established itself as a long-running corporation.'[8]

Every Dreamer wants to grow to be a Unicorn and then a Market Shaper. Every Market Shaper wants to have the spirit of a Dreamer. Is it harder for a startup to grow or is it tougher for a large organisation to be nimble? How much of the organisation is focused on creating the focus for the customer?

The founders are often people who have very strong technical skills (most are engineers). They have been trained to think in binary terms and human beings are anything but binary. So, what they get right are all the tangible aspects of the business—funding, technology and sales. They miss all the intangible elements that drive growth.

Beyond financial capital, they rarely focus on human capital strategies. Most founders know that they need to hire people and have strong talent acquisition teams, but rarely invest time or resources in managing the talent and culture of the Dreamer. When people work together, they have to craft roles, boundaries and hierarchies. Most founders know how to build a product. They do not know how to build an organisation. Growth creates complexity. Roles, boundaries, hierarchies and understanding motivations of people helps build organisations. Dreamers have to keep one eye on the future and build an organisation that is ready for the high-octane growth that they will experience as Unicorns. An old saying in the army was, 'Train intensively during peace times, if you don't want to bleed in war.'

1. Roles: Many co-founders and founding teams are made up of friends who have gone to the same college and have similar educational backgrounds. They become a bit like The Beatles—all four band members could sing. The roles are rarely sharply defined. Each one pitches in to perform every function. As the business grows, this becomes a source of confusion. The team members of the startup have to seek formal or informal approval of each founding member regardless of his/her competence. Dreamers have to often pivot their entire business multiple times to finally discover the exact product-market fit that makes their business grow. It is important to take the time periodically to define the roles. Roles create certainty, but when the context changes, it needs to be redefined. When the business outgrows the competence of a team member, it is hard to let go of the person because the roles don't have clear outcomes that are redefined with each pivot. It is common for founding teams to carry incompetent 'friends' who do much damage to the organisation. In the absence of clear roles, loyalty wipes out the need to upskill and stay competent enough to deliver the role as the business scales. When the founders let go of an outside hire for not delivering, the rest of the organisation wonders why the same yardstick is not applied to the roles held by the founding team members.

2. Boundaries and hierarchies: When roles are defined, they need boundaries. While boundaries decide what is acceptable and what is not, the hierarchy helps to clarify how things will get decided when people disagree. Startup founders rarely have a CHRO in the early days who can define roles, boundaries and organisation structures, not just for the current size of the business but also for the organisation that they want to become and which will continue to retain speed and agility. Human relationships work best when boundaries and hierarchies are defined. A boundary helps establish accountability. Resource allocation can be done to match the deliverables expected of a role.

Dreamers survive on short sprints and projects. As the organisation grows beyond the founding team, decisions can no longer be taken over a drink shared in the evening. Startups are famous for breaking up marriages and friendships. When a newly married founding team member wants to spend the weekend at home, the others feel let down. Employees in Dreamer teams often have to make difficult choices. They have to choose between a spouse and 'frelleagues' (friends who are colleagues).

Dreamers rarely define how decisions will get taken if everyone disagrees. A group of friends sitting around a coffee table with their laptops do not need hierarchy (though it still gets informally defined). When a group of friends with similar backgrounds challenge each other, after days and nights of intense debate, some method of resolving the impasse has to be agreed upon, without which bitterness creeps in, especially if someone more vocal manages to push through their decision about someone else's function. Hierarchy is about planning for the future when the Dreamers will have to bring in specialists (e.g. CEO, COO, CFO and, God forbid, a CHRO) into the organisation. That is when the roles, boundaries and hierarchies really come in handy.

3. Varying motives: The founder are often driven by the dream that brought them together. Hitting that exact unmet need of the consumer is the biggest motivator of the founders and the early founding team. It is no surprise that the founders are usually customer-obsessed. For most entrepreneurs, money is like the report card. It tells that that they are moving towards their goal and the product that they created has found an ever-growing market. They are therefore often disappointed to see a large exit of people after an IPO or after their employee stock ownership plans (ESOPs) have vested. The founders kick themselves for believing that these people were consumed by the same dream that motivated the founding team. Even more heartbreaking for the founder is when people of the founding team express their desire to gain some visible signs of hierarchy and success that act as signalling devices to society. It is even more heartbreaking when some of the founding team members quit after a massive payout. Unscrupulous founders have been equally guilty of verbally promising equity to team members and then refusing to honour the commitment and offering to convert them to ESOPs with vesting periods spread over the next few years. Equity in a company is different from ESOPs. Direct equity means you own a percentage of the company, which may or may not have a waiting (vesting) period and you receive the money in three or four instalments.

ESOPs are given to employees as part of their overall compensation package. It is a right to buy a certain number of company shares at a fixed, throwaway price with a number of performance clauses and vesting periods and non-compete clauses thrown in. Being unaware of human motivations creates challenges of talent retention. The core goals, values, drivers and interests that determine what we desire and strive to attain could vary for every person. They range from recognition, power, aesthetics, money, altruism, affiliation, tradition, security, science and work culture.[9]

Case: Nutrikraft Sustainable and Profitable, But Not a Unicorn

Nutrikraft grew but never became a Unicorn. Yet, they had what many Unicorns, despite billion-dollar valuations, do not have. They were a 'sustainable' and 'profitable' company with a turnover of Rs 1,000 crore. This is their story as told to me by 'NK'—a co-founder of Nutrikraft. NK did not want his name revealed.

When three IIM graduates left their job in 2004 to start Nutrikraft, the combined capital they started with was Rs 100,000. Banks would not fund them without the collateral of assets. No venture capitalist or private equity firm wanted to invest in their firm. Raising funds was hard in 2004. Their product, chicken feed, was seen to be a commodity. This private limited company had three shareholders and all of them were operating shareholders.

Before starting Nutrikraft, they were all working with a large Indian company and had been bitten by the entrepreneurial bug. Nutrikraft was built with the learnings they had gathered from their previous employers.

In 2018, Nutrikraft was bought by a large private equity (PE) firm.

Theirs is the classic story of a Dreamer. When they started, they had a common dream. Their key insight was to take a commoditised product and create a branded high-quality product that would capture the market. NK was the largest shareholder and the most experienced of the three co-founders. The two other co-founders, GR and CS, had been his teammates when they were working at the Indian company.

1. Leadership: NK looked back at his journey by sharing some key ideas. He said, 'The co-founders must remember never to bring the leadership team differences to the board. When we run a business, there are bound to be differences in the approach. After all, everyone has different levels of risk-taking. It needs one person to take the final call, but only after each co-founder has been convinced. This is best done in person. I would spend time with each co-founder till all three of us were aligned on the strategy and the choices. I had more experience than the others even when we were working at our previous employer.'

Build trust: Nutrikraft's growth strategy was built on three pillars—cost, quality and branding. 'We had a contract with a European firm to co-brand our product for a few years. We always provided higher quality than our competitors. It lowered our operating margins, but we did not sell on credit. That allowed us the time to build the buyer's trust in our brand. Our goal was to make Nutrikraft synonymous with high quality. When the next rung of leaders saw the company's success, they felt they were right in their decision to join the team of Dreamers. Their confidence kept the team in the field motivated.'

Document future scenarios involving founders: NK spoke about the need to agree in writing how the company will be run. That results in acrimony and misunderstanding in the leadership team. The leaders had a written agreement that they would avoid any 'conflict of interest'. No employee could have business dealings with any organisation where family and friends were involved. They had agreed even before they started the business that should any of the founders quit, they would lose all shares. Every possible scenario from the decision-making process to compensation methodology for every employee (including founders) was agreed upon *in writing*. That document became the living guide of the leaders whenever they came to a crossroads.

2. Talent: 'While hiring for the field staff, we looked at people who were the heads of the family and for whom that job mattered. In setting up factories in different parts of the country, Nutrikraft hired retirees from the same industries as the consultant. These people had thirty-five to forty years of experience in building factories. As long as the person can do the job, and he wants to work to utilise his experience, why not employ a retiree?' NK asked. Their inclusive approach towards talent paid rich dividends.

3. Culture: Nutrikraft did not have separate departments in the organisation. They kept the operating principles to a minimum. 'From day one, we decided that we would not sell on credit. The distributors would pay cash and buy our product. Offering thirty-day credit was the norm in the market, but that would have reduced our cash flow. When we sold the business, there were no debts on our books. We had about six leaders of the business. We met every quarter to focus on quality and cost. When it came to salary and promotions, employees knew that if they felt a decision was unfair, we would have no problem in changing the decision, even after the increment letters had been released to all the employees. I also knew when we sold the business that the next phase of growth would need a very different approach.'

The Nutrikraft story is the typical story of a Dreamer. The co-founders' dream is the basis of the business. When someone joins the team, they operate in a frugal manner. There is a very high sense of ownership in the team. Everyone is driven by a sense of purpose.

I saw the same fervour in Practo—a healthcare startup I consulted with for a year. Their website says it all. 'We are dreamers, thinkers and doers rolled into one. Together, we want to improve the healthcare experience for all humanity.'

If You Are a Dreamer

Leadership

1. The founders must frequently ask if they are the bottleneck and coming in the way of growth of the organisation (they probably are). In the early days, all decisions, big or small, bubble up to the founder/founding team. It is likely that the complexity of the business has outgrown the founding team. Having a coach to address the founding team's personal effectiveness helps. Having a coach and mentor for the leadership team can bring in the 'outside in' view they lack.
2. Communicating the changes and challenges can often cause frequent spells of despair or euphoria. Both may be distractions. Communication strategy and frequency, especially to the employees, needs careful thinking.
3. Personality impacts leadership styles. Building self-awareness can be a powerful way to keep the leadership team in sync with the business growth.

Talent

1. The most complex part of running the business is often the most neglected—the talent strategy. Someone who is great at running the business when there are fifty employees is probably not as effective when they have 100 or 1,000 employees. That includes even the founding team and early-stage employees who joined when the organisation

could not pay salaries. Scaling up the leadership muscle of the Dreamers is directly correlated with their ability to scale up the organisation when they start operating across multiple locations.

2. Invest in building people management skills in everyone before they start leading a team. Teach people how to hire, set goals, review progress against milestones, coach people and take tough calls. Most leaders in Dreamers' teams have had limited experience of running teams. That may reduce the effectiveness of the C-suite as you scale.
3. Upgrade leadership skills. People can become obsolete even in their twenties. The founding team and early hires must reskill themselves. Not having the skills to scale maybe the single biggest barrier to becoming a Unicorn.

Culture

1. In case of Dreamers, the word 'process' becomes a red flag. Those who have worked in large organisations get reminded of the mindless bureaucracy that used to come in the way. Determined to keep their flexibility, Dreamers forget that there is a sweet spot for balancing processes. Freedom without unleashing anarchy and having processes without becoming bureaucratic are tough balances to find.
2. Investing in the technology to manage the employee experience matters as much as having a terrific customer experience. Mobile-based SaaS systems can provide the collaboration, opportunity and flexibility that an ERP system may not.

3. Collaborating with Unicorns and Incumbents may provide great opportunities for Dreamers to build their brand and get access to a larger customer base.

Family Owned Businesses

The Credit Suisse Family 1000 is a proprietary global database of a thousand companies built on a 'bottom-up' basis by Credit Suisse analysts and launched in 2017. More than 50 per cent of the top thirty best-performing family-owned companies in Asia, excluding Japan, are from India.

Family-owned companies have been defined as:

- Direct shareholding by founders or descendants is at least 20 per cent; or
- Voting rights held by the founders or descendants is at least 20 per cent.[10]

Sonny Iqbal co-heads global executive search firm Egon Zehnder's global family business advisory practice. Their research showed that the two big causes of failure of family businesses are the lack of succession planning and patchy corporate governance. Independent directors are often a motley crew of friends and family who rarely engage with the employees of the company or do enough prior homework where they can challenge the choices of the CEO and the leadership team. In some cases, the genuflecting independent directors are anything but independent. The role of the family, the board and management must be laid out because in case of family businesses, the relationships between family members seep into the working of the CEO and the leadership team, as we have seen in cases from Tata

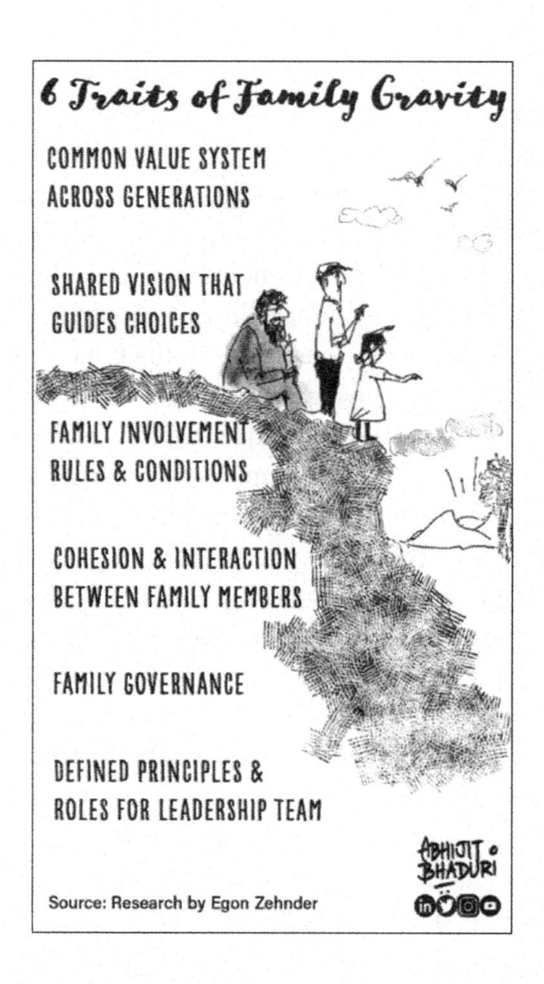

boardroom battles to Singhania succession dramas in recent times. Fiat, the Italian auto group run by the Agnelli family, went through five CEOs and three chairmen in two years before bringing in an outsider to lead it.

What is common to family businesses that stay the course over three to four generations? Egon Zehnder interviewed more than fifty executives at twenty-eight leading family businesses across the Americas, Europe and

Asia, surveyed 4,000 Family Business Network International (FBNI) members and did detailed analysis of fifteen family businesses from a wide variety of sectors around the world.

What makes some businesses last over generations? Egon Zehnder describes it as 'family gravity': the values and priorities that endure across generations.

According to Sonny Iqbal, 'In our research, we found that third- and fourth-generation families had recognised and retained their family gravity.

'Family gravity enjoys a unique position as the strongest force in a family business that impacts perpetuity. It comprises the values and priorities that endure across generations and the way in which these affect relationships, governance and running of the business. Typically, business leaders rely on metrics to help them gauge the performance and direction of their business. Yet, family business leaders have to do more than that. They must also closely observe and reflect upon the dynamics within the family and the relationship between the family and the business with perpetuity as the objective. I refer to this sensitivity for the family-business relationship as family gravity.'

Family gravity has six traits:

1. A value system which unites members across generations.
2. A shared vision that helps the family navigate during periods of high ambiguity.
3. Rules of engagement regarding the family's involvement.
4. Cohesion and interaction between the family members based on mutual respect.

5. Strong family governance that attracts and retains top professionals from every field. This also needs disciplined succession (a particular area of weakness in Indian family businesses).
6. Articulated leadership principles and roles.

Personality is a more accurate predictor of leadership behaviour. Think of any institution and look at how two successive leaders have led a nation, an NGO, a startup or a Market Shaper. The job description remains the same. It is the leader's personality that holds clues.

The Personality of Indian Entrepreneurs

In December 2018, I was invited to speak at 'Demo Day', a huge gathering of Dreamers in Bangalore—the hub of India's startup ecosystem. I shared the research done by Pradnya Parasher on the personality of the Indian entrepreneurs. The research was done in 2012–13, in which 65 per cent of the 256 entrepreneurs who were studied were part of a twelve-week accelerator programme. Their age ranged from twenty-five to forty-five.

1. Very high levels of drive and ambition: They are independent and creative risk-takers. This is what leads them to have an extraordinary opinion about their own capability. On a side note, I have lost track of how many founders model themselves on Steve Jobs—his poor behaviour with colleagues and sartorial sense but not his talent for design and technology. Too little of drive and ambition means you cannot set bold goals. Too much of it and the goals become unrealistic driven by the delusion of infallibility. Narcissism is the dark side of drive and ambition.

'Narcissism—a personality trait encompassing grandiosity, arrogance, self-absorption, entitlement, fragile self-esteem, and hostility—is an attribute of many powerful leaders. Narcissistic leaders have grandiose belief systems and leadership styles, and are generally motivated by their needs for power and admiration rather than empathetic concern for the constituents and institutions they lead. However, narcissists also possess the charisma and grand vision that are vital to effective leadership,' say Seth Rosenthal and Todd L. Pittinsky.[11]

2. Creative, edgy and restless: Dealing with standard practices and procedures is tiresome for Dreamers. Scaling up is by definition all about having standard approaches that anybody can replicate with some training. They resist supervision and help in ideas they know nothing about. Their restlessness leads to many ideas being incubated but without having closure and are marked by poor execution. New hires into startups spend days together trying to learn what should be a standard operating procedure. Creative ideas and vision have to be balanced with powerful execution. That needs clear rules, boundaries and operating procedures. Too many rules and approvals reek of bureaucracy. Too little of it is chaos. A balance has to be found.

3. Distracted by new ideas: Entrepreneurs are easily distracted by the next shiny object. They start and stop new product lines so often that execution suffers. There is a thin line that divides brilliance and temperamental narcissism. A frustrated employee of a well-known fintech startup said, 'He doesn't know what he wants—even if he does, he doesn't have the time to tell us. No one can tell you how many businesses or projects or service lines our company has. Only he can tell you for sure. Sometimes, I doubt if he knows it either.'

For many Dreamers, lack of leaders at multiple levels, no investment in building soft skills and inability to build a culture that makes the growth sustainable is a missed opportunity. Having the right co-founder can be the antidote that Dreamers miss.

How to Pick a Co-Founder for Your Startup

Professor Adam Grant says, 'Liking someone is not a sign that you'll like working with them. Having similar interests doesn't mean you'll have similar goals or working styles. Choose collaborators who share your values and complement your skills.'

According to some estimates, almost 40 per cent of the startups get formed between friends. When businesses are built on the basis of friendship, the results are often disastrous.

Friendships can be formed through social interactions. Your golfing or tennis buddy may not be your best business partner. Watching the patterns during work collaborations can provide vital clues. Does the person work well with people? How does the person behave when they fail? Is the person continuously learning and reinventing their expertise? When there is group work to be done, does the person do their share of work or do they shirk? Does the person consistently go above and beyond when they work on a task?

Professor Grant summarises, 'If you have enjoyed working with someone before, then there is a great possibility that you will collaborate well as Dreamers. You can get to

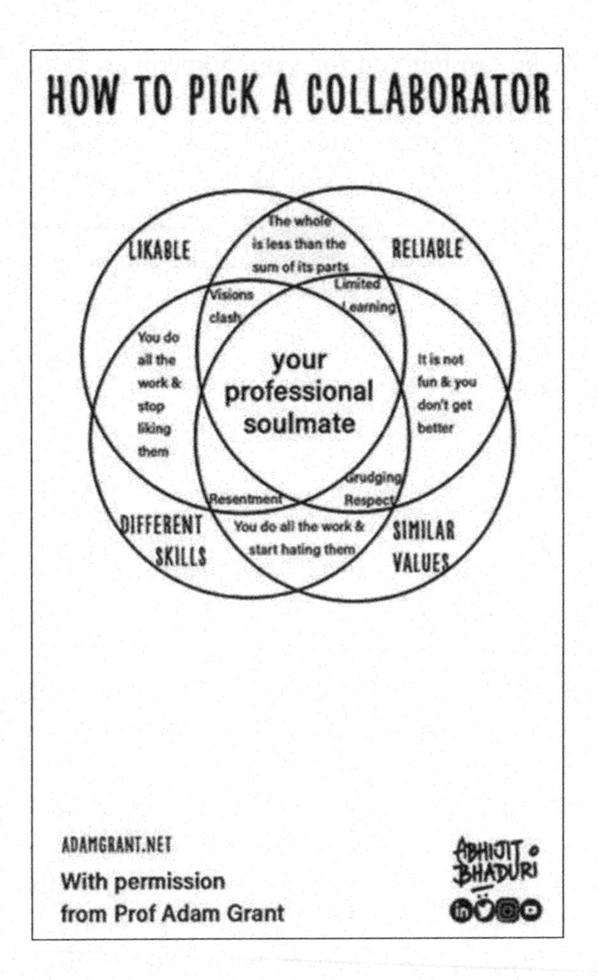

know a friend well through hanging out socially. But you can only get to know a cofounder well by collaborating. By working together prior to founding a startup together, people are able to answer some fundamental questions:

Do we share a core set of values?

Are our working habits compatible?

What are our comparative strengths and weaknesses?

How will we handle conflict when it inevitably arises?'[12]

THE UNICORN

The Dreamers that manage to survive the initial period of trials and tribulation are rewarded by the next phase of growth. They become Unicorns—a phase that can be best described as the scariest roller-coaster that you have ever ridden. Every Market Shaper was also once a Unicorn. So were most Incumbents. Taking the product to multiple geographies needs a new set of leaders at each level and location where the organisation intends to operate who reinforce a culture that creates inclusion (an important element as the business opens up new offices) without compromising on innovation. A Unicorn has its impact in a few markets. A Market Shaper changes the way people live and work across age groups and countries. Sometimes the line is blurred.

1. Take it global: But being able to grow the user base outside of the home turf is an important metric the Unicorns have to keep in mind. As Starbucks has expanded its market to other geographies, thanks to its brand power, its international business grew to 30 per cent of its $26.5 billion in revenue outside the US. The revenue from its international markets is growing faster than the US market. Starbucks runs more than 30,000 stores in eighty markets.

2. Leverage digital experiences: In case of Nike, the growth from its international operations contributes almost 60 per cent of the revenue. Nike learned from the virus-related shutdowns in China in the first few months of 2020. In Greater China, Nike's revenue was more than $1.68 billion. Nike quickly partnered with Adobe to use the Adobe

Experience Manager and recreate an in-store shopping experience. Consumers pay for the experience. Nike knows that.[13]

There's a Unicorn Who Is Probably a Market Shaper Already

That Unicorn has to be e-sports. Some describe it as the future of entertainment. Esports (also known as electronic sports, e-sports, or eSports) is a form of sport competition using video games. Fortnite is an online survival video game, developed by the closely held Epic Games and released in 2017, that has been at the epicentre of this growth. Fortnite players use 'V-bucks'—virtual currency used by Fortnite players for in-game purchases on gaming consoles, PCs and Macs. In mid-August 2020, Apple and Google removed Fortnite, one of the world's most popular video games, from their app stores in an escalating battle over the fees they charge developers to distribute their software and process in-app purchases. When Market Shapers pick battles with a firm, it is a sure sign that another Market Shaper has jumped into the swimming pool.

Esports started to hit the mainstream news in 2019 with big-prize pool tournaments like the $30 million Fortnite World Cup (2019) and the $34 million Dota 2 International 9. But this is a movement that started sometime back. Some trace it to Korea during the time of the Asian financial crisis in 2007 when unemployed people were looking for things to do while out of work. That coupled with faster internet speeds, cheaper data, cloud storage, better hardware and software proved to be a terrific fuel that has made esports a hypergrowth model.

The Economist compares it with traditional sports like tennis and argues why Fortnite could be included in the Olympics. 'There are perhaps only 200 tennis stars in the world who can make a living from playing in tournaments. By contrast "League of Legends", a fantasy e-sports game played by teams of five, supports over 1,000 on good wages. Its World Championship final last year was watched by 44 million people.'[14]

League of Legends players in America are guaranteed a minimum salary of $75,000—most make close to $400,000. The challenge for the esports industry is to build in checks and balances that plague anything that scales up. In 2014, #stopgamergate trended on Twitter to highlight the plight of women in what was then a $70 billion industry.

The Unicorn's Nemesis: Building a Culture of Inclusion

The gaming industry was accused of discrediting or intimidating outspoken critics of the male-dominated gaming culture by calling for death threats and sexual assaults against the women who spoke up.

In 2019, the gaming industry experienced its own version of #MeToo. After more than seventy allegations surfaced on Twitter in June 2020, one of the CEOs of a gaming company stepped down. This is a challenge that will not go away.

Even a virtual world needs to be inclusive and safe for everyone. The leaders of these companies and prominent gamers, influencers and advertisers will all have to work to address these talent challenges. It may be tempting to view them as outliers whose dissenting voices must be silenced. But dissenting voices often serve as the true north that must guide leaders.

Francoise Brougher had run a $16 billion ad sales business and managed thousands of people at Google. At Square, she had successfully ramped up revenues and been involved in the IPO process. 'Although 70 per cent of Pinterest's users are women, the company is steered by men with little input from female executives. Pinterest's female executives, even at the highest levels, are marginalised, excluded, and silenced. I know because until my firing in April, I was Pinterest's chief operating officer.'[15]

Uber's culture under Travis Kalanick was the textbook version of what needs to be fixed—from misogyny and sexual harassment to questionable ethics, Travis approved of it all. 'Always be hustlin' was his slogan to justify it all. Zuckerberg prided himself with statements like 'Move fast and break things'. Today, people wonder if 'things' refers to free speech and democracy as Facebook gets accused of profiting from hate.

Blinded by the market cap and initial success, the leadership team in Unicorns starts to believe their own marketing slogans (which continues to haunt them for years). Google continues to be reminded about their slogan, 'Don't be Evil'. They coined it with the aim of taking a jibe at Microsoft, and today, the same slogan breeds cynicism when they are accused of misusing data.

McKinsey found that high-growth companies offer a return to shareholders five times greater than medium-growth companies. Second, growth predicts long-term success. 'Supergrowers'—companies whose growth is greater than 60 per cent when they reached $100 million in revenues—are eight times more likely to reach $1 billion in revenues than those growing less than 20 per cent. They say, 'Software and online-services companies can quickly become billion-dollar giants, but the recipe for sustained growth remains elusive.'[16]

Without building a culture of inclusion, the Unicorn remains glued to the clearances given by the core founding team. That comes in the way of Unicorns building leadership capability at the grassroots. It is always tempting for a very successful company to try to replicate the business model and culture of the home base even when it moves to a different geography to set up shop. It believes that if things have worked so well at home, there is no reason for it to not work in the rest of the world. A household name in consumer goods in India lost precious time when the US headquartered company failed to understand why a baseball superstar needed to be replaced by some cricketer ('What kind of a game is that?') called Tendulkar for the ads in India! They found the answer but not before they lost precious market share.

Unicorn Numero Uno: Paytm

One97 Communications does not ring as much of a bell as the audio sound that suggests 'Paytm Karo' (use Paytm). Paytm's growth from being a recharge platform to a payments bank is the subject of a case study published by Harvard Business School. Paytm is the short form of Pay Through Mobile. Paytm, started in 2010 is an e-commerce website as well as an app that lets users pay online for many services like prepaid and postpaid mobile recharge, booking flight, bus and train tickets, and paying hotel, broadband or electricity bills with many cashback offers, gift vouchers, etc., using a mobile number. But what made Paytm take off was the demonetisation of Rs 500 and Rs 1,000 bank notes that took place on 8 November 2016 in India.

The founder Vijay Shekhar Sharma explained it by saying, 'Paytm's growth is divided into three phases—first three years of finding the right product-market fit; the next was revenue and monetisation; and the last phase will be about profitability and free cash flows.'

1. Speed builds scale: Paytm's ability to move rapidly and continuously expand its offerings has been the reason for its success. It started off in 2010 as a prepaid mobile and direct-to-home (DTH) recharge platform. By 2013, it had added data card, postpaid mobile and landline bill payments. By January 2014, the company had launched the Paytm Wallet, which the Indian Railways and Uber added as a payment option. Between 2015 and 2016, it added education fees, metro recharges, electricity, gas, water bill payments, tickets for Indian Railways, movies, events, amusement parks, flight ticket bookings and Paytm QR.[17]

2. Increase in customer base: In twelve months, Paytm's user base increased ten times from 11.8 million in August 2014 to 104 million in August 2015 and then doubled again to 200 million.

3. Competition beyond peers: In April 2016, National Payments Corporation of India launched Unified Payments Interface (UPI), which is an instant real-time payment system developed by facilitating interbank transactions. The interface is regulated by the Reserve Bank of India and works by instantly transferring funds between two bank accounts on a mobile platform. More than 155 banks were already using UPI as of May 2020.[18] Besides UPI, which threatens Paytm's growth, competitors include Google Pay and PhonePe from Walmart-owned Flipkart, who have deep pockets.

Though digital payments are still expected to grow to $1 trillion by 2023 compared to $200 billion in 2018, according to a 2018 Credit Suisse report, digital wallets, where Paytm has established a monopoly, may soon become obsolete. Then there is the additional threat that WhatsApp may launch payments through its platform.

The challenge of Paytm is that it is still seen as a one-man show. It is extremely creditable that Sharma took the Dreamer to a $16 billion valuation. Yet, corporate governance structures are weak and the cracks typically show when the headwinds come up.[19]

Mercurial temperaments can wreak havoc on the teams that are executing stuff on the ground. Paytm launched a credit card called the Paytm First Card, issued by Citibank, with much fanfare early last year. (Paytm First is a loyalty programme the company runs, bundling various services/memberships under a single subscription.) Things were going along fine till the two companies got into some negotiation on the charges. Sharma decided to drop the alliance cold, leaving a bunch of executives to take the heat.[20]

Success is much harder to manage than failure. The leaders of many Unicorns are punch-drunk with their own success. They become intolerant of any criticism. The other leaders avoid speaking truth to power and rocking the boat. Addressing the intangible elements like culture, talent and leadership styles while keeping the DNA of a Dreamer alive, will help Paytm become a Market Shaper.

Unicorn No 2: Oyo

Founded in 2013 by Ritesh Agarwal, then a nineteen-year-old student, Oyo set out to organise India's budget hotels, which have traditionally been small, family-run enterprises. Flush with funds from Softbank, Oyo has been the second biggest decacorn (more than $10 billion valuation). Oyo wanted to expand globally and had at one stage more than 1.2 million rooms in eighty countries listed. It employed more than 20,000 people. Eighty per cent of Oyo's employees had been at the company for less than a year, and so training has been a challenge.

Oyo has more than 19,000 rooms in 250 plus hotels across more than 30 states in the US. It has invested roughly $300 million since it formally launched there in June 2019. In January 2020, the *Financial Times* reported about Oyo laying off one-third of its staff in the US and more than 2,000 people in India.[21]

The New York Times wrote a scathing report about the culture at Oyo. They were accused of listing properties that they were no longer eligible for, and there were complaints about delayed payments.[22]

The handful of people at the top have been there from the beginning. But the three growth drivers were held back by a lack of depth in leadership, a talent strategy that wasn't carved out before expanding to a new geography and a situation where 80 per cent of the hires have spent less than twelve months at Oyo and created the perfect recipe for the Unicorn to flame out like a meteor.

Blind ambition breeds a culture that can overpower the need to be inclusive and fair—seen as luxuries that a

Unicorn cannot afford to waste time on. The reset in the business canvas because of the pandemic is an opportunity for Oyo to fix its culture and build local management talent. A deeper investment in the intangible elements like building trust, creating ethical models of partnership and building ethical leadership practices at all levels will rekindle brand Oyo.

Dreamer to Unicorn: Automation Anywhere

Automation Anywhere Inc. is a global leader in robotics/AI automation. The company was founded in 2003 in Baroda/ San Jose with four co-founders playing a pivotal role. They have 2,000 employees present in 40 countries. The company did a Series B funding in February 2020 valuing it at $6.8 billion.

Milan Sheth, executive vice president (EVP) of the company said in an interview, 'The company's first decade focused on the US market and serving product needs in mid-sized enterprises. As it grew in size and product portfolio expanded it had to make changes in what they would look for in each hire. They wanted to retain the agility and hunger of an early stage startup and continue to innovate. But they also wanted to hire people who strengthen a culture of agility even as they built a business that could scale up.'

With every new geography that got added, the teams from various countries had to be assimilated. 'Eventually only a successful project will create a happy customer. You have to build a culture of speed and an organisation structure that is simple enough to be effective without sacrificing speed. That is the only way to grow from a Dreamer to a Unicorn,' said Milan.

Culture Building—Start with the Leadership Team of the Unicorn

When the organisation transitions from being a Dreamer to a Unicorn, the level of complexity grows exponentially and at a lightning speed. The combination of these two things often renders leaders and the entire organisation incapable of succeeding as a Unicorn.

A Dreamer's success depends on the ability to pivot and experiment. The key skill is the ability to handle ambiguity and not have the fear of failure. It needs people with resilience who can repeatedly pick themselves up as they hit a wall. The Dreamer's talent strategy is often limited by cash flow. That also means that they need to go lean if the idea does not find takers. That is the time when leaders have to take accountability.

Assess the Leadership Team

1. *The leadership challenge changes from Dreamer to Unicorn:* The founder and the team of trusted old-timers are often the biggest stumbling blocks for the growth of the business. Loyalty proven by tenure often overrides competence in several organisations. Every leader who is successful in a Dreamer organisation is not necessarily suitable when the organisation hits scale. A person who successfully managed a team of five people may become ineffective with the increase in complexity that comes from even one or two more people. Being a people manager means being able to lead, manage and inspire through personal example. Invest in that training continuously. The

founder may be terrific at building a product but may not be capable of running the organisation. The reverse is also true. A strong leadership team with strong corporate governance processes helps to prepare a Unicorn to become a Market Shaper.

What Does It Mean to Take Responsibility and Accountability?

'At ICICI Bank, K.V. Kamath (MD & CEO) retired six months after we contained the 2008 run on the bank. But we were not out of the woods yet. In mid-April 2009, Kamath called me and told me, "Ram, I take full responsibility and accountability for the crisis. Tell the board that I will not take any pay rise or even a single stock option. I leave it to you, the senior leadership, on what you want to do."

We all followed suit and did not take a pay rise, bonus or stock option that year. Kamath was of the firm view that when the shareholders had seen an erosion in value, we, their custodians, should not seek to harvest value. Remember, we all had many more years to go and make up for it, but for Kamath it was his last year. He put the shareholders ahead of himself. That is taking full responsibility and accountability in a crisis.'

—K. Ramkumar, Founder and CEO, Leadership Centre and was then the CHRO of ICICI Bank*

2. *Communicating good news and bad:* The founders have to constantly communicate with their teams (especially when there is bad news) and build the practice in the rest of the team members. Most of them are outstanding individual contributors with limited leadership skills (even though they

*Story of K.V. Kamath courtesy: Founding Fuel and K. Ramkumar

lead large teams) who have landed up in leadership roles and have to teach themselves to play a different role if they have to build an organisation that can scale. You cannot have the power and privilege of being the leader of an organisation without consciously growing your skills to match the business growth and complexity. Communicating bad news, especially around poor company performance and layoffs, is the acid test of the leadership team. If they ascribe bad news to external factors, you can assume they will usurp all the credit from the team when things go well.

3. *Track the leader's 'air-time' in meetings:* Get someone to track everyone's talking time—especially the leaders'. In meetings, the leader should not be speaking more than 10–12 per cent of the time. Be conscious of how much of what you say as a statement and how many questions you ask. Make sure you have specifically looked out for those who are silent. They have probably listened more. Ask them to share their ideas and have someone summarise the meetings.

Create a Talent Strategy for the Future

1. *Hiring:* The founder's vision is what inspires people to come work for a Dreamer. The founder's vision is what attracts talent. In case of a Unicorn, the employees and candidates must trust the vision of the business. Hiring the right team that can handle scale is a big shift of focus the leaders must be aware of.

2. *Handling red flags immediately:* Designing the right organisation structure is a specialist's job. The organisation

structure impacts the speed of the organisation and accountability. It impacts career paths and the ability to attract talent. It shapes culture. Build structures and processes to handle red flags or early warning signals.

3. *Future-focused skill development:* It is important to have the skills that the organisation will need to scale at the pace it intends to. Being able to manage scale and speed means creating time for each employee to improve their performance at the current level and be ready to deliver adequately at the next higher level. If the leaders are not actively putting away a few days to learn new skills, they will sneer at team members who are. That is an early sign of the talent pool becoming irrelevant.

Your Culture Should Be the Reason to Stay

1. *Are people staying for the golden handcuffs:* The best measure of the culture is to see how long people stay after the ESOPs or equity can be cashed. It is true that each one gets motivated by different things, but people whose sole reason to be in a company is money, have a transactional relationship with the business.

2. *Build strong corporate governance norms:* The number one reason CEOs were ousted from their jobs in 2018 was not poor financial performance, but ethical lapses. More than one-third of the CEOs who left their jobs in 2018 left for 'reasons related to unethical behaviour stemming from allegations of sexual misconduct or ethical lapses connected to things like fraud, bribery and insider trading'.[23]

3. *Encourage diversity at the top:* It is likely that many members of the top team have been friends from day one of the business. Foster diversity in the leadership team—and by that I don't just mean gender, but also people from diverse socio-economic backgrounds and educational experiences. The COO of Hindustan Unilever, Nitin Paranjpe, talks about leveraging technology to build diversity in the candidate pool. The algorithm was able to use almost seventy-four different attributes to screen a million applicants over four rounds using technology. The final pool of candidates that reached the interviewers was very different and diverse in every possible way.*

Case Study: IndiGo—Hiring for Scale

Sukhjit Pasricha was the CHRO of IndiGo from 2013 to 2018. Prior to this assignment, Pasricha had worked with Airtel when it expanded its operations in Africa. I spoke to him about hiring for scale. He said:

> Hire and train to build a cadre of 'professional-entrepreneurs': During the years when I was at IndiGo, the number of aircrafts grew, and with it, the employee strength grew from 6,000 to 15,000. Women made up 43 per cent of IndiGo's workforce. Hiring right is one of the biggest challenges, which slows down the growth of an organisation.
>
> Hiring for scale is one of the biggest areas for the leadership team to focus on. When a company grows from the Dreamer to the Unicorn stage, it does not have enough

*The future of MBA conversation on 30 June 2020 with Founding Fuel people who have experienced what it means to scale. There must be a systematic plan to train up an internal pool of leaders to handle the explosion of scale. While at Airtel, I saw Sunil Bharti Mittal doing this in 2013, when he handpicked Manoj Kohli, the then CEO of the mobile business, and made him the CEO for India business.

So, I believe that when founders look for leaders, they have to look for someone who has managed scale in an organisation that has strong systems and processes in place. When such professional managers have an entrepreneurial streak in them, they run the business with the same passion as a founder. This 'professional-entrepreneur' can put the organisation on to a growth path. Aditya Ghosh, who was the CEO of IndiGo during those years, was such a leader.

What Narcissistic Leaders Can Do To Kill Unicorns

In nine years, WeWork grew from a single office to roughly 527,000 tenants—or 'memberships'—in some 110 cities. The charismatic and narcissistic founder found it hard to handle the success. Adam Neumann, co-founder of WeWork, with his long hair, bare feet, marijuana-smoking, new-age vibe soared high with money from Softbank.

When WeWork's valuation plummeted because of its sky-high losses that were led by vanity projects, Neumann was forced to resign, and its upcoming IPO was withdrawn. *The New Yorker* featured a sharp article about the lack of leadership in the company featured: 'There wasn't anyone else running the company. It was just Adam and his wife.'[24]

The Unicorn's valuation dropped from $47 billion to $7 billion, after a rescue attempt by the Japanese giant SoftBank. The 'reality distortion' effect that Steve Jobs was famous for, was something Neumann had mastered. He boasted of having dazzled Masayoshi Son to part with $4.4 billion in a few minutes.[25]

When WeWork was losing $60 million every two weeks, Neumann bought a Gulfstream G650 private jet for the same amount. In a glaring conflict of interest, he made millions leasing buildings he partly owned, back to WeWork. Poor corporate governance, a narcissistic leader who collects a billion dollars even as he quits the company, leaving numerous employees jobless, should serve as a cautionary tale for leaders.

Narcissistic and toxic leaders have destroyed many Unicorns—from Theranos to Uber. In 2014, the billion-dollar startup Theranos (a combination of 'therapy plus diagnosis') and its CEO, Elizabeth Holmes, were on every magazine cover. Holmes said that she was the female version of Steve Jobs and even dressed like him. She had claimed that her firm had proprietary tech that would make it possible to diagnose multiple diseases from one drop of blood. Her vision was to build a world where 'no one would have to say goodbye too soon'. Her claims and ability to portray herself as visionary genius was just a grand delusion and narcissism. They believe they are superior and are not subject to the same rules and norms. They are more likely to act dishonestly to achieve their ends. They lie intentionally and don't feel shame.[26]

The personalities of leaders shape the culture of organisations and the behaviour of those who work in them. These toxic leaders ensure that divergent voices are silenced and flattery and servility are rewarded. The rapid success of a Unicorn brings out the worst elements of narcissism.

Leaders forget that high growth may have happened for reasons other than brilliance of the leader. Humility helps.

Tomas Chamorro-Premuzic, a personality psychologist, summarises the charismatic-narcissistic style of leadership.[27]

'Leaders are often charismatic, which will make them far more effective. Charisma is mostly an amplifier, so when you have competent and ethical leaders, you want them to be as charismatic as possible. But when they are incompetent or unethical, their charisma will amplify their destructive nature.'

Narcissistic Founders' Checklist

- Everything from the snack served in the cafeteria to the choice of the carpet is decided by the founder. Even when there is a specialist (e.g. CFO, CMO, COO) hired, every decision is signed off by the founder or his 'inner circle' who have learned to second guess what he will approve.
- Every external hire who is hired from a marquee brand is brought in to show the founder that we can hire anyone we want. The inner circle and the CEO will soon start treating the new hire with contempt and openly declare that he/she is 'not as good as was being claimed'. The person is promptly fired for non-performance. The cycle starts again.
- A narcissistic leader takes all credit for the success of the organisation, but makes the mandatory statement, 'I owe it to the team.' All photos in the press and every interview is of the founder.
- The founder believes that he is an expert in all functions, especially in human resources. 'I am the

CHRO' is the reason to never hire one. And if one is indeed hired, the person's decision is always overturned until the CHRO learns to suggest just what the founder wants. Narcissistic founders believe that HR is all about hiring and payroll. They do not invest in developing people and ensure that there is never any succession plan.

- Success is much harder to handle than failure. The founders believe that in order to complete their charismatic appeal, they need to be temperamental and quirky. Changing their mind and going flip-flop leaves everyone confused. When execution suffers, heads roll (not the founder's).

Fireside Chat: Aditya Ghosh

Aditya Ghosh headed India's largest airline, IndiGo, for a decade until he left in 2018. In 2004, Ghosh was working in a law firm that worked with InterGlobe Enterprise. He joined IndiGo in 2007 and in 2008, became the CEO, following the exit of the then chief Bruce Ashby. Ghosh was thirty-two years old and a rank outsider running the incredibly complex business of an airline.

He says, 'To the best of my knowledge, IndiGo is the only airlines of its size in the world that does not have a union. For three consecutive years between 2016 to 2018, they kept salaries flat in response to cost pressures, but continued to win awards for being an awesome employer brand (based on employee feedback).

IndiGo's marketing spend was approximately 1 per cent of the revenue line. Compared to that, Kingfisher Airlines spent 11 per cent on marketing. Ghosh was obsessed with building the organisation's culture. He operated out of two offices in Gurgaon. For three days a week, he was in the Support Centre office where his room was on the same floor as the HR team. The other two days were spent at iFly—the Learning Centre of IndiGo.

Ghosh explains it by saying, 'I am obsessed with people processes—how they are hired, onboarded and trained. Or even the alumni group. They are all things that I am fascinated about.'

IndiGo was the only Indian airline to report a profit even in 2013 when high global fuel prices and a weakening rupee had wreaked havoc on the industry. When Ghosh left, IndiGo had close to 40 per cent market share. There was no doubt that IndiGo was a Unicorn. It was trying to extend the routes beyond India to other countries.

Ghosh left IndiGo to join Oyo—another Unicorn. In a freewheeling interview, I spoke to him about what explains the rapid growth of an organisation from being a Dreamer to a Unicorn.[28]

Leadership, Talent and Culture

1. Culture is the secret sauce. The product, service and business plan are all impacted by the culture. In a regulated industry like the airlines, the operating manuals are no different from one airline to the other. The culture is the differentiator.
2. Culture is the muscle memory of the organisation. It is what we do without even thinking about it consciously. It is what is celebrated, punished/rewarded and noticed.

3. The leader's role is to drive the culture by being consistent and leading by example. An organisation's culture is driven by its leaders. When the leader changes, the culture of the organisation also changes. When employees say that 'things have changed', they are talking about the change in the organisation culture. Even in a promoter-led organisation, a true leader shapes the culture. Three qualities show preparedness for the leader's role—humility, experience and curiosity.
4. India is a country of 1.3 billion people. Yet employers worry about the lack of talent. The consumer has changed, their needs have changed, but our talent has not kept pace. The leader has to build a culture that picks up fresh talent and turn them into the talent that they need. In 2009–10, IndiGo realised that the number of pilots is less than the number of planes in the world. If there was a shortage, then there would be collective bargaining, cost increases, etc. In the middle of the recession, IndiGo decided that by 2015 they would be self-reliant about this skill (of a pilot) but would still bring in some external hires to keep the culture fresh. Hundred per cent of the first officers came from IndiGo's cadet pilot programme, which was creating sixty new first officers every month. Twenty-two to forty first officers were getting upgraded every month. Ninety-nine per cent of lead flight attendants were 'Made in IndiGo'.

Ghosh's involvement with IndiGo started when he was in the law firm that was helping the promoters set up an airline in India with a $5 million kitty and a $45 million debt. In

2008, IndiGo Airlines was launched with nineteen aircrafts that connected nine cities. Eleven hundred employees celebrated when they made $300 million in the first year of operations. In 2018, when Ghosh left, the Dreamer had become a Unicorn (it had a market cap of $8.5 billion and was flying to almost 10 countries). They were flying to fifty destinations with 250 aircrafts and 20,000 employees. IndiGo won several awards for being a great place to work and for being a great employer. This is probably the best example of leadership and driving the culture that builds talent, which in turn produces great leaders at every level.

The leader sets the pace for change in any organisation. When the leader changes, the culture changes. Reed Hastings of Netflix agrees, 'Culture helps a company to scale.'

When a UNICORNS starts attracting political attention, it means it has the ability to become a MARKET SHAPER

Market Shapers: Impact Beyond the Organisation/Industry or Even Country

The world's 500 largest companies generated $33.3 trillion in revenues and $2.1 trillion in profits in 2019. Together, Fortune Global 500 companies listed in 2020 employ 69.9 million people worldwide and are represented by 32 countries. The ten biggest companies of the world by turnover were:

1. Walmart
2. Sinopec Group
3. State Grid
4. China National Petroleum
5. Royal Dutch Shell
6. Saudi Aramco
7. Volkswagen
8. BP
9. Amazon.com
10. Toyota Motors

In this list, the most remarkable factor to note is the rise of China as the land of the biggest corporations. The second, third and fourth companies in the top ten list are all Chinese. In the first Fortune 500 list in 1990, there were zero companies from mainland China. World trade now represents 59 per cent of the output. It is a $14 trillion dollar economy that is a Market Shaper—a tag that cannot be denied.[29]

Dreamers, Unicorns, Market Shapers and Incumbents are just four metaphors to describe the pace and scale of impact.

Case: TikTok

Could an app that lets users make fifteen-second videos threaten national security? Is TikTok a Unicorn or a Market Shaper? Let us unpack this.

TikTok is a Market Shaper with 2 billion downloads and the ability to attract attention of multiple heads of state and CEOs of mutiple Fortune 500 corporations. They make it possible for anyone (even a new user) to become a Power User in no time. The algorithm creates an 'individualised' user experience according to their tastes and preferences. The short videos ensure that the user can quickly switch to another video if they don't like what the algorithm recommends. TikTok videos work through the community of creators. Users can collaborate with strangers to create 'duets'. Any user can use the video or soundtrack of another user and create their own content. Being able to build

human connections with strangers is addictive. The user is not limited to only the people they know. An uninitiated user can garner millions of views as easily as an influencer with an army of followers. Unicorns become Market Shapers by leveraging intangible elements like user experience, creativity and emotions. The user is at the center of the business. The data they collect about each user from billions gives them the power that makes governments and data privacy groups sweat. Market Shapers have to continuously earn the trust of their stakeholders and assure them that they will not weaponise the data they are gathering about billions of people.

By being a fully video-based app and being available in fourteen Indian languages, TikTok bypassed the literacy divide. It reached hundreds of millions of first-time internet users in Tier II, III, IV and even Tier V towns. In fact, some of the most interesting trends and hashtag challenges that take the world by storm actually originated in TikTok India. A song lip-synced by a goat herd gathered thousands of views, and created an outlet for the creativity and inclusion of the non-English speaking population that makes up 90 per cent of the 1.3 billion people.

A wide user base is also the cause of the vulnerability of a Unicorn/Market Shaper. Changing political equations often creates tensions that impact the business. In June 2020, India decided to ban fifty-nine Chinese apps citing concerns of data privacy and national security. That could mean a $6 billion setback for the parent company Bytedance, a privately held company in China with a market cap of $100 billion.[30]

As this book goes to the press in September 2020, the world seems to be heading for a split in the internet (should we call it the 'splinternet'?) and in the world of tech between the US and China. This is the tech version of the Cold War. Regardless of what happens to TikTok or other Chinese apps, it will be all about winning trust.

Since 1995, China's share of world GDP at market prices has risen from 2 per cent to 16 per cent. Tech companies like Alibaba and Tencent have customer bases in China that have more customers than the population of many countries. The messaging app WeChat is deeply entrenched as a combination of a messaging app and a financial instrument with data that makes everyone drool. Plus their proximity to the Chinese State makes it hard to bypass as just another business behind the Chinese firewall.

Does a Company Have a Passport?

In a boundaryless world, it is still possible to put up fences and prevent people from travelling to other countries for work, but the digital world is boundaryless. Electronic banking makes money and investing boundaryless. When there is rise in jingoistic sentiments, we have to pause and ask, 'What is an "Indian" company?'

Flipkart was founded in October 2007 by Sachin Bansal and Binny Bansal, who were former Amazon employees and took the same idea and cloned it in India. Flipkart was operating through a complex business structure which included nine firms, some registered in Singapore and some in India. Does that make it an 'Indian business'? Flipkart raised funding from Tiger Global (part of Naspers Group), Iconiq Capital, Accel Partners, Morgan Stanley Investment Management, Singapore sovereign-wealth fund GIC and almost forty other investors. They were eventually acquired by Walmart—a firm headquartered in the US.

Does Flipkart have an Indian passport?

The Market Shaper's Challenge: Build Trust with Stakeholders

In March 2019, the Boeing 737 MAX passenger airliner was grounded worldwide after 346 people died in two crashes—the Lion Air Flight 610 on 29 October 2018 and Ethiopian Airlines Flight 302 on 10 March 2019. Boeing claims to have solved the software glitches that caused the crash. To get the flights off the ground may be more complex than simply fixing the software bugs. Countries are unable to agree on which pilots would certify that the planes are safe to fly. The pandemic and stalled air travel between countries is making an already wobbly sector even more shaky. Aerospace company Airbus aims to cut 15,000 jobs given the pandemic challenges. Will the pandemic give Boeing an advantage, or will it snuff out the aviation industry?

Don't Profit from Tragedy

Facebook and Google together own 80 per cent of the digital marketing revenues. More than 750 companies including Coca-Cola, Walgreens, Best Buy, Ford, Adidas, Hershey's and Unilever have already temporarily paused their advertising on Facebook and its subsidiary Instagram. They are concerned about Facebook's stand that they support free speech and are unwilling to moderate content that they see as hate speech.

It is easy to run a clever ad campaign about a social cause that people care about. But it places the brands under scrutiny and holds them to higher standards. Declaring oneself a supporter of social justice makes a brand an endeared one, but it also places them under the microscope of stakeholders. The 2017 Dove ad in the US and the UK showed a black woman removing her brown top, revealing a white woman underneath. The Dolce and Gabbana social media campaign, created in Italy for the Asian market, featured a Chinese model attempting to use chopsticks to eat Italian food, while wearing D&G clothes. Fair & Lovely was introduced in the market way back in 1975. For decades, the brand was a symbol of the aspirations of Indians. It was meant to make the skin appear a few shades lighter. In 2020, Hindustan Unilever had to rename it Glow and Lovely. But keeping the production unchanged while changing the name builds distrust. Even a Market Shaper gets swayed by the economics of the decision than the emotion.

Being a Market Shaper means you have to go beyond shareholder interest and address issues that are impacting society. When Apple refuses to unlock an iPhone that could give the government access to a criminal's data, they build trust.

Facebook has been accused of letting its platform's reach be used to repeatedly compromise on individual's data privacy; election interference; the massacres in Myanmar. The algorithm is designed to serve up more divisive, outrageous and polarising content because the truth is often boring. Conspiracy theories, hatred towards certain religions and ethnic groups have led to elections being rigged and extremists coming to power. When asked about

Facebook, Instagram and WhatsApp all being used by authoritarian regimes to spread lies and violate the rights of certain groups, Zuckerberg has said that the solution lies in spreading 'more information'. Big Tech is more powerful than any government. Given that most law makers are fairly clueless when it comes to their understanding of technology, the lobbyists paid by Big Tech shapes the legal framework in most countries. The polarisation is so strong that friends, relatives and classmates exit WhatsApp groups. Anyone whose views differ from ours is subject to trolling, death threats and assaults fomented by social media. Profits and growth cannot be the only gods we worship; leadership is about making ethical choices. When *Fortune* described Sandberg's fall from grace as a leader, they advised, 'True equality means leaning in to power—and bearing the full weight of the repercussions for using it unwisely.'[31]

Experience Disruptors are the new Market Shapers

Experience disruptors are people who are trying to disrupt competition by looking for not just a product-market fit, but an 'experience-market fit'. These are people who run a B2B business with a B2C mindset. They remove friction from the buying process or even the returns process. Their customers become their greatest evangelists. The software company Atlassian does not have salespeople. The CEO of Hubspot explains the five ways in which experience disruptors challenge conventional B2B marketing and sales.

Adobe has an entire conference aimed at experience makers. They are changing how people 'watch, buy and invest'.[32]

Designing experiences need people who understand emotions. They understand the digital space and how they can keep the customers and consumers enchanted. They have the ability to change emotions. They make you feel valued and special.

Regulation Has Its Challenges

One person's terrorist is another person's martyr. In some cases, governments are not willing to keep waiting. Google, Amazon and Facebook face proposed European rules aimed at curbing their alleged anticompetitive behaviour, making them pay more taxes and compelling them to shoulder more responsibility for illegal content. GDPR fines are related to how companies obtain consumers' consent to use their data and how long the firms retain personal data. Enforcing the rules is a burden on governments because it is an additional cost. The European Union privacy regulators are worried about doing this with limited funds at their disposal. That is coupled with the challenge that the best brains would rather work for a Market Shaper than the government.

Most lawmakers do not understand how to handle cyber challenges. If the criminal is in country A and hacks someone in country B whose bank account is in country C but the bank's servers are in country D, which country's law would apply? By the time the regulators agree on the response, the criminals have often fled to craft another scam.

Is regulation good for the business? Regulation creates a level-playing field. While the Market Shapers are always under the watch of the users and are subject to frequent trials by media, the same does not apply equally stringently to the Dreamers or smaller players in the unorganised sector. Regulation, if enforced stringently, creates a level-playing field. It also puts the bigger players at the same level as the smaller-promoter-driven startups.

'India's Amazon Will Be an EdTech Company'

'India's Amazon Will Be an EdTech company' says Gaurav Munjal of Unacademy, India's second largest EdTech startup after Byju's (valued at almost $11 billion). Eruditus, Vedantu and Toppr are snapping at the heels of Unacademy. Education in India is estimated to be $135 billion.

The view is shared by Blume Ventures, which is amongst India's leading early-stage venture funds and investing in tech-led ventures across sectors. This section draws heavily on the data shared in the Blume Ventures EdTech report.[33]

The reasons for EdTech's growth in India are many:

1. *Staying relevant is the individual's responsibility:* Employees are more open to investing their own funds in upskilling their profiles through online classes, where the burden earlier was borne by their employers. We are seeing

the impact of this in the sharp growth in B2C corporate-learning providers such as Coursera, Udemy, Simplilearn, Upgrad, etc.

2. *Education drives social mobility:* Indian parents across the economic spectrum are willing to supplement the school system by paying for coaching classes in soft skills and the core subjects that will help their wards secure admission in a good undergraduate degree. There is a gap in what the students want and what the school or college can provide. New-age skills like robotics, vedic maths, legal studies and coding—what we call 'neo-academic services'—are being demanded by parents. This is driven both by pressures of increasing competition and exposure to Western education. Since most schools are not equipped to provide these services (lack of teachers, content, etc.), this has made way for EdTech.

3. *Earning and yearning:* Each year, about 6.3 million undergrad students graduate but only 0.3 million white-collar jobs are created. Almost 12 million out of 30 million white-collar jobs are government jobs—most of which are allocated based on performance in an exam. Test preparation becomes another opportunity. People who are employed invest in upskilling themselves and spend money on 'yearning skills' like hobbies and languages.

4. *The BYOD moment in learning*: Just as businesses have moved to 'bring your own devices (BYOD)' policy, allowing employees to bring their own hardware to work, the same is happening in the space of learning. Professionals are looking for marketplaces for quality mentors or industry leaders so that they can learn from leaders in a given field.

For example, learning painting from a famous painter or marketing from a CMO of a company. This model can also be extended to networking and finding mentors.

COVID grew both the markets. Those who were laid off have invested in upskilling themselves and those who have stable jobs have invested in 'yearning' skills. A thriving EdTech can make India the skill-building capital of the world.

It is easy to learn from your failures if you attribute it to your choices.
It is easy to learn from successes, if you attribute most of it to other people

Note the Pattern

It is not just organisations that grow up to be Dreamers/Unicorns/Market Shapers/Incumbents. It could be a country. A Dreamer like Estonia has created an entire country that is digital first. What if Estonia becomes a country that provides e-governance services to other countries some day? As we have seen with organisations, it is not about the ability to sort out the problem as it is about building trust with the stakeholders.

When the Leader becomes narcissistic and self-obsessed, it is not good for the organisation. That is just what has happened to Silicon Valley. If there is a place which is a

Market Shaper, it is Silicon Valley, home to several Dreamers, many Unicorns and Market Shapers. It is also the graveyard of many Incumbents that were once Market Shapers or Unicorns. It is looked at as a place that rewards unabashed greed. Much like what led to the crash of Wall Street, Silicon Valley's lack of social conscience will likely lead to its decline.

Those with graduate degrees in AI can earn $5 million to $10 million a year. People complain that such pampering has eroded tech's work ethic, with employees focusing on free lunches and other perks. Ecosystems of talent plus funding and diverse, world-class universities are all essential ingredients of a Silicon-Valley-like culture. In Africa, 300 innovative hubs in the main cities, especially in Kenya, South Africa, Nigeria, Egypt and Morocco, are all coming together. India has Bangalore, Delhi and Mumbai as its innovation hubs. Hollywood, Wall Street and the Valley have their share of toxic masculinity and entrenched sexism. More than half of the top American tech companies were founded by immigrants or the children of immigrants. Only a mere 2 per cent of venture-capital funding went to female founders' startups last year. Talent has always been Silicon Valley's blind spot.[34]

When leaders lose track of talent, there is an exodus. That is just the moment Silicon Valley is experiencing. Silicon Valley itself could become as irrelevant and thereby become an irrelevant Incumbent. Economists call it 'techsodus'![35]

According to the *Financial Times*, during the pandemic, the Market Shapers in pharmaceutical groups grew while searching for the COVID-19 vaccine. The Market Shapers among tech giants rode the trend of working from home.

A Unicorn like Zoom added $47 billion to its market cap and became synonymous with videoconferencing. Retailers grew because they stayed open to provide necessities. Adobe added $40 billion fuelled by a 50 per cent rise in PDF documents used. Trust is a big business opportunity.

The five biggest gainers in market cap (as calculated till 19 June 2020) were all Market Shapers. Amazon added $401 billion, Microsoft added $270 bilion, Apple added $219 billion, Tesla added $108 billion and Tencent added $93 billion. The next five were Facebook ($85 billion), Nvidia ($83 billion), Alphabet/ Google ($68 billion), PayPal ($65 billion) and T-Mobile ($60 billion).[36]

All of them are Market Shapers. They understand how to navigate the new world. That is not what they learned once the pandemic hit. They have been doing it for years. They have been innovating.

It is an uncertain world. Dreamers become Unicorns. Unicorns keep growing and become Market Shapers. Fortunes change and the Unicorn becomes an Incumbent. Business history is littered with examples of Market Shapers becoming irrelevant. Then there are inspiring stories of an Incumbent reinventing itself by becoming a Dreamer. The journey from Dreamer to Market Shaper is shorter than we think.

The Biggest Market Shaper Ever

The greatest Market Shaper in business has to be COVID-19. Its impact is global and has challenged every leader be it heads of governments, organisations or households. It forced people to question the feasibility of their business model. Every purchase was questioned and every employee's contribution was scrutinised. The world of work survived without an office. Some industries thrived because of the culling of competition.

The four stages of growth should actually be looked at as fluid states. A Dreamer can become a Unicorn as it expands beyond the headquarters to some more geographies, maybe inside the country or even outside. When it begins to change the way people live and work, it becomes a Market Shaper, but then its biggest threat is not from other competitors but from governments and its own employees when it loses trust.

The pandemic has claimed a million lives around the world. When a country declares that they have a vaccine ready, people wonder if the news is politically motivated. Trust is the first casualty. It is the first emotion humans experience. It is the time for everyone to build trust in the world.

References

1. There is a detailed explanation of Erikson's framework given here. https://www.simplypsychology.org/Erik-Erikson.html
2. The screaming headline raises hopes until you see the numbers. https://fortune.com/2020/05/18/women-ceos-fortune-500-2020/
3. Radha Radhakrishnan in *Reputation Today* shares examples. https://reputationtoday.in/next-phase-of-brand-communication-journey/
4. Will there be fully autonomous ships navigating high seas? https://podcasts.apple.com/in/podcast/economist-radio/id151230264
5. Read about Digital Therapeutics and what makes it a 'drug'. https://a16z.com/2020/06/21/16mins-videogame-fda-prescription-digital-therapeutics/
6. Legend goes that the drummer could not hear the singing and had to play the beat by watching the singer's body movement. See for yourself. https://youtu.be/jenWdylTtzs

7. Wasserman, Noam. *The Founder's Dilemmas: Anticipating and Avoiding the Pitfalls That Can Sink a Startup*, Princeton University Press
8. A rocker's guide to management contrasts The Beatles and Rolling Stones. https://www.1843magazine.com/features/a-rockers-guide-to-management
9. It is useful to understand the values that drive the founder. They impact the rules and reward systems of the business. https://www.hoganassessments.com/assessment/motives-values-preferences-inventory/
10. Credit Suisse Family Owned Businesses found some surprising results. https://www.credit-suisse.com/about-us-news/en/articles/news-and-expertise/the-family-business-premium-201809.html
11. Research on narcissism is complex. If the focus is self-aggrandisement (esp common in male leaders), it could be a warning sign. https://www.sciencedirect.com/science/article/pii/S1048984306001111
12. Don't start a company with your friends, says Adam Grant. https://www.linkedin.com/pulse/20141015114155-69244073-don-t-start-a-company-with-your-friends/
13. Great digital experiences drive sales. https://www.adobe.com/au/experience-cloud/articles/great-content-mind-shift.html
14. Citius, Altius, Fortnite. https://www.economist.com/leaders/2020/06/27/why-the-next-olympics-should-include-fortnite
15. The Pinterest workplace is toxic. https://medium.com/@francoise_93266/the-pinterest-paradox-cupcakes-and-toxicity-57ed6bd76960
16. It is easy for tech companies to hit a billion dollars but sustainability is hard. https://www.mckinsey.com/industries/technology-media-and-telecommunications/our-insights/grow-fast-or-die-slow
17. Paytm demonstrated its breakneck speed is seen by the number of services they kept adding. https://en.wikipedia.org/wiki/Paytm
18. UPI can be a serious threat to Paytm. https://www.npci.org.in/product-statistics/upi-product-statistics
19. Paytm's weak corporate governance structure has been written about often. Here is one more. https://www.livemint.com/companies/startups/and-now-paytm-faces-its-moment-of-truth-11578503275841.html
20. Failure is hard to handle. But success is even harder. Read this and decide for yourself. https://themorningcontext.com/will-the-real-vijay-shekhar-sharma-please-stand-up/
21. Oyo's business was shaky even before Covid struck. See this. https://www.ft.com/content/9934b808-42ac-11ea-abea-0c7a29cd66fe
22. The toxic culture of Oyo was reported by more than one global newspaper. https://www.nytimes.com/2020/01/02/technology/oyo-softbank-india.html
23. Strong corporate governance builds trust—a necessary condition of growth. https://www.strategy-business.com/article/Succeeding-the-long-serving-legend-in-the-corner-office

24. The rise and fall of WeWork. https://www.newyorker.com/culture/culture-desk/the-rise-and-fall-of-wework
25. Adam Neumann's tale should be a cautionary tale for everyone who believes that a leader must be charismatic & larger than life. https://www.nytimes.com/2019/11/02/business/adam-neumann-wework-exit-package.html
26. The toxic leadership style creates a culture that destroys psychological safety. https://www.gsb.stanford.edu/insights/how-narcissistic-leaders-destroy-within
27. Narcissists are obsessed with fame and success. Psychopaths don't care about the means used and have no remorse about breaking rules or using others. https://www.forbes.com/sites/tomaspremuzic/2020/07/05/are-narcissistic-leaders-as-confident-as-they-appear/
28. Interview with Aditya Ghosh on 04-05 July 2020
29. The *Fortune* 500 Global list. https://fortune.com/2020/08/10/global-500-companies-china-business-cross-border-trade/
30. Bytedance could lose $6 billion. https://www.livemint.com/news/india/tiktok-ban-in-india-bytedance-could-lose-rs-600-crore-11593656151668.html
31. Sheryl Sandberg has lost her personal credibility with a long list of poor judgement calls taken. https://fortune.com/2018/11/28/sheryl-sandberg-facebook-russia-women/
32. Adobe Experience Makers. https://theblog.adobe.com/cast-your-vote-experience-makers-redefining-how-people-watch-buy-invest/
33. Blume Ventures EdTech Report. https://docs.google.com/presentation/d/1P1S_dubRQmqZk45xgkbQiYI2gxAbDRVgT6kRCy6dPzE/edit?usp=sharing
34. Talent has been Silicon Valley's blind spot. https://www.linkedin.com/posts/abhijitbhaduri_silicon-valleys-blind-spot-talent-silicon-activity-6351286568141053952-KMVl/
35. Silicon Valley stands to lose ground as an ecosystem. https://www.economist.com/briefing/2018/09/01/silicon-valley-is-changing-and-its-lead-over-other-tech-hubs-narrowing
36. Prospering in the pandemic lists just what has not just grown but thrived when others have been decimated. https://www.ft.com/content/844ed28c-8074-4856-bde0-20f3bf4cd8f0

13

Epilogue: The Twilight Zone

Hindustani classical music has ragas that are designated for each hour of the day. There are ragas that are sung at dawn and dusk. These are ragas meant for the twilight zone when the darkness and light wrestle with each other. When the sun wins this battle, it signals a new day. When darkness wins, the night begins. It is the twilight zone in music. Much like what we are going through is the twilight zone in the world of work.

The Job Itself Is Changing

Truck drivers in India are on the road for days. They drive for days together and are away from home for long stretches. They miss important social occasions of their family members. Eating at roadside hotels impacts their health. Truck drivers are referred to as the 'thirty-seventh caste' in a caste-conscious society.

Rivigo, an Indian startup in logistics, introduced the 'relay system' where their truck is driven by different drivers for short distances (so that they can be back home in a day). The truck travels towards the destination, while the driver does not. This simple reimagining has made it possible for drivers to work for eight to nine hours like people from any other profession. They drive one for a few hours and rest up before driving back home to join their family for dinner.

Rivigo rebranded the role as a 'truck pilot'. Even the HR team was rebranded as the 'Organisation and Business Engine (OBE)'. One of the major tasks of the OBE team at Rivigo is building scalability towards creating lasting business impact through lean, smart and driven teams. Rivigo uses fuel analytics, route planning and human behaviour analysis to eliminate tasks like auto-alert systems and intelligent decision systems.

In the US, the $800 billion trucking industry is seeing some convulsive changes. For the last ten years, the average distance being driven by a truck driver has been shrinking. That impacts their wages because they are driving for lesser number of kilometres and hours. The rise of e-commerce means that the focus is a lot more on last-mile delivery and not the long distances that drivers have been at the wheel.

Being a driver for last-mile delivery means the focus is on customer interaction and handling goods, which needs a new set of skills that the drivers need. The lack of drivers with these skills makes it one of the 'hybrid jobs' where the talent pool is very low. Add to it the high cost of recruitment, training and safety for a role that sees a lot of attrition, and we have the perfect recipe for automation.[1]

Does that make a watertight case for driverless trucks? Four thousand Americans die in truck-related collisions every year, and human error is responsible for many of them. Self-driving trucks will certainly change lives. That goes double for the nearly 3.2 million people currently employed as delivery and heavy truck drivers.[2]

This in some sense is the world of work. The roles are changing and needs new skills. The work itself is getting automated. Driverless trucks will reduce the human toll but will push many towards unemployment. Those are the complex challenges we have to face. It is truly the twilight zone for everyone.

No One Was Spared

The world of work had a Before Corona (BC) era and what we will see is the After Disruption or Destruction (AD) era. We are going through a time of churn when a lot of destruction is happening. Any industry that brought people together collapsed. Aviation, car rental, hotels, restaurants, conference providers, entertainment and event managers all saw their businesses collapse. Businesses that have lived for more than a century like J.C. Penney (1902) and Hertz Car Rentals (1918) filed for bankruptcy. With it, millions of people lost jobs, took salary cuts and saw their savings evaporate in a few weeks.

It is as if a giant tsunami demolished the world of work as we have known. The world of work will never go back to the Before Corona days. If your world of work has been impacted, this is the time to look at your skills portfolio. Continuous learning, risk-taking and living with ambiguity will be standard features of the world of work.

Think skills, not jobs: Hiring across sectors will be muted for a while, but there is high demand for several cutting-edge skills in every sector, especially tech jobs. If you have been impacted by the recent slowdown, stop waiting for another job to replace the one you have lost. Think of your skills and who can benefit from your skills. Talking to a coach can help you identify possibilities. After that conversation, recraft your LinkedIn profile to appeal to those employers.

Invest in learning new skills: Talk to search firms and headhunters and ask them which skills are most in demand. They can also tell you which sectors are hiring for skills that you have. Educational degrees and previous experience are becoming less valuable than the ability to learn. There are online courses available for just about any skill that you wish to build. Invest in the skills that the marketplace needs. Be prepared to step out of your comfort zone and change cities or sectors or take a cut in money if that helps you get started on a new path.

Become a freelancer: Think of your hobbies and all those plans you made over the years. Maybe you wanted to start a YouTube channel or teach someone a skill. Create a marketing plan to launch Brand You. Build a personal brand that tells potential buyers about your uniqueness. I know of a recruiter who left a stagnant career in a large IT firm to start a career as a stand-up comedian. I know of a doctor who is now a famous singer. Now, a martial arts sensation, she left a thriving career as a marketing head of a large firm to pursue her passion. You could be the owner of a boutique café or a dance studio or a fitness guru. The personal brand will become more important as the people look to take their talent to their audience. The organisation will no longer be an intermediary to help someone reach their audience. While there is a lot being written about 'work from anywhere', we have to remember that it is a luxury for a handful of knowledge workers. The vast majority of the world's workforce have no opportunity yet to be part of the digital world. Hopefully, technology will help create a more inclusive world of work.

Each one of us is now in the twilight zone of our careers. We can choose to see it as the dusk as the sun begins to set. It could also mean the darkness is fading as the eastern sky signals the beginning of a new day.

References

1. The $800 billion trucking industry is changing. As is the role of the driver. https://play.acast.com/s/theeconomistmoneytalks/moneytalks-tikfortok
2. What does the driverless truck mean for drivers? https://www.wired.com/story/what-does-teslas-truck-mean-for-truckers/

Acknowledgements

In 2016, two big things happened in my life. I wrote a book called *The Digital Tsunami* and after seven years as the chief learning officer of Wipro, I started my own leadership and talent advisory firm called Abhijit Bhaduri & Associates. I have been lucky to have worked with iconic organisations across sectors and geographies. From Fortune 500 companies to startups and unicorns, I have had a chance to learn from many iconic leaders. Many ideas have their roots in conversations I have had with them. I have worked—both as an employee and as an advisor—with companies that are global benchmarks in talent management.

Pankaj Bansal, the co-founder of PeopleStrong, deserves a special mention in making this book happen. He gave me access to the organisations and their customers who have undertaken digital transformation with PeopleStrong.

In 2019, PeopleStrong partnered with me to create a podcast that ranked No. 1 on Apple Podcasts. Just Google 'Dreamers and Unicorns by PeopleStrong' and listen to episodes that feature Pankaj Bansal, Anita and Harsha Bhogle, R. Balki, Renuka Ramnath, Joshua Karthik, Anuj Kacker, Shantanu Moitra, Ravi Venkatesan, Pratik Kumar and Sairee Chahal. It was the star cast of guests that made the podcast go viral. This book generously draws on those conversations.

The Society for Human Resource Management (SHRM) is the world's largest HR professional society, representing 285,000 members in more than 165 countries. Thanks to Achal Khanna, CEO, SHRM India & Business Head, Asia Pacific and MENA for giving me access to SHRM's white papers, journals and library, which is a treasure.

Thank you, Pradnya Parasher, for all the research on personality and judgement by Dr Robert Hogan. Dr Tomas Chamorro-Premuzic (Manpower Group) for sharing his insights on narcissistic leaders.

Thanks, Deepa Narayanan, for helping me combine three different manuscripts to let *Dreamers and Unicorns* evolve from that cocoon. Thanks, Apoorva Chaudhary and Kamakshi Pant (PeopleStrong), Rashmi Sharma (Unilever, Vietnam), Vishal Naithani (ex-Oyo), for the support in research and fact-checking. Ester Martinez of *People Matters* and Chitra Narayanan of *Business Line* for letting me take some ideas from my columns. Thanks, Rani Mani, for inviting me to join the influencer programme at Adobe. It is a textbook example of how an influencer programme should be run. You will see references to many of the influencers like Goldie Chan, Sofiya Deva, Kathleen Hessert, Lee Odden, Peter Shankman, Ian Gertler, Ross Quintana, Cathy Hackl, Kelly Hungerford, Winnie Sun, Amber Osborne, Kate O'Neil, Sarah Evans, Kerry O'Shea Gorgone and the rest of the gang.

Thanks, Kanishka Gupta, my literary agent, who thought the book deserved to be taken by the best publisher.

Karthik Venkatesh for editing and shaping the post-COVID manuscript that you are reading now. Thanks, Rajinder Ganju, for the typesetting and layout. *Dreamers and Unicorns* was all set to be printed in January 2020. By April 2020, I knew the manuscript needed to be rewritten.

A big thank you to these leaders who shared their insights and wisdom so generously: Aditya Ghosh, ex-Indigo and now Oyo; Ananth Narayanan, ex-Myntra; Ani Banerjee, VMware; Bill Fischer, IMD Lausanne; Biplob Banerjee, ex-Domino's; Dinesh R., Oyo; Dr Ralph Christian-Orr; Dr Santrupt Mishra, Aditya Birla Group; Dr Henri Lipmanovicz; Indrajit Ghosh, Founding Fuel; Jai Krishna, Amara Raja; John Justice, ex-Microsoft; Leena Sahijwani, Tata Group; Mahesh Samat, Walt Disney; Manish Dugar, ex-Practo; Manish Sabharwal, Team Lease; Manu Narang Wadhwa, Sony Pictures; Nigel Paine, former CLO, BBC; Rahul Jagannathan, ex-Urban Ladder; Rajita Singh, Broadridge; Ram Kumar, ex-ICICI; Ramesh Menon, Murugappa Group; Sanjoe Jose, Talview; Sanju Saha, Smith Nephew; Satyajit Mohanty, Crompton; Saurabh Govil, Wipro; Sonny Iqbal, Egon Zehnder; Shashank N.D., Practo; Sukhjit Pasricha, Kotak Mahindra Bank; Varun Sood, The Morning Context.